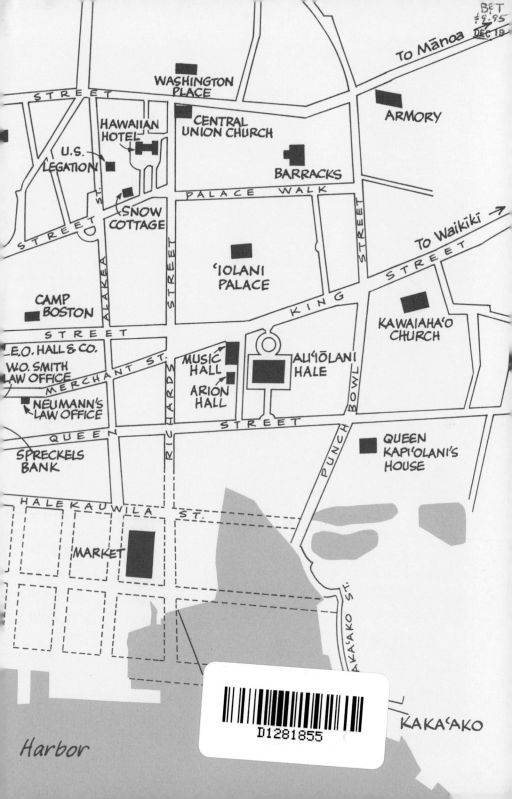

BET
$9.95
DEC 19

To Mānoa

STREET

WASHINGTON
PLACE

ARMORY

HAWAIIAN
HOTEL

CENTRAL
UNION CHURCH

U.S.
LEGATION

BARRACKS

PALACE WALK

SNOW
COTTAGE

STREET

STREET

ʻIOLANI
PALACE

To Waikīkī

STREET

STREET

KING

CAMP
BOSTON

KAWAIAHAʻO
CHURCH

STREET

E.O. HALL & CO.

W.O. SMITH
LAW OFFICE

MERCHANT ST.

MUSIC
HALL

ALIʻIŌLANI
HALE

ARION
HALL

NEUMANN'S
LAW OFFICE

RICHARDS

STREET

QUEEN

PUNCH BOWL

QUEEN
KAPIʻOLANI'S
HOUSE

SPRECKELS
BANK

HALEKAUWILA ST.

MARKET

KAKAʻAKO ST.

KAKAʻAKO

Harbor

For Whom Are the Stars?

FOR WHOM ARE THE STARS?

Albertine Loomis

The University Press of Hawaii
and
Friends of the Library of Hawaii

Library of Congress Catalog Card Number 76-16778
ISBN 0-8248-0416-3

Composition by Asco Trade Typesetting Ltd., Hong Kong
Manufactured in the United States of America

Book design and endpaper maps by Dave Comstock

An informal history
of the
overthrow of the Hawaiian monarchy in 1893
and the
ill-fated counterrevolution it evoked

CONTENTS

ILLUSTRATIONS

Illustrations

PREFACE AND ACKNOWLEDGMENTS

Source material for the 1893–1895 period in Hawai'i is abundant. I began my research more than thirty years ago, when I first visited these Islands, by reading *Hawaii's Story by Hawaii's Queen*. Spellbound by the grievous and tragic tale, I realized nonetheless that the book gave but one view of a complicated story, and began in such time as I could save from other activities to seek a fuller understanding.

While still living in Michigan, I spent three more summers in Hawai'i—in 1953, 1955, and 1958—reading for the most part books and documents in the Bishop Museum Library, in the Hawaiian Historical Society collection at the Mission-Historical Library, and in the Archives of Hawai'i. I remember gratefully the help that was given me by librarians Margaret Titcomb, Willowdean Handy, Sophie Judd Cluff, and Helen Lind, and archivists Maude Jones and Agnes Conrad and her assistants. Especially I would mention Henry Choy at the Archives; in 1958 he was sorting and filing papers from the attorney general's office, including the records and correspondence of the marshal's headquarters in the time of E. G. Hitchcock. What Mr. Choy had ready for me each morning was like a new chapter in a detective serial.

In 1955 I had the good fortune to meet Mary Alexander Smith, whose grandfather, W. D. Alexander, participated in and wrote about the events of 1893, and I was allowed to examine Professor Alexander's private papers at her home. The opportunity helped to make that particular summer decidedly rewarding.

In 1956 I spent two weeks in London, reading British Foreign Office files of diplomatic correspondence between British Commissioner James H. Wodehouse in Hawai'i and his superior, Foreign Secretary Lord Rosebery. In the "round room" at the Public Record Office I found two fat, leather-bound volumes of longhand pages, which bore the titles: "Designs of the United States on Pearl Harbor, 1886–1888" and "Designs of the United States on Hawaii, 1888–1898." I do not recall, if indeed I ever knew, the names of persons who helped me there, but I am grateful, especially to the official who admitted me on the basis of a telephone call from the American Embassy, since the written credentials I had applied for did not reach me until I had returned home at the end of the summer.

But I did not always have to go so far afield. At some time during the 1950s I discovered that the University of Michigan has a remarkably complete collection of documents, many of them copies or blueprints of originals held elsewhere, as well as rare books and newspapers dealing with Hawai'i. This is the Spaulding Collection, assembled by Col. Thomas M. Spaulding, for some years stationed in the Islands and an earnest student of Hawaiian history. It was as a memorial to his son Stephen, who died in his sophomore year at the University of Michigan, that Colonel Spaulding gathered and presented to the university library the numerous and varied items that make up the collection.

Here, then, only thirty miles from where I lived, in Detroit, I had access to sources of great value. For one thing, there was a complete file of the *Pacific Commercial Advertiser* (today's *Honolulu Advertiser*) for the years in which I was interested. Many were the Friday afternoons when I shut the door on everything that was then the present and drove at top legal speed to Ann Arbor, to lose myself for most of the next forty-eight hours in a world distant not only in space but in time. There was no microfilm, thank goodness! There were only the old, brown, crumbling pages that had come from the press in Honolulu in a time of crisis. Margaret Smith, librarian, a personal friend of mine, never reproved me for the circle of newsprint crumbs that surrounded my chair as soon as I began tenderly to turn the leaves.

About 1957 there came to my attention the existence of the amazing Emerson papers. A young collector, Robert E. Van Dyke of Honolulu, had discovered this set of original documents having to do with the counterrevolution, and was generous enough to share them with me. It seems that in 1895 Dr. Nathaniel B. Emerson, missionary son, sensitive student of Hawaiian culture, a friend, though not a partisan, of the native people, had intended to write an account of the uprising that tried to restore the monarchy. When many of the participants in that affair were in Oʻahu prison, awaiting trial, Emerson obtained permission from government authorities to go in and talk at length with some fifteen of them. They told him freely their reasons for joining in the movement and their experiences in the field. Emerson also recorded the statements of a few who were on the winning side.

Whatever the reason, Emerson never wrote the story. He locked the papers in a trunk, and apparently they lay there for more than sixty years. His son, Arthur Emerson, since the key was lost, never had opened the trunk, but Robert Van Dyke persuaded him to break the lock. Arthur was neither a historian nor a collector, so he sold the papers to Robert.

It was when I read these priceless individual accounts of what went on at Rabbit Island, at Diamond Head, and at Mauʻumae on the Kaimukī heights that I decided to condense the scope of my narrative. At one time I had intended to begin at Kalākaua's accession, because so many of the problems that culminated in the overthrow had their beginnings in the Merry Monarch's reign. But since the Kalākaua era has been fully and vividly covered by several able writers, I have chosen to begin on the day when Liliʻuokalani surrendered the sovereignty, to go on through the two years when she and most of her people wishfully believed that the monarchy would be restored, and to devote major attention to the attempted counterrevolution, about which comparatively little has been written.

In recent years I have received helpful advice and encouragement from many persons who share my deep interest in Hawaiʻi's most critical years. Among these are Jacob Adler and Alison Kay, officers of the Hawaiian Historical Society, Thomas Nickerson of the Friends of the Library of Hawai'i, and Jane Silverman, State Parks Historian.

For meaningful illustrations I have turned again to Robert E. Van Dyke, who has searched his remarkable collection and has generously provided all of the photographs and sketches used herein. For maps I have relied chiefly on the Archives of Hawai'i and the help of archivist Agnes Conrad.

And now a special *mahalo* to the Hawai'i Foundation for History and the Humanities for its grant in the spring of 1974 to finance the final typing of my much-revised manuscript. The grant was a helping hand, extended to a weary runner striving for the goal-line.

As to the title, "For Whom Are the Stars?" is a line from the ancient Hawaiian *mele*, or chant, "A Song for Kuali'i." It voices the persistent and often painful question as to who shall control the destiny of a nation—a king, a queen, the people of a certain race, or all those who make that place their home.

IMPORTANT CHARACTERS

LISTED BY CHAPTER IN WHICH THEY FIRST APPEAR

Chapter 1

Royalty

Lili'uokalani, Queen of Hawai'i, 1891–1893

Princes David Kawānanakoa and Jonah Kūhiō Kalaniana'ole, nephews of Kalākaua's queen, Kapi'olani, and by royal proclamation heirs to Hawai'i's throne

Members of Lili'uokalani's last cabinet

John F. Colburn, minister of the interior

William H. Cornwell, minister of finance

Samuel Parker, minister of foreign affairs

Arthur P. Peterson, attorney general

Friends and advisers of Lili'uokalani

Paul Neumann, attorney, former cabinet member

Charles B. Wilson, marshal of the kingdom

Samuel Nowlein, captain of the Queen's Royal Guard

John A. Cummins, retired sugar planter

Joseph O. Carter, clerk, Bishop and Co. bank

Herman Widemann, former cabinet member

Dr. George Trousseau, physician to the royal family

Archibald S. Cleghorn, Lili'uokalani's brother-in-law and father of Princess Ka'iulani

Important Characters

Robert W. Wilcox, leader of the Liberal party, self-styled "professional revolutionist," not always a supporter of the queen

Leaders in establishing the Provisional Government

Sanford Ballard Dole, associate justice of Hawai'i's supreme court, president of the Provisional Government

Lorrin A. Thurston, attorney, member of the monarchy's last legislature, prime mover in the overthrow, later P.G. minister to the United States

Samuel M. Damon, member of the P.G. advisory council, later of the executive council

Henry E. Cooper, member of the P.G. advisory council

William O. Smith, law partner of Lorrin Thurston, member of the executive council

John H. Soper, former marshal of Hawai'i (1890–1891), commander of P.G. military forces

Captain C. W. Ziegler, commander of the Honolulu Rifles

Henry von Werthern, commander of the Drei Hundert

John L. Stevens, United States minister to Hawai'i

Captain G. C. Wiltse, commander of the U.S.S. *Boston*

Chapter 2

James H. Wodehouse, British Commissioner and Consul General in Hawai'i

*Commissioners sent to Washington by the
Provisional Government*

Charles L. Carter, attorney

William R. Castle, attorney

Joseph Marsden, agriculturist

Lorrin A. Thurston (already identified, Chapter 1)

William C. Wilder, president, Wilder Steamship Co.

Commissioners sent to Washington by Lili'uokalani

Paul Neumann (already identified, Chapter 1)

Prince David Kawānanakoa (already identified, Chapter 1)

E. C. Macfarlane, businessman (G. W. Macfarlane & Co.)

Chapter 3

John ʻEna, member of the P.G. advisory council
Clarence W. Ashford, attorney, once a leader in the Reform party, now a royalist
Henry Berger, organizer and director of the Royal Hawaiian Band

Chapter 4

John E. Bush, royalist editor of *Ka Leo*

J. K. Iosepa
J. Kaʻuhane
A. Kauhi
J. H. Waipuʻilani

} members of the kingdom's last legislature who adhered to the Reform party and the Provisional Government

James H. Blount, President Cleveland's special commissioner to investigate the overthrow
William D. Alexander, professor at Oʻahu College (Punahou School)

Chapter 5

Albert S. Willis, U.S. minister to Hawaiʻi, succeeding Blount
Sereno E. Bishop, clergyman, teacher, engineer, diarist, and correspondent
Claus Spreckels, sugar planter, financier, friend of Liliʻuokalani
Rear Admiral J. S. Skerrett, U.S. Naval commander at Honolulu
Admiral John Irwin, successor to Skerrett
Carl Widemann, clerk, finance department

Chapters 7–9

Lt. Col. J. H. Fisher, successor to Soper as commander of the republic's National Guard
Edward G. Hitchcock, marshal of the Republic of Hawaiʻi

Royalists in revolt against the republic

Haole leaders:
Charles T. Gulick, business agent and notary public
William H. Rickard, retired sugar planter from Honokaʻa, Hawaiʻi

William T. Seward, Civil War veteran, "secretary" to John Cummins

Thomas B. Walker, son-in-law of Cummins

Hawaiians and part-Hawaiians:

Henry Bertelmann, contractor and builder

George Townsend, watchman and engineer, Honolulu Fire Department

Charles Warren, first sergeant in King Kalākaua's guard

Lot Lane and others of the Lane family

Robert Haku'ole Sylva

J. W. Bipikāne, hack driver, member of the 1892 legislature

John Li'ili'i Kahoeka and his brother Kaulī, caretakers at Mauna Loke, Waimānalo

Others helping the royalists:

Captain Matthew Martin of the schooner *Wahlberg*

Captain William Davis of the steamer *Waimanalo*

George Lycurgus, owner of Sans Souci hotel at Waikīkī

John Wise, friend of Prince Kūhiō

Carl Widemann (already identified, Chapter 5)

Louis Marshall and William H. G. Greig, friends of Carl Widemann

Chapters 10 and 11

For the republic

Robert Waipā Parker, captain of police

Arthur M. Brown, assistant marshal

Tim Murray, officer in the Citizens' Guard

James B. Castle, member of the Citizens' Guard

Alfred Castle, cousin of James B. Castle

Royalists in the field under Samuel Nowlein and Robert Wilcox

Charles Bartow

Joe Clark

Io'ela Kiakahi

Solomon Kūpihea

Robert Pālau

Important Characters

Tom Poole
Pūkila
Hoa Casabianca Ulukou
William Widdifield

Chapters 12 and 13

For the republic

Albert Francis Judd, chief justice
William Austin Whiting, president of the military commission
William A. Kinney, judge advocate

Royalists on trial
(not already identified)

Volney V. Ashford, brother of Clarence Ashford (Chapter 3)
Charles Clark, guard at Washington Place

PROLOGUE

There are many who want to undo history, to roll back events to a time when they feel things were right. In Hawai'i they long for 1777 (before Captain Cook), for 1818 (when Kamehameha I still ruled), for 1845 (when the king owned all the land), for 1883 (when Kalākaua crowned himself and his queen in a splendid ceremony in front of a new 'Iolani Palace), or for 1892 (the last full year that Hawai'i was a monarchy).

But most of us are forced to admit that history is not a clock that can be set back a decade or a century but one that ticks on relentlessly while we strive to shape an endurable present and mold an acceptable future.

The old-time chant of Kupake'e, translated by Mary Kawena Pukui and quoted by Elizabeth Green Handy, says it well:

> There is no going back; ways now are different. . . .
> Look forward with love for the season ahead of us!
> Let pass the season that is gone!*

*In Handy and Pukui, *The Polynesian Family System in Ka'u, Hawaii* (Wellington, N.Z., 1958), p. 252.

I

That, of course, does not mean that history is useless. History can harm us if it is read with anger and bitterness, if it is viewed as a suit for damages, with the historian as either a prosecuting attorney or a counsel for the defense. And history can hurt us if we let it blur our perception of today's urgent problems or dampen our courage to wrestle with current wrongs.

History, rather, must be read and written with compassion and with awe, with an understanding of man's weaknesses and blundering as well as of his idealism and intense loyalties.

In that spirit it seems right to retell the story of those two heartbreaking years in Hawai'i's life (1893–1895), when history's verdict seemed to hang in the balance, and to recall the exultation and the despair, the hopes and the doubts, the pride and the pain of the days when men whose culture, for more than a century, had had little use for kings and queens contended with those who instinctively revered, cherished, and trusted the highborn. This contest, which ended in the annexation of Hawai'i to the United States in 1898, is a significant part of the story of how Hawai'i has become the Fiftieth State.

Once earlier, in 1854, Hawai'i had stood at the brink of annexation. Then Kamehameha III, perplexed and distraught by the attempts of Frenchmen and Britishers to dominate his little kingdom and by threats of revolution within Hawai'i and of filibustering assaults from California, seriously considered yielding his sovereignty to the United States. He directed his minister of foreign affairs, Robert Crichton Wyllie, to negotiate a treaty with David L. Gregg, American representative. The United States, according to the treaty worked out by these men, was to admit Hawai'i to the Union as a state and make an annual payment of $300,000 to the Hawaiian royalty who would lose their status.

There was opposition from many quarters. British Consul General William Miller strove to convince the king and chiefs that political and social ills were rife in the United States—"slavery, race prejudice, hatred of aristocracy, crime and corruption, vigilantes and lynch law"—in other words, that America was not the noble nation some Hawaiians had come to believe it was.

The heir apparent, Prince Alexander Liholiho, and many other chiefs also tended to think ill of America; and Kamehameha III, who still had faith in the Great Republic, was a dying man.

He had not yet brought himself to sign the treaty prepared by Wyllie and Gregg when his illness suddenly became acute, and his death occurred on December 15, 1854.

Hawai'i remained an independent kingdom, under Kamehameha IV, Kamehameha V, Lunalilo, Kalākaua, and Lili'uokalani, and the trend through these administrations (with the possible exception of Lunalilo's brief reign) was toward a strengthening of royal power and prerogative. But by 1891, when Lili'uokalani came to the throne, the issue was sharply drawn between those persons, mostly foreigners or of foreign parentage, who believed that government was responsible to the people through the legislature, and the queen, who held her cabinet ministers responsible to herself alone. Lili'uokalani admired Queen Victoria, whom she had visited in 1887, and aimed to be like her. But she seems not to have understood that in England the question of governmental responsibility had been settled in Parliament's favor years before, and that the beloved queen reigned but did not rule.

So 1892 was a year of repeated crises, of clashes between the legislature and the monarch, and in January of 1893 the hundred-year-old monarchy was overthrown in a "bloodless revolution."

Much has been written, and very ably, about the crucial reigns of Kalākaua and Lili'uokalani, not so much about the years between the overthrow and annexation, and very little about the attempted counterrevolution in January 1895. Here, then, is that story. It is a sad story, so sad that we could scarcely bear to think about it, did we not know that Lili'uokalani, when annexation was an accomplished fact, declared herself a loyal American and called on her former subjects to do likewise; and that Prince Kūhiō, after traveling far and wide in search of a place where he would rather live, since Hawai'i was so changed, came home to serve his people with distinction in new ways.

Many other Hawaiian patriots in the end accepted history's decree, conquered their bitterness, and found they could sing "The Star-Spangled Banner" almost as fervently as "Hawai'i Pono'i." Somewhat typical, perhaps, of these reconciliations is that of Io'ela Kiakāhi, a leading monarchist in the 1895 counterrevolution, with the pastor and members of his church, who had supported the Republic of Hawai'i.

The Io'ela story as told by his *hānai* daughter, Edith DeMatta,

3

is that one Sunday after long absence from Kawaiahaʻo, Ioʻela, in hostility and defiance, rode his horse straight up the front steps of the old stone church; that unperturbed members, gathering for the service, called out, "E Ioʻela, Aloha!" and invited him to hitch his horse and come in for worship; that Ioʻela, overwhelmed by the cordiality though apologetic that he wore his work clothes rather than his "Sunday best" yielded to their urging, forgot his grudge, and resumed his role as a vigorous but gentle deacon, again and again exhorting the Sunday school youngsters to be proud of their Hawaiian heritage.

On her sixty-second birthday, September 2, 1900, Liliʻuokalani wrote in her diary:

How sad (and yet I gave my consent) to have the old Royal Hawaiian Band who are now the Government U.S. band come and serenade me on this occasion. . . . My consent is the sign of healing over of ill will of all past differences caused by the overthrow of my throne and the deprivation of my people of their rights. Tho for a moment it cost me a pang of pain for my people, it was only momentary, for the present has a hope for the future of my people.

Today, descendants of those on opposite sides at the time of the overthrow join in the restoration of ʻIolani Palace and the reactivation of the Royal Guard. Today Hawaiʻi sensitively refrains from celebrating August 12, that day of mingled joy and desolation when the Hawaiian flag came down and the Stars and Stripes went up over ʻIolani Palace, but makes a festival of Kamehameha Day and observes Kūhiō's birthday as a state holiday.

And today Hawaiʻi sees, perhaps more clearly than many parts of the United States, that the equality proclaimed in America's Declaration of Independence means not only that common folk are as important as kings and queens, but that those whose heritage is Polynesian or Oriental are as precious in the scheme of things as those whose remote ancestors were Anglo-Saxon.

For whom, then, are the stars? Let us hope they are for all Hawaiʻi's people, whatever their ancestry, and especially for those who can remember the bitterest yesterdays with tenderness, because they were able to live through them and "go forward with love for the season ahead."

I. TWILIGHT OF THE MONARCHY

At dusk on January 17, 1893, Liliʻuokalani surrendered the sovereignty of Hawaiʻi. She wrote: "I yield to the superior force of the United States of America. . . . I do under this protest and impelled by said force yield my authority until such time as the United States shall . . . undo the action of its representatives and reinstate me. . . . "

So ended the Hawaiian monarchy, and so closed four days of extreme tension and mild turmoil.

On Saturday, January 14, at noon Liliʻuokalani had prorogued the kingdom's legislature and gone to ʻIolani Palace to proclaim a new constitution. Hundreds of native Hawaiians in gala attire— especially the members of the political association Hui Kālaiʻāina— had gathered to hear the expected proclamation. But the queen's cabinet had refused to endorse the document. In the Blue Room of the palace the four ministers had said a nervous but insistent *no*.

Liliʻuokalani was a woman of determination and independence, yet she felt, apparently, that she must have the approval of her cabinet in abolishing Hawaiʻi's former constitution and substituting one that would increase the power of the Crown. In the closing hours of the 172-day legislative session she had used all her political skill and all her royal influence to rid herself of a cabinet she knew would not agree to the constitutional changes she proposed. Skillfully she had lined up enough votes against the George N. Wilcox cabinet to bring about a vote of no confidence. Then she had appointed men she believed would do her bidding: Samuel Parker, minister of foreign affairs; William H. Cornwell, finance minister; Arthur Peterson, attorney general; and John F. Colburn, minister of the interior.

But on January 14, when she summoned them to endorse the new constitution, she found them opposed—fearful of the political consequences of the move she contemplated. Let the legislature expire quietly, they argued, and leave them in office during the two-year interval before the next biennial session. Eventually, perhaps, there would be a safe time for a new constitution.

The queen could not agree. She showed anger and threatened to denounce them to the assembled populace. But she did not prevail. Two of the ministers scurried downtown to the office of Lorrin Thurston, leader of the opposition party, and asked the handful of politicians gathered there: What shall we do? Shall we resign? No, said the Reformers. We will support you in your opposition to the queen—even to the point of declaring her in revolution and unseating her.

On that Saturday, the people who had gathered on the palace lawn sweated and fidgeted and wondered at the delay. At mid-afternoon Lili'uokalani, now calm but infinitely sad, addressed her subjects from the upper balcony. Speaking in Hawaiian, she dismissed the crowd, telling them "to go with good hope" and not to be troubled; "within the next few days coming," she promised, she would proclaim the new constitution they so earnestly desired.

So the queen had retreated. But the Reform party had not. As Saturday afternoon wore on, angry haoles packed the law office of W. O. Smith, a block down Merchant Street from the palace. There were more of them than could get into the narrow room where discussion seethed, and some waited anxiously in the street

6

for word of decision. Indoors, a paper passed from hand to hand, filling up with the names of those who would fight, if necessary, to prevent the queen's coup d'état.

There were rumors that Lili'uokalani, to gain her ends, would use force, that Marshal Charles B. Wilson already had engaged a number of extra policemen, that the queen had tried to get the Hawaiian leader Robert Wilcox to take charge of the palace artillery. Someone said it might be a good idea to bring the United States marines on shore from the U.S.S. *Boston* before any serious trouble began—"to protect life and property."* Someone else started to draw up a form that the cabinet might sign to request such a troop landing. A third person, more given to parliamentary procedure than the rest, moved the formation of a "committee of public safety" to bring order out of this energetic chaos. The motion carried with a shout.

But, although they appeared unanimous in their exuberance that January afternoon, these men were not of one mind. A few of them—who, like ministers Colburn and Peterson and attorney Paul Neumann, looked strangely out of place in this Reformers' gathering—were thinking only of forcing the queen to retreat. The rest were telling themselves that royalty had defied them once too often, that this must be the final clash that would settle matters for all time. By her attempt against the constitution of 1887, they were saying, Lili'uokalani really had abrogated the monarchy, clearing the way for provisional government and annexation to the United States. They exulted that the queen's favorites, the very cabinet they had so deplored and resented only yesterday, had precipitated the crisis by refusing to do the queen's bidding and now perhaps would take the lead in rallying the community against her.

But Colburn and Peterson had no intention of overthrowing the monarchy. Even after the meeting broke up, leaving a committee of thirteen to supplement enthusiasm with strategy, the ministers thought the chief problem was how to persuade Lili'uokalani to turn back. They knew well her tenacity of purpose. They knew she had pledged herself to accomplish on "another

*Both Great Britain and the United States had for a decade made a practice of keeping warships at Honolulu to protect their citizens in case of trouble.

'Iolani Palace and grounds as seen from the corner of Hotel and Richards streets, 1893.

day" what she had been unable to do today, and that the members of the Hui Kālai'āina—even now enjoying a *lū'au* at the palace— would urge her on to early action. They knew that they, as the ministers who would not sign, were being blamed and berated in a dozen quarters of the town. But they still thought that the irate Reformers would help them put the imp back into the bottle.

How wrong they were Colburn and Peterson saw next morning when the irrepressible Thurston, arriving on horseback, routed them out of their beds at 6:30 to report progress. The Committee of Public Safety, he told them, had declared un- animously that "the solution of the present situation is annexation to the United States." A subcommittee to consider means, es- pecially military means, had met until a late hour at his own house. A host of citizens stood ready to support the cabinet in declaring Lili'uokalani in revolution, the throne vacant, the monarchy abrogated. If the ministers would lead, the committee would back them; otherwise the committee would act alone.

The harassed ministers asked for time to consider and to consult their colleagues. Thurston urged them to act for themselves if Parker and Cornwell held back. He reminded Peterson that he must still have in his pocket the appeal to United States minister John L. Stevens to land the *Boston's* troops; it had been turned over to him yesterday to deliver. Thurston warned once again that the Committee of Public Safety would not delay for their answer, but he told them where they could reach the committee at ten o'clock if they cared to.

All that Sunday, Peterson and Colburn, Cornwell and Parker hurried about Honolulu, asking, "What shall we do?" They called on Marshal Charles B. Wilson and about a dozen other men they considered influential, conservative, and friendly to the queen. Most of these consultants thought a public proclamation by Her Majesty relinquishing her project of a new constitution would satisfy the dissidents. Wilson and one or two others said, "Declare martial law. Arrest those who are planning revolution."

But could the cabinet ministers who just the day before had sought the help of these citizens against the queen now send the marshal to jail them as traitors? Not unless they were willing to be denounced for their change of face and have all their questionable actions of yesterday exposed. Yet theirs was the executive power, and whatever was done to curb the growing threat must bear their signatures. Were he ever so well armed, eager, and confident, the marshal could not move without their directive.

By evening they had convinced themselves that conciliation and appeasement were the better part of patriotism. They drafted a proclamation and had it set in type, so that, as soon as the queen had signed it, hundreds of copies could be run off and distributed. They authorized a mass meeting of loyal citizens at two o'clock on Monday afternoon to counter one that the Committee of Public Safety had called for the same hour. And they sent Parker and Peterson to the American legation to find out what Minister John L. Stevens would do for them if they were faced with an armed revolt against the throne. The messengers reported that the United States minister had told them in his usual blunt fashion that he would do nothing to help "that scoundrel Wilson."

For Lili'uokalani, Sunday was a tense, unhappy day. Charles Wilson had warned her that grave trouble was brewing and had urged her to call in her cabinet and stiffen their will to resist. But she had had enough of the cabinet on Saturday; today she sent for a group of native pastors, seeking to be comforted by their Christian counsel and sustained by their Hawaiian loyalty, but nothing— not prayers nor righteous anger nor elaborate self-justification— banished the cold, clutching fear that numbed her.

It was a relief to have Samuel Parker come in while she was at breakfast on Monday. Of the four ministers, Parker had been the least rebellious. Now he laid before her the printer's proof of the statement she must approve. Her friend J. O. Carter had written it. Her name already stood there in capital letters, followed by the names of the ministers.

Reluctantly she agreed. The short declaration gave assurance that "any changes desired in the fundamental law of the land will be sought only by methods provided in the Constitution itself." Like Kalākaua, the brother she had so often condemned for his weakness, Lili'uokalani had had to retreat. But that this method would check the headlong annexationists seemed doubtful even then; and by noon Charles Wilson, still denied authority to use his police or the government troops, reported that his efforts to talk the Committee of Public Safety out of its revolutionary course were futile. He had forbidden the committee's mass meeting, but he knew full well that words would not stop the gathering.

By two o'clock Palace Square was filled with Hawaiians and part-Hawaiians, and less than two blocks away the armory was packed with haoles. Speakers at the square thanked the queen's followers for their quiet and orderly conduct and exhorted them, in the light of Her Majesty's proclamation, to continue it. The assembly passed with a lusty shout of "'*Ae!*'" resolutions that accepted Her Majesty's pledge and gave "cordial support to the administration."

But in the armory there were resounding noes as speaker after speaker asked, each in his own way, "Shall we believe the queen's promise not to do it again? Shall we accept her retraction?" There were resounding ayes when the vote was taken on the resolutions that "condemned and denounced the action of the queen and her supporters," endorsed the work of the Committee of Safety, and empowered that committee to "devise such ways and means as may be necessary to secure the permanent maintenance of law and order and the protection of life, liberty and property in Hawaii."

Though the words "dethronement," "abrogation," and "annexation" were not spoken publicly, the community, both in and out of the mass meeting, knew what was intended. That morning, while the Committee of Safety met within a stone's throw of the station house, Marshal Wilson had called Lorrin Thurston into the hall to say, "I know what you fellows are up to, and I want you to quit and go home," to which Thurston had answered, "We are not going home, Charlie. . . . Things have advanced too far." And fifteen minutes later Governor Archibald Cleghorn had come to say, "I do not blame you for what you are proposing to do to Liliuokalani, but I wish . . . to have you take into consideration the claim of my daughter, Princess Kaiulani." Thurston had replied with unwonted gentleness, "You know my regard for Kaiulani, Mr. Cleghorn . . . but . . . matters have proceeded too far . . . . We are going to abrogate the monarchy entirely, and nothing can be done to stop us." Cleghorn had bowed his head and gone quietly away.

Since Sunday morning the Committee of Public Safety had been scouting the community to discover what arms and men it could muster. Charlie Carter, dressed "as usual all in white" and mounted on a "tall single-footer, bay with black points," had ridden from house to house like an Island Paul Revere, telling fathers and mothers that their sons would soon "have to show of what stuff they are made." Telephones rang day and night. If anyone, whatever his politics, thought the resolutions adopted at the armory as innocuous as they sounded, he was both deaf and stupid.

Lili'uokalani's friends, who brought to the palace word of the afternoon's events, knew what the resolutions meant, yet they still counseled caution. Perhaps the monarchy could not be saved by concession and compromise as in 1887; even so its partisans must not precipitate bloodshed. So they advised; all but Marshal Wilson, who, raging inwardly, stripped the town of its peacetime patrol to concentrate his forces—regulars, reserves, and volunteers —in the impregnable station house, hoping that soon the cabinet would sanction resistance.

A few minutes before five o'clock Herman Widemann and Dr. George Trousseau brought news to 'Iolani Palace. Finding Lili'uokalani alone in the Blue Room, they described the scene at Brewer's wharf—American marines and bluejackets landing in boats from the *Boston* with artillery, musicians, and hospital corpsmen. On shore they were forming in squads and marching up Fort Street. What did this mean? The queen never for a moment doubted that her enemy Minister Stevens had brought the men ashore to help seize her kingdom. This was what she long had feared from the Americans. But there must be no fighting, no Hawaiian blood vainly spilled. "Tell the people to be quiet," she directed, and her friends went out to counsel peace.

Hearing the drums, Lili'uokalani stepped out to the balcony and saw the sailors coming along Merchant Street. In the center of town some marines had been detached, one squad being assigned to guard the American consulate, another sent up Nu'uanu Avenue to the legation. The rest of the battalion paraded through Palace Square into King Street, giving Her Majesty, as they passed, a royal marching salute—arms port, colors drooped, a ruffle on the drums.

Late that evening, after camping uncomfortably on the J. B. Atherton lawn for several hours, the men went into quarters at Arion Hall, *makai* (toward the ocean) of the opera house and ʻ*ewa* (west, toward ʻEwa) of Aliʻiōlani Hale. Landed by order of Captain Wiltse, who twice had gone on shore himself to size up the situation before acting on Minister Stevens' advice and his own confidential instructions from the Navy Department, the battalion was charged with protecting the United States legation and "the lives and property of American citizens," and assisting in the preservation of public order. They were not to take sides in the brewing conflict, their officers had been instructed, but to deal firmly with arson or robbery or violence in dark streets and out-of-the-way hedgerows. So the officers pored over the Honolulu maps that Minister Stevens with difficulty procured for them, marking those areas where Americans lived. The fire patrol stood ready for action, and the guards cocked their ears for alarms. What they heard, however, was the Royal Hawaiian Band, finishing the moonlight concert in the hotel grounds two blocks away, where Honoluluans, native and haole,★ strolled and flirted, gossiped and applauded just as they had on any other bright, sweet-scented evening.

There were many to testify afterward that the town was quiet that night, even though at a late hour some hoodlums burned up the arbor in Emma Square. But here and there within the placid houses there was turmoil of spirit. It was one of those nights when sleepless men toss under their mosquito nets or pace their verandas, forced to choose, as paths part forever, which way they will go. On this night Judge Sanford Ballard Dole, who believed passionately in wise and stable government, yet was loath to end the Hawaiian monarchy, would decide to resign from the supreme court and accept leadership and high office in the movement

★ In this book most Hawaiian words are italicized. A few are not—those like haole (Caucasian), poi, hula, and lei, which occur so frequently and are so familiar as to be truly a part of the English language.

toward annexation. John H. Soper, a man of limited military experience, with grave doubts about the whole action, would decide to become commander-in-chief of the revolutionary forces —that is, if his friend Judge Dole took the presidency. Samuel M. Damon, a man of gentleness and goodwill and a close friend of the queen, would decide to go into the advisory council and participate in the dethronement.

Joseph O. Carter, uncle of the fiery Charlie, would choose, despite family ties, to remain the queen's firm supporter and trusted adviser. John A. Cummins, who frequently had been counted a Reformer in politics, would decide to be loyal to the Hawaiian part of himself and to his *ali'i*, his chiefs. Robert Wilcox, who in the last six years had been for and against Lili'uokalani, for and against the Reform party, for and against annexation, yet always enamored of revolution, would decide to remain neutral until he saw how this thing was going to come out.

Henry von Werthern, who cared nothing for either Reform or royalty so long as he could relieve the unemployment and poverty of his fellow Germans in the organization known as the Drei Hundert, having been sought by both sides, would choose for himself and his shooting club the haoles' bread and butter rather than the monarchy's poi. And United States Minister Stevens, an ardent expansionist, an experienced and conscientious diplomat, who had been beset for two days by calls for help from both parties and had approved Captain Wiltse's decision to land the troops, must decide just what to require of a new government before recognizing it as de facto.

As for Lorrin Thurston, when he got home just before dusk on Monday afternoon, he collapsed and sent for a doctor. An attack of grippe before Christmas had left him in no condition to cope with the constant strenuous exertion since Saturday. Ironically, though he would compose the proclamation of the new order and dictate it from his sickbed to his law clerk, the prime mover of the overthrow would not be present at the simple ceremony next day by which the Provisional Government superseded the Kingdom of Hawai'i.

If Lili'uokalani had succeeded in promulgating her constitution, it would have been Hawai'i's fifth. Kamehameha III and his chiefs gave the kingdom its first one in 1840, and a remarkably liberal and well-designed document it was. But by 1852 legislation and custom had made the 1840 instrument "distinctly out of date." A commission appointed by the king (Dr. Gerrit P. Judd, a former missionary; John 'Ī'ī, a Hawaiian leader; and Judge William Lee, a nonmissionary American) drafted a new one. Extensively amended by both houses of the legislature—the Nobles and the House of Representatives—it was signed by Kamehameha III on June 14, 1852.

Kamehameha IV, on taking office, paid tribute to his predecessor in these words: "He gave us a Constitution and fixed laws; he secured the people in the title to their lands, and removed the last chain of oppression. He gave them a voice in his councils and in the making of the laws by which they are governed."

But Kamehameha IV did not live easily with the constitution of 1852. Repeatedly during his reign attempts were made to alter its provisions. A part of the contention centered around the unrestricted manhood suffrage granted in 1840 and retained in 1852. In August 1862, two of the king's ministers, Robert Crichton Wyllie and David L. Gregg, in a minority report in regard to some proposed amendments, said: "The present Constitution is a failure. It does not meet the necessities of the people, or the wants of the country. . . . While it professes to recognize the principles of a Constitutional Monarchy, it attempts to sanction the most radical ideas of Democracy." Even so, the constitution of 1852, with only minor changes, lasted twelve years.

When Prince Lot came to the throne in November 1863 as Kamehameha V, he would not take an oath to support the constitution of 1852. Instead, he called for a convention "for the purpose of consulting on the revision of the Constitution of our Kingdom." When the convention deadlocked, the king dismissed the delegates and, on August 20, 1864, signed and promulgated a constitution embodying his own ideas. The most drastic change from the constitution of 1852 was the institution of property qualifications for representatives and for voters. It was decreed at this time, too, that the nobles and representatives of the people should sit together in one chamber and be known collectively as the legislative assembly, an arrangement that made for firmer royal control.

Early in the reign of Kalākaua, in 1874, an amendment, adopted by the legislature in accord with provisions in the constitution itself, removed the property qualification for voters. Kalākaua's critics complained that the king, from this point on, exercised control of the enlarged electorate by the distribution of free liquor at election time and by the presence of his soldiers and often of himself at the polls to overawe voters. This and other complaints against the king led eventually to the "revolution" of 1887. Reform-minded citizens of Honolulu, largely haoles, demanded that the king dismiss Walter Murray Gibson as prime minister, accept a new cabinet recommended by the so-called reformers, and sign a constitution embodying "reform" principles. The constitution, drafted in a few days by a small committee working round the clock, was presented to Kalākaua on the afternoon of July 6. He signed it that evening.

This document corrected a number of abuses that the constitution of 1864 had permitted. By it, as one of its authors put it, the king was "reduced from the status of an autocrat to that of a constitutional Sovereign." Ironically, one of the provisions most resented by many of the Hawaiian people was the restoration of what both Kamehameha IV and Kamehameha V had advocated, namely, the property qualification for voters.

Lili'uokalani was in England, attending Queen Victoria's Diamond Jubilee, when the 1887 revolution took place. Then and after her return to Hawai'i she criticized her brother for yielding to haole demands. When she came to the throne in 1891, she took the prescribed oath to support the constitution, but it cannot have been long before she regretted having done so. In *Hawaii's Story by Hawaii's Queen*, published in 1898, she mentions the names of several of her friends and advisers who proposed that she give the kingdom a new constitution. Later, *Hawaii's Story* relates, petitions began to pour in through the Hui Kālai'āina. "It was estimated by those in position to know", the queen wrote, "that out of a possible nine thousand five hundred registered voters, six thousand five hundred, or two thirds, had signed these petitions. No true

Hawaiian chief would have done other than to promise a consideration of their wishes."

The proposed new constitution consisted of parts cut from the constitution of 1864, attached to mutilated pages of the 1887 document, which the queen and many others scornfully called "the Bayonet Constitution." New provisions were written in at the suggestion of Charles B. Wilson, Samuel Nowlein, Joseph Nawahī, and William White. On January 14, 1893, a neatly prepared copy was given to the Hui Kālai'āina for its leader to carry in a ribbon-tied parcel to the ceremony of promulgation.

If successfully promulgated, the consitution of 1893 would have given the sovereign the power to appoint members of the House of Nobles for life, to dismiss cabinets at will without having to secure a vote of no confidence by the legislature, and to make executive decisions without the "advice and consent" of the cabinet. It would have abolished the property qualification for voters and done away with the curious custom of "denization," which gave the vote to male residents of Hawai'i without requiring them to be naturalized. Also it would have limited the term of supreme court justices, formerly appointed for life, to a mere six years. Thus the queen sought to increase her own power and that of the native people, while clipping the wings of the haoles.

Haole residents—Hawai'i-born, naturalized, or merely "denizens"—recalling the Kalākaua years and the agonizing conflicts of 1892, believed that such a constiution—and they knew all too well what it contained—must not be allowed to become the basic law of Hawai'i. And so the battle lines were drawn, and men took desperate and determined measures for what they thought was right.

It was on Monday evening, after she had seen the American marines march past the palace, that Lili'uokalani made the hard decision: to yield and avert bloodshed. Her personal motto was *'Onipa'a* (steadfast), and she had tried to live up to it throughout her public life. But certain childhood memories drove her to compromise. In 1843 at the age of five she had witnessed the restoration of Hawaiian sovereignty by British Admiral Richard

Thomas. Then right had prevailed, and she believed it would again.

On July 31, 1843, history records, Admiral Thomas summoned to a spot on the dusty plain east of Honolulu the soldiers and chiefs and people to watch the lowering of the Union Jack, which had flown over the Islands for a little more than five months, and the raising of the Hawaiian ensign. England had repudiated Lord George Paulet's seizure of the kingdom in February and now was restoring the sovereignty to the young king, Kamehameha III.

The ceremonies were unforgettable. Early rain had laid the dust, but by ten o'clock the weather had cleared and the jubilant crowd had gathered. Three fieldpieces fired seven guns apiece, combining to offer a royal salute to the Hawaiian flag. Three vessels in the harbor shot off twenty-one guns each, and the two forts, one at the shore and one on Punchbowl, saluted likewise. English soldiers performed symbolic maneuvers, showing humility and acceptance of defeat. "Rebel" Hawaiian soldiers, who for five months had of necessity obeyed Paulet, went to the king's house to receive forgiveness, to kiss the monarch's hand, and to swear anew their allegiance.

Missionary E. O. Hall had composed a "Restoration Anthem," and later in the day the children from the Chiefs' Children's School gathered with a large group of foreigners and chiefs to sing it at the top of their lungs. Next day there was a dinner at the king's residence, where "thousands of natives" dined and celebrated. Most impressive of all, perhaps, was the thanksgiving service at the stone church, when the young king spoke the memorable words, *Ua mau ke ea o ka ʻāina i ka pono* (The life of the land is perpetuated by righteousness). The little girl who attended all these festivities in the company of her teachers, Amos Starr Cooke and his wife, Juliette Montague Cooke, and of some sixteen other royal children, members of the school, could never forget a single detail, especially since year after year on the anniversary of Restoration Day the wonderful story was retold.

When artesian water became available for sprinkling lawns and nourishing greenery, the arid spot where the flag had been raised in 1843 was converted into a handsome park and named Thomas Square. The words Kamehameha III had spoken in the stone church became the motto of the kingdom, to be graven on cornerstones and memorial plaques.

Righteousness in 1843 had meant official patience, devout prayer, and trust in God. Now, fifty years later, did it not mean the same? The queen decided that it did.

The monarchy came to an end at half past two on January 17. On the steps of Ali'iōlani Hale, the government building across from the palace, Henry Cooper read the proclamation, his hand shaking, his voice steady. The document reviewed twenty years of conflict between the Crown and "the people"; it declared the "Hawaiian Monarchical system of government" at an end and a Provisional Government established "for the control and management of public peace . . . to exist until terms of union with the United States of America have been . . . agreed upon;" it listed an executive council of four and an advisory council of fourteen; and it asked all government officers except the queen, her cabinet, and her marshal "to continue to exercise their functions and perform their duties."

There were many words and few to hear them. The founders of the new state had walked unarmed and unnoticed through the streets to take possession of an almost deserted building. In the offices a few subordinates were at their desks, and the chief clerk of the Interior Department surrendered formally to Mr. Cooper's demand. Royalist Charles McCarthy, detailed by the government to oppose the revolutionists, waiting in vain for the government soldiers the marshal had promised him, could only shrug and turn away. But for the moment the new government, too, was without military support; it had appointed three o'clock as the hour of rendezvous at Ali'iōlani, and not until Henry Cooper was reading the preamble did its troops start arriving from the armory on the double. These were largely the old haole rifle companies from the turbulent days of Kalākaua. Long since disbanded, they nevertheless responded with alacrity to the call of their former officers. By the time the reading was finished, thirty of the Drei Hundert (so called though there never were three

Ali'iōlani Hale and Music Hall, from 'Iolani Palace, early 1890s.

hundred in the club) had formed in the front yard, and soon the new government had a guard of sorts around its headquarters.

But the only shot of the revolution had already been fired. At the corner of King and Fort streets, a little after two o'clock, a wagonload of guns had been in transit from E. O. Hall's hardware store to the armory. A native patrolman, one of a group watching the intersection, put his hand on the horse's bridle and ordered the driver to stop. John Good, the guard atop the load, shot the policeman through the shoulder. While fellow officers turned to help the wounded man, the wagon rattled away toward its destination as if the devil were after it. In a hack, seized without formalities, two policemen gave chase. At the corner of Beretania and Punchbowl streets they encountered a rifle company on its way to the government building. Captain Ziegler quickly deployed his men across the street between the pursuers and their prey and so prevented the capture of Captain Good and the guns.

Back at Hall's corner a crowd had gathered. Good's patrol shot had called terrified citizens and nervous policemen from all directions to gape at Leialoha's bloody shoulder, as his officer friends helped him toward the station house. Shutters banged into place as merchants and mechanics closed their places of business, expecting momentarily to see Honolulu erupt with warfare. So Queen Street and Merchant were deserted as, a little ahead of schedule but grateful for the diversion, the handful of revolutionists advanced on the seat of government, armed only with their firm purpose and their proclamation.

After that, things happened so fast that no one could be sure later of their exact timing or sequence. Messages flew back and forth among the government building, the station house, the palace, the legation, and Arion Hall in an intricate pattern, tending toward one result—the establishment of the Provisional Government without fighting.

Lili'uokalani, when the news of the coup had been carried to her, sent for Paul Neumann, E. C. Macfarlane, Herman Widemann, Archibald Cleghorn, J. O. Carter, and the young princes, David Kawānanakoa and Jonah Kūhiō Kalaniana'ole. In the Blue Room they sat around the table, where three days before the queen had demanded angrily that her ministers sign the new constitution. Now she seemed calm and relaxed, a little weary, and willing to be advised.

Much later the cabinet came, fresh from a conference with Sanford Dole and his colleagues at their headquarters, and with them Samuel Damon to represent the Provisional Government. Marshal Wilson, the ministers said, still wanted to fight; but because the United States troops doubtless would take a hand if fighting broke out, and because Mr. Stevens had already recognized the new government, they thought the queen would do well to "resign under protest."

The others were of the same mind. Let there be no useless bloodshed. To the filing of a protest Samuel Damon raised no objection. E. C. Macfarlane had said to him at the station house an hour or so earlier, "I know such a protest does not amount to anything, but still . . . you had better accept it." Later a jubilant council member at Ali'iōlani Hale had said, "Let them protest all they want to, just so they give up." But in the thoughts of the queen the events of 1843 were uppermost. To her the surrender must be "under protest" and temporary.

It was agreed. Paul Neumann began drafting the statement as the meeting broke up, and the cabinet waited to carry it to the new government. Words came easily to Neumann, and the words he put together in the early lamplight of January 17 proved to be potent ones—more potent, possibly, than he could foresee.

At his new headquarters Sanford Dole took the fateful paper from the hand of W. H. Cornwell with the remark, "Here is a statement which they wish to file, and I see no objection to acknowledging its receipt." Then he wrote on the back, "Received from the hands of the late cabinet, this 17th day of January, 1893." The surrender crowned with success a desperate gamble. It brought the first moment of relief after hours of almost unbearable tension. Its precise wording, then, seemed unimportant.

But did the Provisional Government mean to concede that the American naval forces had overpowered the monarchy? or that the establishment of the Provisional Government was an act of United States Minister Stevens? or that the United States was to be invited to arbitrate the dispute? Thousands of words of testimony bearing on the implications of Paul Neumann's phrases would be taken thereafter in Honolulu and in Washington, to be studied by an American president, a secretary of state, and a senate, for whom the fate of Hawai'i would become a major political issue.

Lili'uokalani, writing in her diary under the date of January 17, gave credit to her long-time friend Samuel Damon for the leniency of her foes. She noted that she had given up the government at a quarter to six, "but under protest." She added: "Things turned out better than I expected."

At Ali'iolani Hale everything was purposeful turmoil. Throughout the afternoon there had been a steady influx of volunteers—businessmen who had closed up shop precipitately when they heard the shot or got word by telephone, teachers from Punahou and Kamehameha schools, eighteen-year-olds whose parents thought them safely at home, middle-aged veterans who had done their first fighting thirty years before at Antietam or Chancellorsville. Former Honolulu Rifles in their dark blue uniforms and caps mingled with civilian-garbed recruits, marked as soldiers only by the Springfields or Winchesters they carried on their shoulders. Company commanders lined up their rapidly increasing units in the halls or on the grounds, put them through the manual of arms, assigned them to the battle stations they were to take if an attack came, and kept sentries posted at the six gates.

In the legislative chamber, where they would sleep on the floor if they slept at all, the rank and file smoked, swapped news and stories, and tried not to think about the Austrian fieldpieces in the palace grounds across the way, their muzzles pointed toward the government building. Bales of horse blankets arrived, and cases of hardtack and tinned corned beef; then, most cheering of all, a huge urn of coffee from Nolte's saloon. Some of the youngsters could not eat or, having eaten, rushed out to puke into the gutter in a dark corner of the lanai. No one mentioned the *Boston*'s sailors, camped within a stone's throw. Except for sentries, they kept out of sight, the yard of Arion Hall being on the side away from Ali'iolani. There was plenty of talk, though, about Captain Nowlein's Household Guards at the barracks and Marshal Wilson's men at the station house. Part of old Rifles Company A had gone with the royalists, and their onetime cronies knew well enough what tough and determined fighters they might be pitted against.

After dark, when the waiting had grown hard to bear, a Punahou teacher and some of his former pupils began to sing—at first the placid, gentlemanly "Stars of the Summer Night"; then, joined by others, the mildly rowdy "Solomon Levi"; and after that "Mine Eyes Have Seen the Glory . . ." An old man named Rhodes, "who grew roses in Manoa Valley," jumped on a chair and held up his hand for attention. There was a time, he said, when they had sung that song, sitting around a campfire in Virginia, and then the next camp took it up, and then the next down the line, farther than they could see, until they were sure the whole Army of the Potomac was shouting, "Glory, glory, hallelujah!" The voices in Ali'iōlani Hale swung into the chorus again. But the walls of that building are thick, and none of the *Boston*'s bluejackets caught so much as an echo. For "My Country 'Tis of Thee" they stood up and pulled off their hats. Many were choking now and winking back the tears. They had got through the first "verse" when an orderly rushed in from Colonel John H. Soper's headquarters. "Stop your damn noise," he yelled. "The queen has surrendered. Orders are to keep quiet."

A few minutes later a detachment from Company A marched to the station house. Marshal Wilson dismissed his men with a quiet little speech and turned over the guns and ammunition to Commander-in-Chief Soper of the Provisional Government.

When the Provisional Government was two days old, Sanford Dole wrote to his brother George, in California, thoughts he could not confess to his colleagues in Honolulu:

It was with extreme reluctance that I accepted the responsible position which has been accorded me in the new government, and which places me at its head, but the pressure upon me was so strong and in all ways unanimous that it seemed a call to duty I could not disobey.

How I have regretted this whole affair, had I my way about the matter I would have used far more tactful ways than the treatment we have thus rendered. I have reiterated time and again my desire that we hold the power of the throne in a trust . . . in the name of the young princess Kaiulani . . . until she reaches her majority. . . .

I am sorry to say this plan has not met with approval, for all seem to feel that we must be rid of this vile curse of the monarchy forever. I regret that this must be so . . . and I hope that history will bear with us and not be critical for we have done what we know to be right and we are but men. . . .

2. ANNEXATION OR NO?

Two days after the overthrow Lorrin Thurston rose from his sickbed and, taking with him his personal physician, joined four other commissioners—William R. Castle, William C. Wilder, Charles L. Carter, and Joseph Marsden—on the chartered steamer *Claudine*, bound for San Francisco and thence for Washington, D.C. to negotiate a treaty of annexation.

They anchored off San Francisco at 1:00 A.M. on January 27, and Thurston, never one to lose time, went ashore in the harbor boat and hired a boy he found "loafing in the pilot office" to take their dispatches to the morning papers. He himself rang up the *Examiner*, told the news in one sentence, and was gratified to hear a commanding shout: "Stop those presses!"

"It has proved a genuine sensation," William R. Castle wrote afterward. "We are overwhelmed with reporters and telegrams of congratulations."

The San Francisco Chamber of Commerce, meeting that day, passed a resolution favoring the annexation of Hawai'i. At the

Palace Hotel two of the commissioners quickly assembled a dozen important and influential men, including former Hawai'i residents Claus Spreckels, the "sugar king," and Charles Reed Bishop, widower of Princess Bernice Pauahi, to lay news and hopes before them. Spreckels, who in the Kalākaua reign had loomed large in Hawaiian politics, took the floor, so Castle reported, to declare that without his assistance and that of the sugar trust annexation would surely fail, but that he would go in his private railway car to Washington and there bring it to pass—a promise that he did not, however, fulfill.

As the commissioners sped by train across the continent, reporters came aboard at all important stops. On the crowded bus that transferred them from the Northwestern to the Pennsylvania Station in Chicago they had newsmen "sitting in their laps" and "hanging to straps," taking eager notes. They began to see the daily papers and to find them full of the Hawaiian crisis, most of them speaking out in favor of annexation. Atop Wormley's hotel in Washington, D.C., a Hawaiian flag waved in the breeze to welcome them.

On February 4, the day after their arrival at the capital, they had their first interview with Secretary of State John W. Foster, who impressed them as "straightforward and honest" and as favorable to their mission.

All of this was no surprise. It conformed to the predictions that Lorrin Thurston had made almost a year before. Then he had visited Washington as the representative of the small, largely secret, Annexation Club of Honolulu, a group of men who believed that Hawai'i's future lay with the United States and who felt sure that the time was not far distant when Caucasian Hawaiians would end the "corrupt" monarchy and seek annexation. Thurston had been commissioned in the spring of 1892 to get an answer to the question, What would be the response of the government in Washington if Hawai'i came asking admission, either as a state or as a territory, to the great American union?

"If conditions in Hawaii compel you people to act as you have indicated, and you come to Washington with an annexation proposition, you will find an exceedingly sympathetic administration here." This is the message Thurston brought when he

27

arrived back in Honolulu on June 4. He had not seen President Benjamin Harrison, but he had talked with Senator Cushman K. Davis, a member of the Senate Committee on Foreign Relations; with Representative James H. Blount, chairman of the House Committee on Foreign Affairs; with Secretary of the Navy B. F. Tracy; and with Secretary of State James G. Blaine. It was Tracy who had brought him the encouraging message from the president.

Secretary Blaine was ill and unable to keep a second appointment he had made with Thurston. To that fact history owes the seven-page letter dated San Francisco, May 27, 1892, in which Thurston, on his way home, spelled out his thoughts about annexation. Stable government, Thurston told Blaine, was the foremost desire of the "substantial people having at heart the permanent welfare and progress of the islands." And stable government, he believed, could not be had under a native monarchy; in fact, it could be had only by "union in some form with the United States or England." "Every interest," he wrote, "political, commercial, financial and previous friendship points in the direction of the United States; but . . . a union with England would be preferable to a continuance under existing circumstances."

Thurston then outlined the means he thought could be used to bring matters to a head, provided the United States was in a responsive mood. In winning over the common natives he predicted there would be no great difficulty. Some of their leaders already favored annexation—in part because they were out of favor with the queen, and in part because under annexation they anticipated that manhood suffrage would replace the existing property restrictions. (This doubtless was a reference to Robert Wilcox and John E. Bush, though their views were not nearly so clear and consistent as Thurston represented them to be.) By working through these leaders and by holding out to the common people the hope of economic betterment as a result of annexation, Thurston believed a majority of the native people could be won over.

In the course of the next few months he hoped to secure the appointment at the Islands of a cabinet "committed to annexation," proceed with the "education" of the Hawaiians, win "the adhesion of as many native leaders as possible," and have the legislature adjourn in August or September instead of being prorogued. This maneuver would allow the House to reconvene on its own volition without being called into extra session by the queen. Then, when the time was ripe—perhaps in December when the American Congress had expressed itself in favor of annexation—Thurston proposed either to submit the question to the Hawaiian people in a general election or to take action in the reassembled legislature.

Long afterward, in writing about the Annexation Club of 1892, Thurston said, "Our object was not to promote annexation, but to be ready to act quickly and intelligently, should Liliuokalani precipitate the necessity by some move against the constitution, tending to revert to absolutism or anything of that nature." By the time he wrote these words he seems to have forgotten the plan of action he had outlined to Secretary Blaine—a plan no important detail of which he was able to carry out. So little did this *kamaʻāina* —this "child of the land," born and bred in the Islands—understand the hearts of the Hawaiians, and so firmly did he believe that union with the United States was Hawaiʻi's destiny and a priceless privilege, that a bit of encouragement in Washington had sent him off into a dream world where peaceful change, motivated by "hope of economic betterment" and accomplished with general goodwill, would solve everything.

Thurston's dream faded quickly after his return. By the end of the summer of 1892 it was blurred beyond recognition. But while the details of his plan lay forgotten in State Department files, the object of the trip to Washington was no secret from any of the interested parties in Honolulu. For royalists it was a threatening shadow that hung over the last and longest legislative session of the Kingdom of Hawaiʻi; for those who believed in annexation the messages Thurston had brought home in 1892 were heartening and reassuring.

By early 1893 the situation at the United States capital had changed radically. In November, Republican Benjamin Harrison, seeking reelection to the presidency, had been defeated by Democrat Grover Cleveland, who would take office on March 4, 1893. Negotiations for annexation had now to be conducted with a lame-duck secretary of state and, when concluded, submitted to a lame-duck Senate for ratification. Under the circumstances

Thurston and his colleagues thought it advisable to make many concessions.

When the commissioners expressed their desire to have Hawai'i annexed as a state, Secretary Foster advised that the immediate agreement deal only with the fact of annexation and not with the form of the prospective government. Other matters, such as the obligation of the United States to lay a cable to Hawai'i and to dredge and develop Pearl Harbor, were likewise reluctantly omitted from the draft. The treaty contained no guarantee that the system of contract labor, so important to the sugar industry in Hawai'i, would be allowed to continue or that the bounty being paid to United States sugar growers would be granted to those in Hawai'i. "We all agree," Castle wrote in his day-to-day account, "to the short and concise treaty necessary to get action by the Senate." Once the Islands were annexed, Secretary Foster assured the commissioners, Hawai'i would be treated as an integral part of the nation, entitled to have its special problems carefully and deliberately considered by Congress and the administration.

So the commissioners and the secretary signed the treaty—a hand-written document as protocol required—inscribed on blue-ruled and blue-bordered paper, and on February 15 President Harrison sent it to the Senate with his recommendation that it be speedily ratified.

Only now did the commissioners' euphoria begin to vanish. More and more antiannexation sentiment started to appear in the press. More and more voices were saying that the men from Hawai'i had "stolen" the country they were offering to the United States. Other voices cried out that the whole thing was a "job" put up by the sugar trust, to get a bounty for Hawaiian growers. Moreover, the Senate found itself in no mood for action. Democratic members began to hear from President-Elect Cleveland that he wished them to delay.

The commissioners, who once had envisioned themselves returning triumphantly in a body to announce the "good news," drifted home, one by one or two by two, to admit to their colleagues in the Provisional Government that the day of annexation seemed a long way off. Much as they hated to admit it, they were forced to recognize that the change in attitude of the American press and people had resulted, at least to some degree, from the effective presentation of the queen's case by her chosen commissioners.

To send her own commissioners to America, Liliʻuokalani mortgaged her three homes—Hamohamo at Waikīkī, Muʻulaulani at Pālama, and Washington Place—to the Bishop Bank for a total of $10,000, and cashed the postal savings accounts of her two little wards, Kaipo and ʻAimoku. She was not the reckless spendthrift her brother Kalākaua had been, but she was always generous in her charities, lavish in her entertaining, and, her opponents said, unstinting in her use of money to gain her political ends. January 17 had found her in debt and without ready cash; but Samuel Damon, vice-president of the bank, arranged the loan.

For her delicate errand she chose Paul Neumann, as a haole unexcelled in legal acumen, and Prince David Kawānanakoa, as a youthful and winsome member of the house of Kalākaua. Her letter to President Harrison, dated January 18, taken by the *Claudine*, had begged him to defer action on the Hawaiian question until "a statement of the true facts" could be laid before him, and then to "judge uprightly and justly" between herself and her enemies. She had asked for passage for her envoys on the *Claudine*; but, since the Provisional Government had said no, she had had to dispatch them by the *Australia*'s regular sailing on February 2.

It was not so much from the Republican president that she hoped for consideration as from the Democratic president-elect, who would take office on March 4. In 1887, on her way to England, Liliʻuokalani had been entertained at the White House. Remembering that gracious occasion, she felt that Grover Cleveland, now elected for a second, noncontiguous term, was truly the "great and good friend" who would intercede for her. Her letter to him was one of the papers Paul Neumann carried. Another, more important, was Neumann's own précis, as he called it, of the case against the United States minister. This, with its charges of collusion between Stevens and the "revolutionists" and its thesis that without the *Boston*'s troops there would have been no overthrow, was to become in the months ahead the basic document for anti-expansionists on the mainland and royalists in the Islands in their campaign to defeat annexation.

Neumann, however, talked very plainly to his client. Her

chances of restoration, he said, were hardly worth mentioning. He would do what he could for her in that direction, but he must go armed with power of attorney to relinquish her claims in return for the best financial settlement he could get for her and for Ka'iulani. He drew up the document and the queen signed it. Later, according to her diary, she wrote him not to use it.

By the *Australia*, Lili'uokalani had sent out still another appeal. Addressed, through British Commissioner James H. Wodehouse to "Her Most Gracious Majesty, Victoria, Queen of Great Britain and Ireland and Empress of India," it read:

> In reliance upon the friendship so often expressed by You for myself, my house and my people, I prefer my present entreaty for Your mediation. . . . I can assure Your Majesty that the movement against me is not supported by my people. . . . I have sent a commission to Washington to obtain redress . . . and beg that You and Your government grant me Your friendly intercession.

The answer, Lili'uokalani directed, was to be sent to Sir Julian Pauncefote, British minister in Washington, so that "Mr. Neumann . . . might become acquainted with its contents while there." In due time the British Foreign Office informed Major Wodehouse that "the Queen has opened the Queen of Hawaii's letter and returned it without comment." The official reply, when it came, said simply that Her British Majesty had "referred it to her advisers." And there the matter ended.

With Paul Neumann and Prince David on their mission to the United States went E. C. Macfarlane, former cabinet minister and special friend and associate of Princess Ka'iulani's father, Archibald Cleghorn. Some royalists thought that Macfarlane went primarily to present the princess' claims to succeed her aunt, and this may well have been the case, since Cleghorn, who contributed largely to the cost of sending Macfarlane, had little patience with the deposed queen.

"I have never given the Queen anything but good advice," Cleghorn wrote on January 28, 1893, to his daughter, at school in England. ". . . if she had followed my advice she would have been firm on her Throne and Hawaiian Independence safe, but she has turned out a very stubborn woman and was not satisfied to reign but wanted to rule. If she had followed in the example set her by Victoria, she would have been respected by all good people."

Again he insisted in a letter dated February 8: "I cannot make her out. She has no one to blame but herself for the loss of the monarchy. She might have been firm on her throne if she had left a good cabinet alone, and she had a good strong one with [George N.] Wilcox, [Peter C.] Jones, Mark K. Robinson, and Cecil Brown."

And on March 9 he wrote, "We *cannot have any more Legislatures like the last* and we must have good ministers. I am afraid if your Aunt goes back the same trouble would come again."

Cleghorn and some of Lili'uokalani's other critics would doubtless have better understood her behavior during the long legislative session of 1892 if they had been able to read her private journal, available today in the library of the Bishop Museum. It reveals much of what lay back of her political maneuvering in the last months of her reign, especially her unfortunate involvement in the "lottery question."

In *Hawaii's Story by Hawaii's Queen*, Lili'uokalani, in a chapter titled "The Crimes I am Charged Withal," defends her signing of the lottery act in January 1893, on the ground that she had no choice. The constitution of 1887, she maintains, granted the sovereign no veto power, but this was not the case. Article 48 of the much-resented constitution provided for the return of a bill to the legislature with stated objections if the monarch disapproved the act, and for the passage of a bill over a veto by a two-thirds vote if the legislature was so disposed. Article 48 also provided:

If any Bill shall not be returned by the King (sovereign) within ten days (Sundays excepted) after it shall have been presented to him, the same shall be a law in like manner as if he had signed it, *unless the Legislature by their adjournment prevents its return, in which case it shall not be a law.* [italics added]

The lottery bill of 1893 was passed on January 11, only three days before the date set for prorogation. If Lili'uokalani had not liked the bill, she had only to hold it until after January 14, and it would not have become law.

In the same chapter in her book the queen refers to a supreme court opinion in Kalākaua's reign that the king could not refuse to sign a measure unanimously recommended by his cabinet. She thus implies that her signature was forced by her ministers. But the G. N. Wilcox cabinet, still in office when the lottery bill was passed, was emphatically opposed to the measure and would not for one minute have pressed Liliʻuokalani to approve it. Many voices called for a veto. A group of church women that included Juliette Cooke, Liliʻuokalani's teacher at the Chiefs' Children's School almost half a century before, visited the queen to tell her that they were counting on her to say no to the lottery. Liliʻuokalani was gracious and spoke with special tenderness to her life-long friend Mrs. Cooke. But she promised only to do what seemed to her to be right. And what she did was to sign the bill. The reason for this action is to be found, not in her book, but in her journal. For months she had been under pressure, not only from some of her subjects, but, in a devious way, from the lottery promoters themselves.

The lottery story, so far as Liliʻuokalani is concerned, began on July 7, 1892. That was the night of Her Majesty's ball for the members of the legislature. After the dancing was over—the lancers, waltzes, polkas, gallops, and a minuet—and the "tasty and bounteous supper" had been served in the state dining room, she retired, so the journal says, to her bedroom "at 1:30 o'clock." At two, Miss W____ brought her cards.

This is not the first time the journal speaks of the queen's German teacher, Fräulein Wolf, who by shuffling and drawing from the pack could, so she asserted, read the past and predict the future, but it is the first time the medium's cards revealed anything about the lottery.

She told me that at ten next morning [that would be July 8, the day the entry was written] a gentleman will call on me with a bundle of papers where it would bring lots of money across the water.... She says I must have the House accept it, it would bring [$] 1,000,000.

Fräulein's cards went further. They advised the queen about cabinet choosing. Although the Samuel Parker cabinet, then in office, bade fair to remain so for some time, Fräulein suggested several replacements, using only initials and leaving the queen to identify the men referred to. Three of these Liliʻuokalani was not to appoint; they "wanted to snatch the crown from her head." From among five others four might be selected, for

. . . they will make a good cabinet [the entry continues, quoting Fräulein] but you are going to appoint and the house will reject, you send down again and they refuse, but you must be firm, after that everything will be alright.

3:30 A.M. [the diary goes on] I retire and Miss Wolf [this time Fräulein's name is written in full] goes home. . . .Woke at 8—Miss W__ came at 9—till 10. When she felt the man was in the house I sent her home. 10:25—sure enough—the man came up with the bundle of papers and spoke of lottery. How strange she should have told me.

In the journal the man is named only as T. E. E., and since no one with these initials appeared openly as a lottery promoter, it is better, perhaps, not to try to identify him further. He had come in behalf of those who, forced to cease operations in Louisiana, had come to Hawaiʻi and interested several Honoluluans in seeking a gambling franchise. The queen told him to send her a copy of their proposal. "I wonder how all will end," she concluded the July 8 entry.

After that, as the days sped by and the need to deal shrewdly with the legislature mounted, Liliʻuokalani's sessions with "the little lady" became ever more frequent. Political advice came mixed with bits about a fortune waiting in Austria to be claimed by the family of Liliʻuokalani's late husband, John Dominis, and with numerous trifles about the queen's friends and associates. "I believe her predictions," Liliʻuokalani wrote on August 16, "for all she has told me has proved true."

If today's reader of the diary seeks something beyond a medium's occult powers to explain what seemed so baffling and exciting to Liliʻuokalani in the summer of 1892, let him note that among those known to be working with the lottery's foreign promoters was Samuel Nowlein, captain of the queen's Household Guards and a resident at the Royal Barracks, just across from the *mauka* (mountain-ward) gate of the palace.

The lottery scheme, as Mr. T. E. E. explained it to Liliʻuokalani

35

in subsequent visits, appeared to be a most benevolent one. In return for the franchise, the company proposed to pay the Hawaiian government $500,000 each for railroads on Oʻahu, railroads on Hawaiʻi, and the improvement of Honolulu's harbor; $175,000 for the encouragement of industries; $25,000 for the encouragement of tourist travel and immigration. Here, it seemed to the queen, would be the answer to many of Hawaiʻi's financial problems—an answer that would make the government independent of local bankers and taxpayers.

Somewhat more than a month later the choice of a successor to Attorney General Whiting, who resigned, became a matter of concern. The diary tells how matters were arranged.

Aug. 27 ... Mr. E__ will call at 10:30 tomorrow. What he proposes [I am] to accept. He will say that I should say to them [her supporters in the legislature], I would not nominate Mr. N [Neumann] until you all vote for this H. L. Bill and they will promise to.

Aug. 28 ... 10:30 A.M. Mr. E. did call as she said, and he did suggest all that she predicted he would. He had been working very hard.

Aug. 29 ... 10:A.M. Mr. Parker and Mr. Spencer both came in. I told them I would only accept Mr. Neumann as A.G. on certain conditions—and they consented. The H. L. Bill will be brought in by Mr. W. White. Mr. E. came in all worn out. I told him not to trouble himself any more, that it will end all right.

At the opening of the legislature Liliʻuokalani had faced the problem of keeping in office a cabinet that would protect Marshal Charles Wilson in his job and approve a new constitution when the time came. Now, influenced by what seemed to her supernatural guidance, she had taken on the added burden of maintaining in power a cabinet favorable to the lottery. So she braced herself to appoint and let the House reject, to send down names again and let them refuse, until in the end they gave up and allowed her to have her way. At least that is what Fräulein's cards had said would happen.

At this point—the end of August 1892, when Representative White of Lahaina had just introduced the lottery bill—to the bewilderment and regret of those who seek to follow these tangled strands, Liliʻuokalani apparently stopped keeping her diary. Blank pages stretch from here to the end of the calendar year. Not until January 17, 1893, the day when the monarchy ended forever, did she begin again, in a new book. Why? The question is as useless as it is tantalizing. But certainly history is the poorer for want of the queen's personal view of those tempestuous days from September 1, 1892, to January 14, 1893, when, flushed with victory in the parliamentary struggle, she prorogued Hawai'i's longest legislature.

Coming up in early September for its first reading, the lottery bill did not rouse much support. Its opponents decided that there was nothing to worry about. But on January 10, when prorogation was in sight, the lottery bill suddenly was called up and passed its second reading, 20 to 17, even with some of the queen's partisans absent. Final passage was now inevitable. Seeing this, Reformers Thurston and W. O. Smith led the fight to incorporate safeguards against default or chicanery by the promoters. Next day the vote on the amended bill was ayes 23, noes 20.

To insure the implementation of the lottery act and to prepare for a new constitution, Lili'uokalani now sought to rid herself of the Wilcox-Jones cabinet. But, though twenty-three votes were enough to pass a bill, now that several Reform members had left for their homes it would take, as the supreme court had ruled, twenty-five—a majority of the whole membership—to put out the cabinet. The queen and her supporters must, in one way or another, persuade two more House members to change sides.

Twenty-four hours later the two had been won over. There were plenty of rumors as to how it had been done. Waipu'ilani, Iosepa, Ka'uhane, and Kauhi, the four Hawaiians who refused to desert the Reform party, were said to have been offered, and turned down, large bribes. Lucien Young, an officer on the U.S.S. *Boston*, later described in his book *The Real Hawaii* a meeting in the suburbs of Honolulu, in which, under the auspices of an unnamed Irishman, food and drink, persuasion and hard cash were used to open the eyes of Hawaiian members to their "true interests."

A Reformer wrote afterward that the queen had "gone down on her knees" to one Hawaiian. She was said to have placed 'ilima leis around the shoulders of those who were to make and second the want-of-confidence motion. It was widely believed that a haole's vote against the cabinet had been won by the promise that his father-in-law would be called on to form the next cabinet.

Whether any of this is more authentic than the counter-charges that the Reformers earlier had used bribery to keep this same Wilcox-Jones cabinet in office is difficult to say. But whatever the means, whoever the agents, the necessary votes were lined up. At the afternoon session on January 12 Representative Kapahu's want-of-confidence resolution against the Wilcox-Jones cabinet carried, 25 to 16.

The cabinet was out, and the House immediately adjourned. Lili'uokalani seemed to have won everything. She still had her trusted marshal. She had the lottery that would, she believed, enrich Hawai'i. She had ready for appointment a cabinet of her own choosing, men whom she thought she could count on to support her policies. All that remained, she must have told herself, was to keep her promise to her native subjects and grant the new constitution they had prayed for—a constitution that would, by restoring to the Crown some of its former prerogatives, increase the political power of the Hawaiians and clip the wings of the haoles.

But Fräulein's cards had not prepared her for the untoward events of January 16 and 17.

When Archibald Cleghorn, baffled by Lili'uokalani's conduct, wrote to Ka'iulani on January 28, he sounded not only critical of his sister-in-law but somewhat pessimistic about the monarchy's chances of survival. "Anyway my dear daughter," he wrote, "you may think that it is best you should not come to the throne. You may be happier in private life and so be an example to your people. . . . You have no lack of friends."

And again on February 8: "I . . . hope you will not worry. You are young and have all the world before you and are liked & respected by all the best people here. The P.G. are friendly to you and you may be a happier woman without being a ruler. I would much rather you should be . . . like Queen Emma & Mrs. Bishop [Princess Bernice Pauahi] than like some others. I think if your dear mother was alive she would say the same."

The first word to Cleghorn from his emissary E. C. Macfarlane was far from heartening. Macfarlane wrote on February 24 from Washington, D.C., of "the general satisfaction with which the Annexation question was received with the people and the press of the U.S." The commissioners of the Provisional Government, he said, had made rapid headway since their arrival and "the Annexation fever" had taken hold of the people to such an extent that it seemed to be a foregone conclusion that it would meet with little or no objection and must receive the endorsement and support of both houses of Congress. "You may imagine my surprise—I may say consternation," he continued, "when I saw that the President and Secretary of State had committed themselves to this course [recommending ratification of the treaty] and rushed through the negotiations without first hearing from the Queen's representatives."

Even this disheartening letter, however, showed Archibald Cleghorn that he had chosen an able and energetic person to present the monarchy's case. Macfarlane lost no time in quitting Washington, where matters seemed so hopeless, and descending on New York City, where he interviewed the editors of all the leading newspapers. Soon he was able to send some clippings to show that editorial opinion was swinging to the side of caution and delay in the matter of the treaty.

All of my conferences [he reported] were with the responsible heads of the several newspapers. I went straight to headquarters. The World, Herald, Nation, Harper's Weekly ... Mail & Express (Times and Tribune were against us, so I left them alone) & other New York newspapers which I have seen later from time to time ... are editorially fighting the treaty on the grounds that any attempt to rush it through the Senate at this time would be hasty, ill-advised and piratical.

Then back to Washington Macfarlane went, to work among his political friends and those to whom he brought letters from New York adherents. A little later he and Prince David Kawānanakoa tried to see President-Elect Cleveland but decided in favor of sending a message to him through his secretary, lest Cleveland resent their urging him to interfere in what was not yet officially his business. Paul Neumann's précis of the queen's case, however, was duplicated and sent to Cleveland, to the chairman of the

Senate Committee on Foreign Relations, and to fifteen senators.

On March 1, 1893, the Princess Ka'iulani arrived from England, accompanied by her guardian, Theo H. Davies, Davies' wife and daughter, and a chaperon-companion, Miss Whartoff. Several observers, including royalist Macfarlane and his adversaries Thurston and Castle, thought that this move did the princess' case no good, since the coming of Davies, formerly British commissioner in Hawai'i, suggested England's interference in an American dilemma—an interference likely to arouse resentment against the monarchy rather than sympathy for it.

Prince David, after a brief and formal meeting with Ka'iulani at the Brevoort House in New York City, told reporters in Washington that the princess, "under the thumb of Theo H. Davies," was working in the wrong direction—that is, against the interests of Queen Lili'uokalani.

But the whole approach of the Davies party was so low-key in New York, in Boston, and finally in Washington, and the manner and appearance of Ka'iulani so charming—the princess had brought with her thirteen trunkfuls of elegant hats and gowns—that in general the press treated it more as a colorful feature story than as a political ploy. But it was while the Davies party was in the United States capital that President Cleveland, having been inaugurated on March 4, withdrew the annexation treaty from the Senate and, a few days later, announced his intention of sending a personal representative to Hawai'i to investigate the overthrow of the monarchy and the establishment of a provisional government. That was big news in all the papers.

Before leaving Washington, Theo H. Davies paid unexpected tribute to the "revolutionists." "One of the saddest features of this matter," he said, "is that it has been presented as a plot and a conspiracy of bad men. It is not that. It is the blunder of good men, men to many of whom I would entrust my dearest interests. They have been goaded on by misrule into injustice, forgetting that injustice is no remedy for misrule."

3. INTERIM

In Honolulu the two weeks after January 17, 1893, were as peaceful as any that city had ever known. Martial law, enforced by mounted patrols, kept the night streets orderly and quieted the gong of the Chinese theater, much to the delight of dwellers in Pālama. The American troops moved from their cramped quarters at Arion Hall to set up "Camp Boston" in a fine old house and grounds on King Street. Colonel Soper took over the barracks and disbanded the Household Guard, allowing the queen to retain sixteen men as a guard of honor. Already, Liliʻuokalani had moved to Washington Place, and the government authorities had begun an inventory of the contents of the palace.

At one of its first sessions the Provisional Government canceled the controversial lottery contract, and the government's new marshal, urging on the native police force he had inherited from Charles B. Wilson, began a campaign to rid the city of the illicit *che fa* banks. Gamblers, it appeared, would be reduced to betting on whether the *Claudine*, speeding the annexation commissioners to San Francisco, would make the passage in eight days or less.

Except for the *Claudine*, which had been chartered by the Provisional Government, the interisland steamers plied their customary routes, carrying word of the momentous changes in Honolulu—word that was received everywhere with the same outward calm that prevailed in the capital. The royalist politicians, Hawaiian and part-Hawaiian, were as stunned as if they had just been thrown from their horses; they could make no plans; they could only wait to see how soon annexation would arrive, and to know what their opportunities would be under the expected regime.

But by the last of January there were signs that the P.G. honeymoon was about to end, that the new tenants in Aliʻiōlani Hale faced some vexing and complicated problems. For one thing, the volunteer army had grown restless. Most of the recruits, being business or professional men, wanted to be discharged before their personal affairs fell into utter chaos. The Drei Hundert, on the other hand, not only hungered for permanent employment at good pay, but sought fantastic bonuses in recognition of their timely help—one of their leaders suggested a gift of sixty acres of land for each of them—and for lucrative offices in the government as the spoils of victory. From the first, the executive and advisory councils had agreed to keep in the civil service all, or nearly all, of the incumbents. They required only a simple oath of allegiance, which most of the officials and employees appeared ready to sign. But the Drei Hundert proclaimed loudly that without them there would have been no revolution, and demanded the sacking of former royalists to make room for them in the police and postal departments, in the customhouse, and in the offices of the Interior Department and the Treasury. Otherwise, their spokesmen said, the government would find itself deprived abruptly of their extremely valuable services.

Clearly, the military forces must be reorganized, for, although there was surface calm in Honolulu, wild rumor had it that as soon as the warship *Naniwa* arrived from Yokohama, there would be trouble, and maybe violence, because of the demand of the Japanese for the franchise. It was not impossible, alarmists said, that the Mikado's government would strike a bargain with the queen's supporters, that the plantation workers would rise and restore Lili'uokalani, who would in return grant them the right to vote.

Once again help was sought from Minister Stevens, who on February 1 proclaimed a United States protectorate over the Hawaiian Islands "but ... not interfering with the administration of public affairs by the Provisional Government." Twenty-five marines took charge of Ali'iōlani Hale, on whose tower the Stars and Stripes replaced the Hawaiian flag. Citizen soldiers returned to their neglected business affairs, and only such members of the revolutionary army as would sign the pledge of allegiance were inducted into the regular force. Most of the Drei Hundert, still grumbling, joined permanent Company F; the only alternative was unemployment.

"*Aloha nui*, Uncle Samuel," said the *Liberal* of that date, cordially. "Walk in, and make yourself at home.... We are waiting to clasp hands, upon terms of equality with our forty-four sisters across the sea. For Heaven's sake, Uncle Sam! after having thus excited our hopes, do not leave us in the lurch by with-drawing from the scene. Stay with us, and let us stay with you. Hawaii will show herself a loyal and dutiful member of your family."

The *Bulletin*, too, hailed the protectorate, which would, it said, "guarantee peace and security, under the reign of which the industry and commerce of the country can resume its even flow," save the taxpayers "a large expense for keeping watch and ward against any outbreak," and do away with the "necessity for haste in negotiations at Washington for the settlement of ... a perma-nent form of government."

But British Minister James H. Wodehouse was not pleased; he wrote in protest to President Sanford Dole. And when Lili'uo-kalani drove by Ali'iōlani Hale, she refused to look at the American flag. "Time may wear off the feeling of injury ...," she wrote in her diary, "but my dear flag—the Hawaiian flag—that a strange flag should wave over it. May heaven look down on these missionaries and punish them for their deeds."*

By February 1, the battle for the minds of the Hawaiian commoners had been joined. On the outer islands native pastors, almost to a man, accepted the verdict against Lili'uokalani. Told that she had signed unrighteous bills into law and had sought to increase her own power at the expense of her subjects, they agreed sadly that Hawai'i would be better off when, in a few short weeks, it became part of the great American Republic. But they could not carry their congregations with them. In some places they were driven from their pulpits or shut out of their chapels. For the most part the people simply stayed away from the sermons or listened in sullen silence and thought what they pleased.

Often they gathered clandestinely in meetinghouses to pray for the restoration of the queen, and the natural leader where the Christian minister had been discredited was the pagan priest, or *kahuna*. Some worship of the old Hawaiian deities, some trust in familiar spirits had long existed side by side with Christianity. Often a Hawaiian believed in both—Christianity for his soul and the old pagan ways for his body. Sometimes while petitioning the missionaries' God for eternal life, he carried hidden a wooden fetish to ward off the death that some enemy, with the help of another fetish, might be bringing upon him. Now that the message of the preacher was unwelcome, he listened only to the *kahuna*.

In Honolulu at the old stone Kawaiaha'o Church, where a

---

*Lili'uokalani and her supporters always referred to the party that opposed her as "missionaries." Officially, the name of this political faction was the Reform party. It came into being in 1887 and included a few, though not many, native Hawaiians. Some, though by no means all, of its members had missionary connections. Of the twenty-four men who held office in the Provisional Government, either in the executive council or the advisory council, seven were sons or grandsons of the American Board missionaries. They were all island-born and therefore citizens of Hawai'i. Three others were also Hawai'i-born of American parentage; eight were American citizens, who as "denizens" had voting privileges in Hawai'i; three were Scotch, one German, one English, and one Canadian.

Aside from the ten who had lived all their lives in Hawai'i, the duration of residence of these officials ranged from four to forty-two years, with an average of about twenty years.

haole pastor, a son of the Mission, had preached for almost thirty years, a substantial core of Hawaiians accepted the changed order, albeit with sorrow and heartache. Here Lili'uokalani, when she was a princess, had played the organ and directed the choir; and later, though she liked to worship sometimes at the Anglican cathedral and sometimes at Kaumakapili in western Honolulu, she had sat in the red plush box pew reserved for royalty. After January 17, 1893, the royal pew went unoccupied, and the queen transferred her allegiance to the Episcopal church, whose rector continued to pray for her publicly each Sunday.

At Kaumakapili all was strife and confusion. The followers of the Reverend Waiama'u, who accepted the overthrow, sought to oust Deacon Alapa'i, the queen's friend and supporter, on charge of heathenish practices. On four successive Saturdays a jury of native elders heard testimony. But, though Alapa'i's wife was known as a *kahuna* who kept an *'unihipili*,* the decision went in the deacon's favor, and he continued to foster royalist sentiment in the congregation. For weeks, to the dismay of those who lived within its sound, the Kaumakapili bell tolled each morning between four and four-thirty to call members to prayer for restoration.

Lili'uokalani recovered quickly from her bewilderment and sent out messages and agents to tell her people not to despair. Help was certain to come for her cause, she assured them, and when she was restored she would reward all those who had stood by her.

At first there was some talk in the outlying districts about Ka'iulani. If Lili'uokalani had done wrong, as the haoles said she had, let her give way to the young princess. Let the haoles set up a regency—under an American protectorate, if need be—until the princess was of age. Then let her be crowned queen of Hawai'i. So the people heartened each other, not knowing that Sanford Dole had recommended this very plan to his colleagues in the movement against Lili'uokalani, and that the revolutionists had rejected it flatly. If Ka'iulani had had an American instead of a British father, Dole's suggestion might have met with some favor.

---

* *Unihipili* is defined as "the spirit of a dead person, sometimes believed present in bones or hair of the deceased, and kept lovingly."

Dimly aware of the Ka'iulani movement, Lili'uokalani was wise enough to see that if the United States came to the aid of the monarchy, it would be only to undo the acts committed by its representatives, Minister Stevens and Captain Wiltse. If there were restoration, it must be the restoration of what had existed on January 17. Ka'iulani could wait.

In Honolulu six newspapers, in both English and Hawaiian, bombarded the populace. On the morning after the overthrow, the *Advertiser* had exulted:

> Every native-born Hawaiian will be entitled to all the freedom ... and rights enjoyed under the American Constitution.... The United States of America is ... the one country in the world which affords everybody an equal chance. Under its broad aegis this weary nation will at length find peace.

But the *Advertiser* had few readers, and the queen's men, rousing themselves to the campaign, quoted and misquoted dispatches from the mainland to prove that the commissioners who would sign the annexation treaty thousands of miles from Hawai'i had no such noble sentiments about the native's place in the scheme of things.

The *Liberal*, a biweekly, founded by the Robert Wilcox party some months before the overthrow, sprang into the arena as the proponent of immediate statehood, warning, "If such government be not secured at the outset of our career under the stars and stripes, it will not be secured during the life of anyone now living." The *Liberal*'s masthead named Wilcox as the Hawaiian editor and manager; the English section for a few weeks was run by C. W. Ashford. When Ashford resigned, the *Liberal* abandoned the campaign for statehood and devoted itself to deploring the "wrongs" suffered by the Drei Hundert. Wilcox was still making up his mind about annexation.

The *Bulletin*, formerly the organ of the queen's party, followed at first a wait-and-see policy, confining itself to ample news coverage and the mildest of editorial comment. But, as prospects of immediate annexation dimmed, it became more outspokenly royalist.

Ka Leo (The Voice), edited at the house of John E. Bush in

Printer's Lane, was cautious for a time. Like Robert Wilcox, Bush had been in and out of the royalist ranks so often that no one knew where his support could be expected to go. Perhaps Bush himself was in a quandary, for on February 1 he turned the editorship over to subordinates and sailed for San Francisco to assay the temper of the mainland.

The weekly *Kuokoa* (Independent), published in Hawaiian by the Reverend Sereno Bishop and his Hawaiian protégés, stood for annexation; but it appeared to exert small influence. Its circulation fell off, and the subscriber who tore up his copy, threw the pieces into the street, and stomped on them, dramatized, doubtless, the reaction of hundreds of Hawaiians to criticism of the queen and praise of the Provisional Government.

Bilingual *Holomua* (Progress) was uncompromisingly royalist. Every word in either English or Hawaiian was designed to incite the native against what it scornfully called the P.G.—to swell anger and inflame hurt pride until the Hawaiians became forever irreconcilable. The new government, *Holomua* reiterated, had no right to exist; the men who were running it had stolen the country. Any native who gave allegiance to this band of thieves was a traitor to his nation and to his race. A day of reckoning would come for all such people—when the Crown was restored.

To keep *Holomua* going, Lili'uokalani was pouring in her own money, almost bankrupting herself. On the day after editor Henry Sheldon's arrest on charge of seditious libel (the first of several such arrests), she instructed Samuel Parker to sell her shares in the Hawaiian Agricultural Company. They brought her almost $10,000 and eased her financial problem for the moment. But that same morning John 'Ena, a member of the advisory council, warned her that, unless she withdrew her support from *Holomua*, the government would stop her monthly allowance of $1,200 and dismiss her guard. Lili'uokalani told him that she had withdrawn from politics and was living in complete retirement. Nevertheless, the blow fell in March. The men of the council were not disposed to subsidize vigorous attacks on themselves; and a lady in retirement, they decided, did not need a sixteen-man guard at government expense.

As for Henry Sheldon, when he fell afoul of the P.G., he did not want for legal aid. Five attorneys sprang to his defense, one of them the able C. W. Ashford, once a Reformer but now a royalist. By questioning the legislative powers of the combined councils and the validity of the writ, these lawyers soon had the case so snarled that the government was glad to drop it.

The *Hawaiian Star*, destined to be the most boisterous defender of the Provisional Government, did not begin publication until April 1.

The Royal Hawaiian Band, pride of the monarchy, now played for the Provisional Government. Henry Berger, composer, conductor, drillmaster, and for twenty years arbiter of Honolulu's musical destiny, saw nothing political in tubas and trombones. The boys had given a number of concerts—one of them in honor of the birthday of Germany's Kaiser Wilhelm—before anything was said about the oath of allegiance; and even when Maestro Berger first mentioned the requirement, it did not seem much of an obstacle. Plenty of other loyal Hawaiians had signed the oath. But when they thought about it, and especially when they talked with their royalist friends, the boys began to have doubts. Perhaps it was the American flag on Ali'iōlani Hale that helped them to their decision, for it was on February 1, the day that Minister Stevens declared the protectorate, that they marched in a body to Henry Berger's house, collected their pay and stated positively that they would not sign "the document of the enemy."

If Berger was disturbed, he did not show it. Very well, he told them, they were discharged. They could turn in their instruments and their uniforms immediately. The next day, instructed by the government to do so, he began to recruit a new band. In the end, sixteen of his former musicians came back to him, took the oath, and gave him a nucleus for his organization. Dropping the word "royal," they were known officially as the Hawaiian Band, but because many of the newcomers were Portuguese, they were apt to be referred to as the Portugee band. They gave their first concert on February 9 with but eight days' practice and were "enthusiastically encored by a large audience." On the twenty-first they introduced Berger's latest composition, a march entitled "Provisional Government." But it was a long time before even

48

the skill and the strict discipline of the maestro had brought them up to the old standard.

Friends of the monarchy, those men who had advised the band boys to "eat stones" rather than to concede, bestirred themselves to raise a fund to buy new instruments and pay a new director. Calling themselves the National Band, the royalist musicians serenaded Lili'uokalani at Washington Place on March 17, exactly a week after their brasses and woodwinds had arrived by the *Monowai*. They opened with the sprightly "Lili'uokalani March" and closed with the noble "Hawai'i Pono'i." Sentiment almost overwhelmed them, but the notes came out strong and clear; men trained as Berger had trained them do not forget in a month. The queen spoke to them from the veranda, telling them to be steadfast and have faith.

4. MR. CLEVELAND'S COMMISSIONER

Word came in mid-March that President Cleveland would send his own commission to the Islands to find out what had led to the coup of January 17 and exactly how it had been accomplished. Annexation commissioners, returning or writing to their friends, said that was good. Besides former Congressman James Blount, a Southerner, there would be, they had heard, such discerning men as General Schofield for the army and Rear Admiral Brown for the navy.

The Provisional Government announced that it welcomed investigation, that it had nothing to hide and could not but profit by the report of any commissioners the president might send, but annexationists could not altogether conceal their disappointment and chagrin. Girded for only a short run, they faced with misgivings the prospect of plodding on mile after mile toward an uncertain destination.

For the royalists the sky had suddenly brightened. A commission from President Cleveland was exactly what they wanted. Led on by prominent Hawaiian women, Lili'uokalani's supporters thronged into a new patriotic league, with an old name, the Hui Aloha 'Āina (those who loved their country). Parents listed their children, down to infants in arms, and one mother subscribed the name of her annexationist son, believing, perhaps, that she was saving him from the consequences of waywardness. In their enthusiasm the ladies sometimes circulated blank pages, leaving the heading to be filled in later above the signatures. But, though these devices may have inflated rolls somewhat, no one doubted that the *hui* was a large and steadily growing organization. Soon *Holomua* estimated the membership at ten thousand; *Ka Leo* made it fifteen thousand.

John E. Bush, just home from a trip to Washington, mounted the bandwagon. Speaking in Palace Square, he gave his cheering listeners the impression that the expected commissioners—"very favorable to us"—were being sent on his personal recommendation. There was applause when he said, "I have a firm hope that Liliuokalani will be restored." Then, perhaps remembering that he had not always supported the queen, he concluded, "I have declared myself an annexationist provided you consent to it; but, finding you oppose, I have nothing more to do. I am ever with you." Straight from Washington, John E. Bush had brought hope to the royalists. His *Ka Leo* now could set its editorial course with confidence.

But the Hui Aloha 'Āina did not have the field to itself. When it became known that annexation was not assured but must be sold to the new administration through its commissioners, the Annexation League came quickly into being. The promoters rented a suite of rooms on the second floor of the Campbell block and greatly distressed the royalist proprietor by hanging a huge American flag across one side of the building. A "monster" mass meeting convened in the new drill shed next to the barracks to approve a plan of organization and listen to thirteen speeches. Robert W. Wilcox, one of six vice-presidents, acknowledging prolonged applause, said that annexation would mean "liberty and independence and perhaps the salvation of the native race." Mistakenly, he announced himself as the only Hawaiian present, and boasted, "When I begin an undertaking, I will stand to it like a man."

Did Robert Wilcox believe this estimate of his own stead-fastness? Probably. Master opportunist that he was, he never had changed his course without reasons that seemed to him compelling. At the moment he could see himself as the one really farsighted Hawaiian, who would wean his people from the defunct monarchy and nurture them in American democracy. But in a week the arrival of Mr. Cleveland's commissioner had put a different face on matters. In a month the Annexation League had struck his name from its list and filled his place as vice-president. By that time, as he explained years later, he had seen "that the United States meant to do what was right and just," and accordingly he had "decided to become a strong adherent to the queen."

J. K. Iosepa, long a staunch Reformer, followed Wilcox on the rostrum, speaking with dignity and conviction. "When a man is sick and weak, he needs a strong man to take him by the hand and lift him up, and so it is with the native. . . . If Mr. Bishop [the banker] should invite us to be a partner of his, would we not feel rich? So we should now when the United States takes us into partnership. . . . I am today abused because I take up annexation, but . . . I am not going to move back one inch. I stand on this platform and shall stick to it until we reach the hour of annexation."

The applause of the haoles was deafening. Six weeks later Iosepa went with three other Hawaiians to tell President Cleveland's commissioner how he felt about annexation, but the testimony of Ka'uhane, Kauhi, Waipu'ilani, and Iosepa must have seemed to Mr. Blount too unimportant to receive a place in his voluminous report. At least it is not there. As for Iosepa's fellow Hawaiians, most of them hated him bitterly for his stand.

Flags by the hundreds greeted Commissioner James Blount as he came ashore from the U.S. Revenue Cutter *Rush*. Streaming from staffs, draped from windows, suspended above streets, swathing lanais, and adorning the vest pockets of gentlemen and the coiffures of ladies—everywhere there was red, white, and blue. The Stars and Stripes predominated, but the Hawaiian ensign was there too; and for good measure a loyal son of the old sod had flung out at one downtown corner the green banner of Erin. United or divided, peaceful or at swords' points, the people of

Honolulu could always salute a visitor in style, and they did so on March 29, 1893. In white *holokus* and crimson leis, the women of the Hui Aloha 'Āina marched down Fort Street and lined up along the dock, waving small American and Hawaiian flags in a frenzy of welcome. Handsome tricolor badges, arriving from the printer's in the nick of time, adorned the lapels of Annexation Club members, as they too converged on the wharf. Steam launches carried the official greeters, who boarded the *Rush* just inside "Naval Row"—Minister Stevens, United States Consul H. W. Severance, a committee from the Annexation Club, the queen's chamberlain, and the gentlemen of the press. If anyone felt let down on discovering that the commission consisted of just one travel-weary Georgian who politely refused all offers of assistance in locating himself, if anyone wondered what had become of the gold braid and brass buttons, the chevrons and stars that had been promised, such a person concealed his regret and beamed on the unpretentious commissioner as if he had been Mr. Cleveland himself.

Two days later, on April 1, the American flag came down from the government building, the American marines and sailors returned to their ship, and the American protectorate ended. "A glorious sight. It will never come down again," annexationist W. D. Alexander had written when Minister Stevens raised the colors on February 1. But James Blount, whose authority was paramount, said he could not properly conduct his inquiry until he had restored the Hawaiian flag and left the Provisional Government entirely on its own.

The government was equal to the challenge, although its preparations for the transfer were of necessity feverish. Rumors abounded. The royalists or the Japanese or both, it was said, would seize the occasion to rise. And however little truth there may have been in these predictions, Colonel Soper intended to be ready for trouble if it came. On the afternoon of March 31 he ordered his entire force under arms, not only the newly uniformed regulars, but the four reserve companies, the Citizens' Guard—who turned out in their business suits or their shirt-sleeves, muskets on their shoulders—and the single artillery squad with its four big guns. The night was a sleepless one at the barracks. Alarm drills were called, and toward midnight President Dole inspected the troops.

At sunrise American colors broke out all over the town. It was as if the people said, "One flag may come down today; we will raise a hundred in its stead."

Meanwhile nothing Commissioner Blount might say could keep the queen's party from interpreting the lowering of the flag as an American repudiation of the Provisional Government, the first step toward a restoration of Liliʻuokalani. But the queen's spokesmen warned the native royalists that they must not show their joy openly. Since everything was in President Cleveland's hands, loyal supporters of the Crown could best help the cause by proving themselves restrained and law-abiding.

So it was a silent, breathless crowd that, a little before eleven on the morning of April 1, saw the *Boston*'s men mass on the *waikīkī* (east, toward Waikīkī) side of the lawn at Aliʻiōlani Hale and the government troops march in and face them on the *ʻewa*; heard the clear, shrill notes of the bugler's call; saw the Stars and Stripes slide slowly down the staff, and then, in a moment, the Hawaiian flag rise to its place above the tower. Colonel Soper's men fired a salute, and the naval battalion began marching off toward the docks. Unnoticed, Lieutenant Lucien Young folded the lowered flag and carried it with him. There would come a day, he told himself, when it would be raised again in Hawaiʻi.

At Snow Cottage in the grounds of the Hawaiian Hotel, Commissioner James Blount set up his office and worked indefatigably at recording testimony. But had he come to Hawaiʻi as a juror, to hear evidence on both sides of a controversy about which he held no settled views, or as a prosecutor, to work up a case against suspected wrong-doers? No one in Honolulu seemed to be sure, least of all, perhaps, the commissioner himself.

Before he left Washington, Blount had had no opportunity to discuss his instructions with President Cleveland, and he had talked with Secretary of State Walter Q. Gresham, not about the events of January, 1893, but only about the raising of the American flag in a virtual protectorate on February 1. So he could, and did, tell himself that the officials in Washington had open minds and simply wanted all the facts. But Blount was not stupid. He was forced to draw inferences from Cleveland's removal of

U.S. Commissioner J. H. Blount with Mrs. Blount and (left) his secretary, Mr. Mills; at Snow Cottage, July 4, 1893.

the annexation treaty from the Senate and from Gresham's un-concealed disapproval of Stevens' actions in February.

As to his own predilections and prejudices, they are a matter of record only in the testimony he gave a subcommittee of the Senate Committee on Foreign Relations (the Morgan committee) on January 11, 1894, more than six months after he had filed his report. Then, under persistent questioning, he admitted that his reaction to Lorrin Thurston in Washington in the spring of 1892 had been negative—he considered Thurston "an uppish sort of person," engaging in questionable inquiries—and that when he read Minister Stevens' letter of November 1892 (Dispatch No. 74) on the political situation in Hawai'i and the imminence of a crisis, he had not been pleased. (He had seen the letter early in March 1893 when Secretary of State John Foster showed it to some Democratic members of the Senate in the hope that it would influence them to vote for annexation.)

"I did not like the looks of the letter," Blount admitted to the Morgan committee, "but I think they did not make much impression on me. . . . I did not think much about it." Pressed by Senator George Gray, Blount added, "Oh, I rather had an im-pression—it was a vague one—that it [Stevens' letter] manifested some passing beyond the proprieties for an American represen-tative in a foreign country."

In answer to another senator a moment later, Blount said, "I had some apprehension that there might have been something imprudent done there; I had no opinion." The committee was left to draw the fine distinction between "apprehension" and "opinion."

At the outset of Blount's investigation, many of the revolu-tionists believed him to be disposed in their favor. The blow their pride had suffered in the flag-lowering he softened by reminding them that Hawai'i, if it were to negotiate with the United States, must be completely independent. He hinted that he understood many of their problems, and when asked if he had come to restore the queen, smiled as if the question were an amusing absurdity. But soon his genial Southern manner turned a trifle brusque; and after a sumptuous dinner with W. O. Smith and his colleagues in Smith's home—cuisine by Honolulu's prime chef and music by the famed Quintette Club––Blount announced that he would leave the social amenities entirely to his wife for the rest of their stay.

With the royalists it was different. From the moment when the ex-ministers Parker and Peterson called on him that first afternoon at his hotel cottage, he seemed at ease with the queen's adherents. When, on his third day ashore, he received the Hawaiian Patriotic League, it pleased him immensely to see what an urbane and intelligent gentleman John E. Bush was. It delighted him, likewise, to be handed a copy of *Holomua*. He asked to become a subscriber. On the commissioner's fourth day in Honolulu, just before the lowering of the United States flag, Samuel Parker came again, bringing ex-minister Cornwell, and suggested that the three of them have breakfast together and become better acquainted. And so it went.

Not that the commissioner admitted a preference for royalist company. In all that he said he appeared the impartial fact finder, revealing no more of his own opinion than as if he had been the Kamehameha statue in front of Ali'iōlani Hale. But he soon discovered that royalists dropped in casually and easily at the Hawaiian Hotel, where the manager was an enthusiastic supporter of Lili'uokalani, whereas P.G.s came only by appointment. And nothing Blount could do kept the Hawaiians from jumping to their own conclusions about his mission. By April 10 Lili'uokalani was recording in her diary the rumor that "in two weeks everything will be settled and then he [Blount] is going to enjoy a good time."

In interviewing witnesses, Blount used no legal or judicial procedures. He felt, he said later, that he had no authority to administer an oath. Since each person who testified was alone with him, except for the stenographer, there was no cross-examination. Blount was the sole judge of what should go into his report and what, if anything, should be omitted as irrelevant. He alone decided which of the many persons who were eager to talk to him he would receive. On one occasion the Annexation Club proposed to line up some witnesses for him, but, as he told the Morgan committee, he was annoyed by the suggestion. "I am here," he informed the club's spokesman, "to make an investigation for the Government of the United States, and while, perhaps, I will examine some persons you want examined, as a rule I want to direct these examinations and say whom I will examine and whom not."

History, gossip, and invective in abundance came Blount's way as the days went on, and much of this he included in the amazing conglomerate that was his report to Washington. He seems to have worked hardest on answering the crucial question, Did John L. Stevens, United States minister in Hawai'i, participate in the overthrow of Queen Lili'uokalani? He sought to find out exactly how many men each faction had under arms on January 17, 1893, just what messages were exchanged and what conversations held between the leaders of the revolution and Stevens, what instructions the *Boston*'s officers were given about their shore duty, why the sailors were quartered so close to Ali'iōlani Hale and the palace, what the U.S. troops did and didn't do on January 17, and what they would have done if events had worked out differently. He wanted to know at precisely what hour on that Tuesday afternoon Minister Stevens had recognized the new government and whether, perchance, the recognition had been premature. He tried to learn from the queen's last cabinet and her marshal what they had expected or feared from the *Boston* battalion and how their fears had affected their actions. To these ends he directed his questions, deliberately and skilfully, while his secretary took shorthand notes.

By July 1893 he had prepared a report that "proved" what an antiexpansionist president and secretary of state presumably had hoped to hear: that the representative of the United States under a Republican administration had erred, involving his government improperly in the termination of the Hawaiian monarchy. As he wrote in his summing up,

The leaders of the revolutionary movement would not have undertaken it but for Mr. Stevens' promise to protect them against any danger from the Government. But for this their mass meeting would not have been held. But for this no request to land the troops would have been made. Had troops not been landed no measures for the organization of a new Government would have been taken.

The American minister and the revolutionary leaders had determined on annexation to the United States and had agreed to the part each was to act to the very end. . . .

There was one other point that interested Blount greatly: whether the Provisional Government would be willing to submit the annexation question to the Hawaiian electorate and what the outcome of a plebiscite would be likely to be. He found no supporter of the revolution willing to consider such an election and no one on either side who thought annexation would carry if put to a vote. This opinion, Blount thought, greatly strengthened his conclusion that the queen could not have been overthrown without United States intervention and that the Provisional Government probably would collapse if American support were withdrawn.

Demands for a plebiscite had troubled the annexation commissioners from the time they went ashore in San Francisco insisting that the revolution in Hawai'i had been a popular movement against an arbitrary queen. Reluctant anti-imperialists and sanguine expansionists alike had seen in an appeal to the people—to the Hawaiian natives—a means of justifying an act foreign to American tradition. Even President Harrison had asked, rather wistfully, when Secretary Foster laid the treaty before him, whether it wasn't possible to include some words about the will of the Hawaiian people.

No, the commissioners had explained, over and over, the common native did not always know what was good for him and his country. Anti-American propaganda and racial bitterness often had swayed his judgment and would do so again if a vote were taken; the rank corruption that had nauseated honest men in the monarchy's last days would flourish once more and turn such an election into a farce. Besides, the annexationists argued, there were things that might not be settled by counting noses—slavery, for instance, or the isolation of lepers. Though numerically a minority, the supporters of the Provisional Government were an overwhelming majority of the "respectable, intelligent, and property-owning citizens" of the Islands. These men had seen the ship of state about to crash on the rocks and, at great risk to themselves, they had seized the helm, seeking to save all hands on board. Until Hawai'i was moored safely in the harbor of annexation, they would not willingly relinquish control, nor would they consult the passengers about their destination.

Such words, when newspapers and travelers carried them back to Honolulu, excited the native Hawaiians against the government and swept away whatever small chance there might have been of winning their trust and confidence in the new order. Royalist orators easily persuaded their listeners that the intent of the pending treaty was to organize a purely white man's government. In vain the annexationists denied any thought of discriminating against the Hawaiians or of claiming for themselves any privileges not shared equally by the whole nation. In vain they reminded native leaders that it was Liliʻuokalani who had sought to thwart the will "of the people" and to gain for herself alone the power to appoint half the legislature. Their words went unheard. And when it began to look as if the United States did not really want to take Hawaiʻi into its republican family, the Provisional Government was left with a shaky platform and no battle cry. It was to forestall just such a fiasco that Lorrin Thurston had gone to Washington in 1892.

Paul Neumann and Prince David came home on the *Alameda*, arriving on April 7. Liliʻuokalani sent her chamberlain, James W. Robertson, to convey them straight to Washington Place, but so great was the crush of Hawaiians, cheering and smothering "their" commissioners with leis, that the state carriage could hardly get through. All the important royalists gathered in the house—Samuel Parker, whose mortgages were being foreclosed by the Provisionals; E. C. Macfarlane, who had traveled with Her Majesty's envoys while seeking information that would direct his own financial ventures; J. O. Carter, who had found his friendship for the queen a growing handicap in his business relations. For all of them, restoration could not come too soon.

Outside, the people stood for a long time, waiting for the ambassadors' report to filter through to them. When news came, the words were good. Mr. Neumann had talked with the American president, and the president had said that justice would be done. That, of course, meant that Liliʻuokalani would soon be once again the queen of Hawaiʻi. Justice could not possibly mean anything else.

Commissioner Blount found the conduct of United States Minister Stevens extremely irritating. Calling at the legation one day in April, Blount asked some sharp questions. Was it true the minister had sent for Claus Spreckels, the millionaire planter who had come back to Honolulu after the overthrow, and besought him to influence the queen in favor of annexation? Had Stevens said that, since he did not expect to be in Hawai'i very long, he was eager to see annexation accomplished speedily? Had Stevens stated that he thought Blount favored annexation?

Yes, Stevens admitted, he had asked Spreckels to call on him and they had talked about the possibility of winning over the queen. But he thought Spreckels had misunderstood what he said on the other points. Still, his favorable views on annexation were revealed in his published dispatches, and he could never go back on them.

With difficulty Blount held himself in check. It was certainly "very unseemly," he said, for Stevens to be urging annexation while he, the commissioner, was on the ground to inquire into that subject; it "scarcely seemed fair" for Stevens to undertake to form public opinion on the subject when a representative of the president's own party was at hand; in the future whenever it became necessary to say anything about annexation, let the minister refer the matter to him.

To Gresham, Blount reported that the colloquy was "characterized by kindliness on my part, and, so far as I could observe, by courtesy on the part of Mr. Stevens." But if Blount kept his temper, Gresham did not. As fast as mail could travel, came Stevens' recall. Blount was appointed minister. "While your acceptance permanently would greatly gratify the President," Gresham wrote, "your wishes will control."

So far as Stevens was concerned, the brusque dismissal made little difference. He had long since mailed his resignation to Washington and set his departure for the last of May. But Gresham's removal of Consul General Severance at the same time left no doubt that the secretary was in a mood to clean house in Hawai'i.

As soon as he could, Stevens vacated the legation and moved to the Eagle Hotel. There, on the eve of his sailing, he was saluted by five hundred members of the Annexation Club, who, preceded by the band, marched into the hotel grounds and shouted for him to come out. From the lanai "old man eloquent," as his admirers called him, addressed the crowd and was cheered long and lustily. A committee presented the parting gift—a handsome silver service that had cost a thousand dollars, each dollar given by a different person, they told him. It was well that he had made his speech; he was too moved now to say a word. "The old man will be heard when he arrives in the States," predicted one who stood in that crowd. But Lili'uokalani had another thought. She wrote: "Mr. J. L. Stevens ... went back to the United States on the steamer *Australia* with a history which has never been paralleled in Hawaii. . . . May he be made to suffer as much as the many pangs he has caused among the people." The death, by drowning, of the daughter who had been his secretary—an event almost simultaneous with the overthrow—Lili'uokalani considered a judgment from heaven.

Blount's relations with British Commissioner Wodehouse were as cordial as those with Stevens were rasping. The two talked freely and comfortably from the first. Wodehouse explained that he had been annoyed with Lili'uokalani for precipitating the January crisis, that in doing so she had ignored his advice and that of others in the diplomatic corps. Nevertheless, he said, on reviewing the action of Mr. Stevens and Captain Wiltse, he could "only regard it as a filibustering enterprise."

At a time when annexationists, though baffled by Blount's reticence, still thought him probably on their side, Wodehouse confidently predicted, in a dispatch to his superior, Lord Rosebery, that Blount's report to President Cleveland would oppose annexation and advise reinstating the queen. "I may remark," the letter continued, "that my American Colleague and I meet frequently and discuss the 'situation,' and he has encouraged me to express my views on it—of course 'unofficially.'" Wodehouse thought His Lordship would be gratified to know how good an understanding had existed between the two representatives.

Claus Spreckels had been in Honolulu since April 18. In February, when annexation looked certain, he had allowed a mainland newspaper to quote him as favorable; he had even offered one of his ships to transport soldiers to the Islands in case the new government needed them for its defense. But after the proposed treaty was made public, he had had a change of heart. All the safeguards that the commissioners had told him they would insist on for the advantage of sugar planters had been omitted. There was nothing to protect the labor contracts then existing and nothing to guarantee that the importation of contract-bound cane-field workers could continue. The immigration of Chinese laborers was specifically prohibited. Yet after all these concessions the treaty makers had not been able to secure an extension to Hawaiian sugar of the two-cents-a-pound bounty the United States government paid to domestic growers. To Spreckels the whole thing was preposterous. And now that the Cleveland administration seemed reluctant to complete the bargain on any terms at all, he decided that an independent republic would be far better than annexation.

He set out for the Islands certain that he could swing other planters into line. To his amazement not a plantation owner or sugar factor would listen to him. Yes, they agreed, the change to free labor would create problems, but problems nowhere nearly so vexing as those they had all faced in the last few years. Some thought that in the long run free labor, though expensive, might prove more satisfactory than bound. But anyway, what they wanted—first, last, and always—was annexation; and Claus Spreckels, who did not live in Hawai'i but only made money there, could talk until he was blue in the face without winning them over.

Petulantly, Spreckels threw himself into the restoration movement. He called on Lili'uokalani and told her that he personally would see that she was returned to the throne. He would first wreck the Provisional Government by calling in his loans and by forcing some of the key men over whom he had influence to withdraw their support. Thus the government would collapse in short order. Let the queen have ready a new constitution and a new cabinet. Antone Rosa would be a good attorney general; Wilson must go back as marshal; she must do away with Judge A. F. Judd and others like him and have a new supreme court. There need be no fighting. He and Blount would do everything.

Early in December 1892, during the G. N. Wilcox regime, the queen's government had borrowed $95,000 from the Spreckels bank in Honolulu to meet withdrawals from the shaky postal savings system. The notes were for six months, but in February Spreckels had assured the new minister of finance that, if the interest were paid, he would extend the loan indefinitely. Now he notified the executive council that he must have the whole sum on June 1. About the same time the government must find $30,000 to pay the semiannual interest on the London loan, negotiated in Kalākaua's day. The treasury was almost empty, and taxes would not come in until July—if they came at all.

On May 31 Peter C. Jones, who for health reasons had resigned as the Provisional Government's minister of finance, went into the business district of Honolulu determined to raise the $125,000 that would save the government. In a few hours he had succeeded. Fortunately for the Provisionals, sugar prices had risen that spring, brightening somewhat the financial horizon; even so, it was an astounding feat. Again Claus Spreckels had to revise his plans; he was at a loss to understand these P.G.s.

5. HAWAI'I WAITS AND WONDERS

All summer Hawai'i waited to learn its fate.

Honoluluans trooped to the beach resorts for picnics and bathing parties. The rival bands filled the soft nights with Strauss waltzes, Rossini overtures, and Henry Berger marches. On June 11 horses trotted to celebrate Kamehameha Day. On July 4 a parade of antiques and horribles, "literary exercises," boat races, baseball games, and a reception at the United States legation hailed American independence. Royalists and government supporters rowed out in the same boats, smiling and chatting, to dine or dance on board the ships in Naval Row.

Beneath the surface, though, there were worry and foreboding and bitterness more intense than Honolulu had ever known before. Neither Lorrin Thurston in Washington nor James Blount at Snow Cottage could find out what President Cleveland and Secretary Gresham intended to do about Hawai'i. Reports that the United States was about to restore the queen met and mingled all over town with rumors that desperate P.G.s were about to assassinate her. Unrestrained editorials in the *Star* and loose talk among the soldiers kept royalists uneasy. Whispers of monarchist conspiracy, on the other hand, disturbed the government, and direct threats drove Sanford Dole to sleep now here, now there, to evade crackpots. Troops, largely German and Portuguese, patrolled the city and suburbs day and night; their insolent manners and Europe-tinged talk ("Get off mit de bayonet vonce") rasped the nerves of well-bred haoles and stirred resentment in those Hawaiians who once had guarded the monarchy with such genial gallantry.

In June the government occupied 'Iolani Palace and renamed it the Executive Building, while the plaza in front became Union Square. The throne room—stripped of its plush chairs and *kāhilis*, the feather standards symbolizing royalty—became a place of assembly; departments were installed both upstairs and down; the regular soldiers moved from the barracks on the opposite side of Hotel Street to the basement. Everything now was compact and readily defended. Ali'iōlani Hale, across the square, became the Judiciary Building, expendable in case of trouble.

Lili'uokalani grieved at the desecration of the palace, symbol of the fallen monarchy's magnificence. Unable to bear the thought of living there again, she was comforted by Claus Spreckels' promise to build her a far handsomer residence when she resumed her reign.

One day Spreckels stormed into Commissioner Blount's cottage with a placard he had found nailed to the front gate of the big, ornate frame house where he lived on Punahou Street. Underneath a death's head some annexationist wag had scrawled, "Silver and gold are potent, but lead is more effective." Blount referred the matter to President Dole, who assigned police to protect the irate sugar king. Had it not been for the horse racing at Kahului on Maui, Spreckels might have left the Islands at once. As a matter of fact, however, it was a month before he made ready to sail, with Mrs. Spreckels and his daughter, on a ship of the Spreckels-owned Oceanic Steamship Company.

Royalist anger had blazed at the threat to the queen's most distinguished partisan—a threat that seemed to bear out all their fears of P.G. violence. Though they might be shot for it, they told each other, they would honor the *'ona miliona*—the "owner of a million"—at his leaving. Perhaps remembering Mr. Stevens' silver service, someone started a subscription fund to buy the colonel a gold-headed cane. Charles Creighton presented it on deck after the Spreckels party had been photographed and had had their health drunk in champagne. Beaming above his leis, Spreckels made a little speech of acknowledgment.

The cane, it turned out, bore a most interesting inscription: "Ave! Claus! *Morituri te Salutamus* . . . from your fellow citizens doomed also to die at the hands of the murder society of the Annexation Club. . . . *Leben Sie Hundert Jahr und niemals sterben.*" There followed a list of the presumably doomed donors. There were twenty-three of them, and lo! the names of Lili'uokalani and of James Blount led all the rest.

Blount readily convinced the Provisional Government that he had had nothing to do with the gift, and that his name had been used without his knowledge or consent. But the incident embarrassed him painfully and increased his impatience to escape from his ambiguous position. He finished his report and sent if off to Secretary Gresham together with an urgent request to be relieved as soon as possible. But the State Department remained strangely silent.

At length, in mid-August, Blount took matters into his own hands and sailed for home. In Washington he found the explanation—though for the next quarter of a century only a handful of men knew the whole truth about President Cleveland's illness. From June 30 to August 7 the president had been at his Buzzard's Bay home, recovering, it was said, from "an attack of rheumatism" and "the extraction of some teeth"—actually from surgery for cancer of the mouth. When he reappeared in the capital just in time for the special session of Congress that was to deal with the money crisis, Mr. Cleveland's haggard face testified that he had indeed been too ill to think about far-off Hawai'i. With his own nation in the grip of depression, he had driven himself to the verge of exhaustion to prepare a message that would induce Congress to repeal the Sherman Silver Purchase Act and return the country to the gold standard. Until that was done, Commissioner Blount's report would rest in Secretary Gresham's files, and neither the press nor the president would hear a word of it. As to a successor for Minister Blount, that too would have to wait. For a time Rear Admiral J. S. Skerrett, commander of the Pacific Squadron, would represent the United States in Honolulu. So Hawai'i waited.

The *Australia* was due on September 2, Lili'uokalani's birthday. Perhaps, someone must have said, the word would come that day from President Cleveland, and Admiral Skerrett would send his men ashore and reinstate the queen. How appropriate! In a few hours Hawaiians were telling each other that the restoration orders were sure to come by the *Australia*. Quickly they laid their plans to strew a flowery carpet in Her Majesty's path from Washington Place to the throne room. Pink and red hibiscus, white gardenias and ginger, yellow alamanda, fragrant jasmine—her blessed feet would crush them all and their perfume would rise like incense. The ladies of the Hui Aloha 'Āina cornered the flower market; the commercial lei makers had nothing to work with that day.

But the word did not come by the *Australia*. The blossoms wilted, their high mission unfulfilled.

A little later, though, the queen had good news for her people. Before Blount had been gone a month, she had dispatched E. C. Macfarlane secretly to Washington. Now he brought reassurance. He had not seen Mr. Cleveland, but both Gresham and Blount, who had granted him long consultations, had insisted that in due time the United States would right the wrongs it had committed in January. The new envoy to whom the task would fall might arrive any day, certainly not later than the end of October.

Again there was joy among the queen's friends.

Abruptly, near the end of October, Admiral Skerrett received orders to leave Honolulu. He was to take passage with his staff on the next mail steamer for San Francisco, there to join the *Boston* for transfer to the navy's Asiatic station. Skerrett recognized the orders for what they were—a rebuke. He had been too friendly with the Dole government. For the administration's crucial move on the Hawaiian chessboard, Admiral John Irwin would be dispatched from Hong Kong. Exchanging stations with Skerrett, he would be subject in all Hawaiian matters, so his instructions

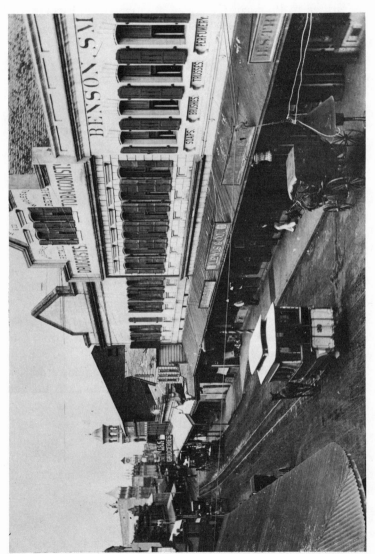

Fort Street about 1895.

read, to the new United States minister—long awaited but not yet arrived.

Back in Washington, on October 13, Secretary Gresham had written to President Cleveland a letter which began: "The full and impartial reports submitted by the Hon. James H. Blount . . . ," and closed by posing the question, "Should not the great wrong done to a feeble, but independent, state by an abuse of the authority of the United States be undone by restoring the legitimate government?" But there was no intention that either capital should hear of this letter until the new minister, Albert S. Willis, leaving Washington that very day, had reached his post and carried out at least a part of his secret instructions.

In his office at Snow Cottage—the same quarters in the hotel grounds that Blount had occupied—Minister Willis welcomed Lili'uokalani. It was the morning of November 13; he had been in Hawai'i a little more than a week and had presented to Sanford Dole his letter of credence and President Cleveland's "renewed assurance of the friendship, interest, and hearty good will . . . for the people of the island realm." Today Consul General Mills, formerly Blount's secretary, now successor to the dismissed Henry Severance, had invited the former queen to a conference. She had come in her carriage, accompanied by Chamberlain Robertson, who straightway was taken into another room. Mills had gone to the front of the house to protect the conference from interruption.

Lili'uokalani knew what the interview portended. For ten months she had waited for the American republic to answer her appeal and restore "the life of the land." They were seated. Minister Willis, a small, bald man with a gray-streaked mustache and a stubby beard, spoke quietly, cautiously. The president of the United States, he said, had important communications to make to her. Was she willing, for her own interest and safety, to receive them alone and in confidence?

"Yes," said Lili'uokalani.

The words went on. "The president sincerely regrets . . . unauthorized intervention . . . with your consent and co-operation . . . the wrong . . . redressed." Lili'uokalani bowed in acknowledgment. Of course she was willing to cooperate.

"The president expects . . . forgiveness . . . magnanimity . . . love . . . loyalty . . . peace, friendship, and good government."

The minister paused. This time Lili'uokalani made no reply.

"The president not only tenders you his sympathy but wishes to help you," Willis went on. "Before fully making known to you his purposes, I desire to know whether you are willing to answer certain questions which it is my duty to ask."

She said, "I am willing." But she was beginning to look troubled.

"Should you be restored to the throne"—he stressed each word, fearing that she might miss the point—"would you grant full amnesty as to life and property to all those persons who have been or who are now in the Provisional Government, or who have been instrumental in the overthrow of your government?"

Lili'uokalani waited a long time to reply. Was she thinking that to "those persons" her brother Kalākaua had yielded, and ever since there had been trouble in the land; that for "those persons" she had appointed cabinets she did not trust and judges she despised; that for them she had withdrawn the constitution her people prayed for and pledged herself to abide by the hated one of 1887; that in spite of all this they had deposed her, driven her from her palace, seized her Crown lands, humiliated her, threatened her, persecuted her friends, tried to sell her country to a foreign government?

At length she said slowly, "There are certain laws of my government by which I shall abide. My decision would be, as the law directs, that such persons should be beheaded and their property confiscated to the Government."

Afterward Lili'uokalani did not believe that she could have said "beheaded." Willis, who had put the word into his dispatch to Washington, was sure that she had.* But whatever word she used, she was refusing to grant amnesty.

*It seems possible that the word "beheaded" in Willis' report to Washington was the result of the minister's error in interpreting his own notes. At least, one may wonder whether the word he jotted down (his stenographer was not present at this first interview) was "banished." Elsewhere Lili'uokalani is quoted as using the phrase "sent out of the country" to indicate the punishment she thought her enemies should suffer. It is not difficult to believe that to a harassed transcriber "banished" may have looked like "beheaded."

"It is your feeling that these people should be beheaded and their property confiscated?" the minister repeated.

"It is," she said, not quite positively. Minister Willis saw that she began to doubt herself.

"Do you fully understand the meaning of every word which you have said to me, and if so, do you still have the same opinion?" he asked.

"I have understood, and mean all I have said," she answered, "but—" There was a little pause, in which she arranged her thoughts. "But I might leave the decision of this to my ministers."

Willis pressed his advantage. It was all-important that he secure the queen's promise as quickly as possible. "Suppose it were necessary to make a decision before you appointed any ministers, and that you were asked to issue a royal proclamation of general amnesty, would you do it?"

She said, "I have no legal right to do that, and I would not do it." Then after a moment's hesitation she went on to explain her stand. "These people were the cause of the revolution of 1887. There will never be any peace while they are here. They must be sent out of the country and punished, and their property confiscated."

Though Willis had now gained the lives of the revolutionists, he had not fulfilled his instructions, which were to save also their property and their right to remain in the community. "Should the queen decline to pursue the liberal course suggested . . . ," his commission from Secretary Gresham read, "you will report the facts and wait further directions."

To the queen he said, "I have no further communication to make to you now, and will have none until I hear from my government, which will probably be three or four weeks."

There was a long pause while they looked at each other. Finally, Willis spoke. Would Liliʻuokalani give him the names of four of her most trusted friends? Within a day or two he might consider it his duty to hold a consultation with them in her presence. She named J. O. Carter, John Richardson, Joseph Nawahī, and E. C. Macfarlane. Then once more Willis cautioned her to hold in strictest confidence the conversation they had just had. During the dreary wait for word from Washington, the Provisional Government must not know of it.

On the sixteenth, Mr. Willis sent off a letter—a full account of the interview, with some comment—which could be expected to reach the capital in about fifteen days, and two telegrams—one in cipher, one not—which with luck would get there in nine. "Views of first party so extreme," said the open message, "as to require further instructions."

The *Alameda*, which carried this correspondence to San Francisco, was the through steamer from Australia; it brought, with other mail from "down under," a Reuter's dispatch from Washington by way of London and Auckland, which said that President Cleveland was drafting a message to Congress "favoring the restoring of monarchy to Hawaii." At first, government circles labeled the story a canard. But at noon the *Star* sent a reporter to question the American minister. Willis would neither confirm nor deny the Reuter report and would not discuss his own instructions, except to say that contingencies had arisen since his arrival that made it necessary for him to wait for further word. Since such word could not arrive for at least three weeks, he assured the *Star* that no action affecting the government would be taken for some time.

So everybody waited in harrowing uncertainty. Royalists, who had been utterly confident when Willis arrived, could make nothing of the delay. Lili'uokalani, the only one who knew, kept her promise to say nothing.

Samuel Damon, who had spoken informally with Willis, found hints of an American protectorate in the minister's guarded words. Sereno E. Bishop believed Willis was "getting new light" but doubted that his wisdom and tact were "adequate to meet the difficulties of his position." Many government supporters, while asserting that the minister could not possibly mean to restore the monarchy, doubted their own brave words. Sanford Dole, saying nothing, watched and wondered whether his government had come to its severest testing.

The *Monowai*, on the twenty-fourth, ended a part of the suspense. It brought papers containing the gist of Gresham's letter to Cleveland and word from Minister Thurston that the Cleveland administration apparently had decided on restoration, though he could get no confirmation at the State Department. As the New York *Herald* of November 8 had put it: "A diplomatic bombshell will burst within the next few days. . . . The bomb will be thrown by an accredited representative of the United States Government . . . against the badly conceived and worse managed Provisional Government of the Hawaiian Islands.

"If Minister Willis and Rear Admiral Irwin arrived in Honolulu on schedule . . ."

The government party meant to have something to say on that subject. More than a thousand haoles met the next evening in the drill shed. As usual there were speeches and resolutions: ". . . we have read with surprise and regret the recommendation of the Secretary of State; . . . we condemn the assumption . . . that the right of the Provisional Government to exist was terminated by [the] refusal to re-submit to the Senate the treaty of Union pending between the two countries; . . . we support . . . the Provisional Government, in resisting any attack upon it. . . ." They were sober and determined. Once they had thought the issue was annexation; now they saw that it was the very existence of their government.

President Dole, inquiring by letter of Mr. Willis whether the newspaper stories were correct, was reminded that a report to the president of the United States from one of his cabinet members was "a domestic matter," which the minister "could not assume to interpret." In an interview with Dole and W. O. Smith, however, Willis expressed sympathy for the Provisional Government in its plight, and regret that he could not speak fully and frankly. There were things not known to his government, and not known to him until he came, that required further instructions, he said. The whole business was "hung up." He would let them know as soon as he could.

They drew their own conclusions. Though they could not guess the reason for the delay, they did not doubt that Willis would move eventually to restore the queen. Would he use force? Would American bluejackets land to drive the government out? Admiral Irwin thought they would. Expecting to be called upon at any moment to give the distasteful order, he told a fellow officer that he had not felt "so deeply, so thoroughly sad" since the bombardment of Fort Sumter.

The executive council issued rifles and ammunition to the

marshal for the Citizens' Guard, rescinded the permission to land men for drill from the United States ships of war, increased the size of regular Company E, ordered the volunteer companies— one each night in rotation—to be quartered in the executive building, and fortified the lower verandas with sandbags.

President Dole met with officers of the military companies to discuss the council's plan of defense. The troops were to "resist until forced to yield," but the government could not ask Americans to fire on the United States flag. Two days later the sergeants of the Citizens' Guard sent one of their number to protest against such weakness. Let there be no yielding, the officers said in their written recommendations. Let the men fire on the U.S. marines if need be. Fortify the executive building thoroughly; wall it round with stones torn from the old, useless barracks. Store provisions and supplies for a siege. Arrest the queen and hold her as a prisoner of state. The government debated for hours and in the end rejected most of the Guard's proposals; but the word went out through Honolulu that the government soldiers, if attacked, would fight to the death. The belligerent sentiments had come, not from the regular army, but from the citizen volunteers—the clerks, the bankers, the schoolteachers, the doctors, the lawyers, the merchants —who stood ready to close down their businesses and lock up their offices at an instant's notice. They had been willing to fight in January, but it had not been necessary then. Now, no doubt, their bravery would be futile; they could not hope to hold out for long against the powerful nation they admired and had sought to join; but they could prove to the world that they were worthy of their American blood. So said the citizens of Honolulu. Sixty-seven-year-old Sereno Bishop, retired minister of the gospel, wrote in his journal, "I suppose a disabled old fellow like me . . . ought to stay by the women and children—but I should like to die fighting U.S. forces on such an infamous errand."

Firmly the executive council now examined government employees suspected of favoring restoration. For months the council had resisted pressure—at first from the snarling Drei Hundert and later from exuberant Annexation Club members— for a wholesale dismissal of royalist incumbents. Unless he entered a conspiracy or ran afoul of the strict antisedition laws, a clerk in the customhouse or an officer on the police force might think as he pleased and still hold his job. Now the *Star* began to shriek about the disloyal ones and to name names.

The questioning went on, and those who would not promise to take up arms to preserve the Provisional Government were turned out of their posts. This was when young Carl Widemann, a clerk in the Finance Department, came to a parting of the ways. He admitted that he would like to have the monarchy back again and that he was opposed to annexation, though he would, of course, submit if the United States decided that way. If there were war, he said, he would not fight against the Provisional Government—at least not as long as he remained an employee of the government—but he certainly would not carry a gun or shoot American sailors to defend it. Next day he was asked to resign; the hard-pressed council dared take no chances. It was the same way with George Smithies, whose father-in-law was the royalist Samuel Nowlein, and with a number of others. Samuel Damon alone opposed the dismissal policy and offered to resign as minister of finance, but at length he accepted the decision of his colleagues and remained on the council. The question of the native policemen was still moot when the *Corwin* came in.

At dawn on December 14 the lookout roused Honolulu with the word that the U.S. Revenue Cutter *Corwin* was off Diamond Head. This was no scheduled arrival. It could mean but one thing—the instructions for which Minister Willis waited, rushed to him by special sailing. Men of both parties hurried downtown to glean what they could, leaving anxious wives to consult each other by telephone. As the pilot boat touched the quay, the captain leaped out, stepped into a waiting hack and drove at a furious pace toward Minister Willis' house. Some observers said that Mr. Blount had come again, but that turned out to be a mistake. The dispatch-bearer merely resembled him in build and grayness.

All that insistent reporters could learn at the legation was that the message was being decoded, a process that would take hours. Whether the minister would make a statement later remained to be seen. But the *Star*'s legman who went to the wharf had better success. Though the *Corwin* had carried no mail, a crew member had an American newspaper. Dated December 4—the day Congress had convened for its regular session—it contained the president's message. By 9:40 the *Star* had an extra on the streets, and everybody who could read English knew that Mr. Cleveland had said, "Our only honorable course was to undo the wrong that had been done by those representing us, and to restore as far as practicable the status existing at the time of our forcible intervention. Our present Minister has received appropriated instructions to that end."

But had the president directed the minister to use force—if not in his original instructions, then by the coded message of the *Corwin*? On the American ships liberty was stopped; the decks bristled with stacked guns, filled cartridge belts, and packed knapsacks, though when asked what it all portended, officers said they did not know. Navy wives who had been living in the city packed their belongings for quick removal from shore to ship, and native royalists stood in crowds on the wharves, expecting a landing at any moment.

The Provisional Government ordered out its reserves and kept in the prisoners who usually worked on the roads. Honolulu's "Black Week" had begun.

"Should the Queen refuse assent to the written conditions you will at once inform her that the President will cease interposition in her behalf. . . . The President feels that . . . we have incurred responsibilities to the whole Hawaiian community, and it would not be just to put one party at the mercy of the other." So read the dispatch brought by the *Corwin*. Mr. Willis decided he must make another effort to persuade the queen.

Since their first interview he had not communicated with her directly, but he had conferred with some of her friends, seeking to find out how far they shared Lili'uokalani's views about the required amnesty. By now he knew that, whatever terms were finally made, a restoration of the monarchy would be followed by a new royalist attempt to overturn the hated constitution of 1887. He saw that a return to the status of January 14 by no means would end turmoil in Hawai'i; that in his quixotic instructions he had brought from Washington, not peace, but a sword. Yet he must do his utmost to fulfill the mission on which Secretary Gresham had sent him.

Of all the tried and trusted friends of the monarchy he had talked with or observed closely, J. O. Carter seemed to Willis to have the greatest integrity and intelligence. Carter also seemed the most likely to soften the queen's resistance. So, when two days after the *Corwin*'s dramatic arrival Lili'uokalani came again to the legation, she brought, at Willis' suggestion, this middle-aged haole adviser, whose close kin were even then arming to prevent her restoration.

Lili'uokalani had had a month to prepare for this interview. She chose her words carefully; and this was well, for Consul Mills was with them, making a stenographic report. She was willing, she said, to grant the enemies of her kingdom their lives, but further than that she would not go. All who had had a part in her overthrow must be sent out of the country and their wealth seized. With their confiscated property she would pay the debts of the Provisional Government, which she agreed the monarchy would have to assume. But the traitors must go. "Their presence and that of their children," she repeated, "would always be a dangerous menace to me and my people."

When Mr. Willis had repeated the president's inflexible demands and Lili'uokalani had again indicated her refusal, the conference ended. That was Saturday, December 16. On Monday morning Minister Willis began drafting the dispatch that would report the stalemate to Washington, but he was not left in peace to accomplish his depressing task. Over Sunday word had got around, and citizens had jumped to the conclusion that Monday was the day. Excitement mounted as the crowd on the waterfront increased. There were native Hawaiians, haoles, and Orientals. Everybody was watching the warships *Philadelphia* and *Adams*— with feverish hope or frantic fear or just plain curiosity. A chance word, a slight incident could have touched off a bloody riot. Twenty-three native policemen, questioned once more as to their loyalty, resigned abruptly, leaving the marshal alarmingly shorthanded. Business places remained closed.

In midmorning German Consul H. F. Glade called at the

legation. "Say something to relieve this tension," he implored Willis. But the harassed minister could only protest that he was laboring to the utmost to arrange matters satisfactorily for all parties. At present he could not reveal anything. Perhaps in another forty-eight hours—.

"In another forty-eight hours you and I will be lucky if our houses have not been set afire," Glade said. He shrugged and departed.

About that time J. O. Carter's telephone call came in. Carter believed that another interview with the queen might get some results, but he thought it most unwise for Her Majesty to be seen in the streets just now. Willis agreed; they made the appointment for early afternoon at Washington Place.

Carter opened the conference with an earnest appeal to Lili'uokalani to show a spirit of forgiveness and magnanimity, else good government for Hawai'i seemed impossible. But it was of no use. The queen would not give an inch. She said again that her people had had all they could stand of interference with their rights. How, she asked, could she be assured that her country would not be troubled again as it had been in the past, if she accepted President Cleveland's terms?

That, Mr. Willis said, was a subject the United States had no right to look into or express an opinion on. At the end of half an hour the minister and the queen were no nearer together than before.

Consul Mills stayed to transcribe his notes and read his report for Lili'uokalani's approval. He told her that the two transcripts—today's and that of the sixteenth—would go forward to President Cleveland. The *Corwin* would sail with them that evening.

President Dole's letter, delivered to the legation that afternoon, did not make Minister Willis any happier.

I am informed [it said], that you are in communication with Liliuokalani, the ex-Queen, with a view of re-establishing the monarchy. . . . Will you inform me if this report is true or if you are acting in any way hostile to this Government.

I appreciate fully the fact that any such action upon your part in view of your official relations with this Government would seem impossible;

but as the information has come to me from such sources that I am compelled to notice it, you will pardon me for pressing you for an immediate answer. . . .

A little before six o'clock J. O. Carter called again to say that Lili'uokalani was now ready to agree to the president's terms in full. Her written pledge of amnesty would be in the minister's hands early the next morning.

Willis canceled the *Corwin*'s sailing orders. Then he replied to President Dole's letter, asking for an appointment the next day. He could now speak plainly to the Provisional Government.

They met at 1:30 on the afternoon of December 19 at the office of the foreign minister—that apartment in the palace that had once been Kalākaua's bedroom and study. Besides Willis and Dole, there were the other members of the executive council —S. M. Damon, W. O. Smith, J. A. King, and F. M. Hatch. Through a thousand words of prepared text, reviewing the issues between the Provisional Government and the queen as President Cleveland saw them, Minister Willis plodded toward his climax: ". . . you are expected to promptly relinquish to her the consitutional authority," and his direct question to the men before him: "Are you willing to abide by the decision of the President?"

"The Government will take the matter under consideration," said President Dole, "and answer you as soon as they are ready."

The answer, written by Sanford Dole and unanimously approved by the executive and advisory councils, reached Minister Willis at midnight on the twenty-third. At 4:00 A.M. the *Corwin* was on her way, carrying to President Cleveland and Secretary Gresham the final blow to their hopes—a dignified but categorical *no*.

For two days after Minister Willis had submitted his question, the pall of Black Week continued to shroud the community. Business remained in abeyance; crowds of the nervous, the sanguine, and the curious still clogged the streets along the waterfront; the American warships still displayed their menacing preparations. No one, probably, but Willis knew that he had no authority to call the troops ashore; that if the government refused

to step down, he must report that fact to Washington and wait—
in heaven's name, wait how long, with the city going distracted?
—for further word from his superiors.

But the *Alameda* was due on the twenty-second; there would
be mail and papers for the news-hungry community. The whole
town would go down, as it always did, to see her come in; and
everybody—all the haoles, at least—would stand around the
post office until the packets were opened. Somebody who had a
newspaper would jump up on the veranda railing and shout out
the headlines to the crowd. People who had letters would tear
them open, scan them quickly, and share passages with their
friends. Long before the seals had been broken on official dispatches,
Honolulu would know how Congress had treated the president's
plans for Hawai'i.

All these things happened as expected, but before a passenger
or a mail sack had left the *Alameda*, as she lay off the harbor in the
sunrise, the message "All is right" was flashed ashore and sped to
the anxious watchers. Lorrin Thurston, they soon found, had
come home to tell them, firsthand, that Washington—and indeed
much of the United States—was in a turmoil of protest against the
president's policy; that the Senate was asking for an investigation;
that henceforth Congress, not Gresham or Cleveland, would call
the tune.

So the only war would be a war of words. Black Week was
history.

A "decent regard for the opinion of mankind" led Sanford
Dole to amplify his refusal to surrender the sovereignty with a
review of the controversy as the Provisional Government saw it.
Accepting the president's decision against annexation as final for
the present, though not for the long term, Dole addressed himself
to what he called the "misstatements and erroneous conclusions"
of Willis' communication of December 19.

"We do not recognize the right of the President of the United
States to interfere in our domestic affairs," he wrote, asserting that
noninterference was not only a principle of international law, but
an avowed tenet of the American Republic since the beginning.
Upon what, then, had the president based his assumed right?

Upon the assumption apparently that the queen's protest, filed with the Provisional Government on January 17, constituted an agreement between the two parties to seek arbitration. Dole marshaled his evidence to show that there had been no such agreement. As for the queen's notice of her appeal to the United States—that document which William Cornwell had brought from the palace to Ali'iōlani Hale as evening closed in on January 17—Dole wrote: ". . . it was a matter of indifference to us. Such an appeal could not have been prevented, as the mail service was in operation as usual. That such a notice, and our receipt of it without comment, should be made a foundation of a claim that we had submitted our right to exist as a government to the United States had never occurred to us until . . . the presentation of the claim of the President . . . by you on December 19."

Then with a deft change of direction Dole set out to show that if the president believed that he had been called upon to adjudicate a dispute, he had proceeded most strangely. ". . . when and where," he asked, "has the President held his court of arbitration? This government has had no notice of the sitting of such a tribunal and no opportunity of presenting evidence of its claims." A detailed and critical discussion followed of Blount's procedures in selecting and examining witnesses. Blount's report Dole had not yet seen, but he quoted the familiar words in which both Gresham and Willis had summarized his allegations "that the movement against the Queen if not instigated was encouraged and supported by the representative of this [the U.S.] Government at Honolulu; that he [Minister Stevens] kept his promise by causing a detachment of troops to be landed from the *Boston* . . . and by recognizing the Provisional Government . . . when it was too feeble to defend itself." Dole denied "specifically and emphatically" the correctness of "each and every one of the allegations of fact" contained in the passage. Then came another of those disarming concessions that a skilled lawyer knows how to make with effect. Supposing that all this were true—that the American forces had illegally assisted the revolutionists and that thus the American government had made itself responsible to the queen—that, said Dole, was a matter for the American government and the queen to settle between them. "This Government, a recognized sovereign power, equal in authority with the United States Government and enjoying diplomatic relations with it cannot be destroyed by it for the sake of discharging its obligations to the ex-Queen."

There was more—about the problems of maintaining stable government in "a community made up of five races, of which the larger part but dimly appreciate the significance and value of representative institutions" and about the incidents and controversies that had led up to the revolution. At the end he said, " . . . we deem our position impregnable under all legal precedents . . . and in the forum of conscience. . . . Our only issue with your people has been that, because we revered its institutions of civil liberty, we have desired to have them extended to our own distracted country, and because we honor its flag and, deeming that its beneficent and authoritative presence would be for the best interests of all our people, we have stood ready to add our country, a new star to its glory. . . . If this is an offense, we plead guilty to it."

This was the statement which Minister Willis received at midnight and sent off by the *Corwin* in the early morning of December 24. At San Francisco the little ship idled off the coast until it could enter the bay in the dark and its captain could forward the dispatches to Washington before any newspaper reporter was the wiser. It became part of the voluminous matter on Hawai'i that Mr. Cleveland laid before the Senate.

The *Alameda*'s budget of news, so heartening to government supporters, shattered the royalists' hopes with terrible suddenness. Through a year of delays and postponements, the queen's friends had never doubted that the United States would reinstate her. To Lili'uokalani herself the betrayal—so she termed the failure to use force—was heartbreaking. Against her better judgment she had promised everything the American president had asked, but she might as well have remained firm for all the good it had done her.

As so often happens when a cause has received a setback, the royalists quarreled among themselves about whom to blame. Some chided the queen for not accepting the president's conditions in mid-November. Some berated Cleveland for not acting months before, while Blount was there. Some, maintaining that the Provisional Government had joined with them in submitting the dispute to Cleveland for arbitration, charged Dole and his colleagues with bad faith in rejecting the president's solution. Some, grieved as they were, thought this the end for the monarchy.

When the news got around that Lili'uokalani had made concessions to Minister Willis, promising amnesty to the P.G.s and a return to the constitution of 1887, the executive body of the Hui Aloha 'Āina met in indignation and addressed a fifteen-hundred-word rebuke to her.

"The restoration being, not a favor, but an obligation of justice on the American Government," the memorial said, "ought to be done without any restrictive conditions, and Your Majesty owes to the Hawaiian people, who have stood by you, to now stand by them and not sacrifice one iota of their rights." She should not have "acceded privately," the document continued, but should have consulted with the representatives of her people; and in the event that she did not consider her present cabinet as speaking for the nation, she was reminded that "the nearest and most authoritative representatives of the people" were the officers of the eight-thousand-member Hui, who had "proved their loyalty . . . and their discretion and trustworthiness."

The undersigned—Nawahī, Bush, Cummins, Bipikāne, Marques, Rickard, Ross, and Seward—hoped that the queen would "excuse this plain talk." They wished to "place themselves on record as having dutifully sounded the alarm," so that they might not be blamed if the members of the Hui got discouraged and apathetic on hearing that their hopes of "a good and stable and just national government" had been frustrated.

Lili'uokalani had known well enough all that the memorial set forth. But she had known, too, that unless she yielded to the American minister's demands, President Cleveland would make no further effort in her behalf. And as to consultation, Mr. Willis had allowed her but one adviser, J. O. Carter, whose counsel she had followed—to no avail.

"Madam does not look well," reported a Washington Place guard who was in the pay of the marshal at this time. It was no wonder.

The last day of 1893 fell on a Sunday. From Washington Place Lili'uokalani could see the "missionary" people flocking to the evening service at Central Union Church to give thanks for their deliverance from doubt and fear. She could hear their hymns of faith and praise; she knew the songs well, for her choir at Kawaiaha'o had sung them in Hawaiian in days gone by. But tonight the P.G.s were not depending on God alone; their watchmen (Lili'uokalani called them spies) were all around—on the corner by the church, in the school yard *'ewa* of her house, in Miller's Lane, over by the Episcopal church—all carrying guns. "Captain Nowlein is quite nervous," she wrote in her diary.

At midnight, after a brief sleep, Lili'uokalani woke to the sound of bells and bombs. Somewhere nearby the National Band —her own loyal musicians—were playing "Hawai'i Pono'i." Again she opened her diary and recorded her thoughts: "Thankful to our Creator for all we have enjoyed during the past and hoping for all that is good for the future. That our Nation may be restored by President Cleveland and Congress is my earnest prayer and of my people to our just Rights."

On January 17, 1894, the Provisional Government celebrated its first birthday anniversary. From early morning, when firecrackers and tin horns roused the populace, till evening, when thousands jammed Union Square for speeches, the day was one of rejoicing. Though annexation might be as far away as 1897 or 1898, the pressure that had mounted through November and December was now relaxed. Only wishful royalists believed that the American Congress would concur in the president's desire to roll back history. So the joyful partisans flung out their flags and decked the capitol grounds with lanterns; the military forces marched; and President and Mrs. Dole shook innumerable hands.

A little more than two weeks later came a royalist anniversary, observed privately but with fervor. It was a year on February 1 since the Royal Hawaiian Band boys had resigned rather than take the oath.

"What can you do to get a living?" Maestro Berger had asked, that day in 1893.

"'*Ai pohaku*! We will eat stones," the boys had cried. Their *kama'aina* friend Ellen Wright Prendergast (Kekoaohiwaikalani), when they told her about it, commemorated their fierce loyalty in a song. "Kaulana na pua o Hawai'i," it began, "Famous are the flowers of Hawai'i." But it did not mean the hibiscus and the plumeria; it saluted those native Hawaiians, who were so steadfast in their love of country that they would not sign the "greedy, grasping document" brought by the messenger of the "evil hearted." It continued:

> We are content with the rocks,
> That remarkable food of the Country.
> . . . .
>
> We will adhere to Liliuokalani
> Until the Crown is again restored.
> This is the end of our refrain
> For the people who love their Country.

One who heard the band boys sing it on the anniversary of their defiance said it had on the Hawaiians the effect of the "Marseillaise" on the French—"exciting and exasperating." The *hula ku'i* business (stamping, heel-twisting, thigh-slapping, dipping of knees, doubling of fists) almost drowned out the words, but the fierce loyalty was written in every shining face. Over and over they beat out the rhythm, thumping their drums and miming their scorn of the "paper of the enemy," of the "heap of government money." It was a pledge renewed. They had not thought it would be so long before President Cleveland kept his word, but they would wait.

To a foreign visitor in the spring of 1894, Lili'uokalani said, "How could I be otherwise than well and happy? I am surrounded by everything that is beautiful—the lovely foliage of the flowers in the garden and the birds that sing so sweetly." And indeed Washington Place, with its magnificent trees—tamarind, ironwood, monkeypod, ylang-ylang, and royal palms; its oleander and lilies, begonias and bougainvillea; its gay-colored crotons and ti; its well-groomed lawns and graveled paths; and its gracious white mansion, offered every comfort an aging body and a tired spirit might seek. Yet Lili'uokalani could not rest.

There were the long periods between mails, when hope

86

battled with foreboding, and the crushing disappointment each time a steamer brought news that was, if not bad, at least not good. There were the money worries, growing more pressing day by day. When she heard that the Provisional Government was ready to pay her a liberal annuity if she relinquished her claims, she must have thought how peaceful it would be to live, retired, with no fretting about cabinets and constitutions, protests and proclamations. But she believed that duty lay elsewhere. She wrote in her diary, "Not a cent will I accept and sacrifice the rights of my people."

Sometimes she sought relief in music, spending hours at the grand piano that had been the gift of her friends. Melodies and words composed in happier days—among them the tender "Aloha 'Oe,"—brought tears of self-pity, and the self-pity turned easily to anger and apprehension. She was sure there were desperate characters among the P.G. soldiers who waited only for a good opportunity to take her life; she knew that the publication of Minister Willis' dispatch, attributing to her those bloodthirsty words she was certain she had never spoken, had brought forth new demands that she be imprisoned or deported; and she feared that there were among her vaunted friends spies in the pay of the government (there were!). She dared not ride out in her carriage, where she could be shot at or kidnaped; indeed she rarely went as far as the Beretania Street gate. But she chatted now and then with her volunteer guards to keep up their spirits and received many visits from royalist leaders.

Cut off from the social and ceremonial activities that she had loved as princess and as queen, she still shared the anxiety, the perplexity, and the quarrels of her partisans, who brought her disturbing rumors, named would-be cabinets, submitted memorials, wrote protests, proposed meetings, sought credentials, and abused each other until Lili'uokalani's head was in a whirl.

More cabinets were made and unmade in the queen's parlor that spring than in the tempestuous session of the 1892 legislature. Must Parker, Peterson, Colburn, and Cornwell—those rascals who had brought on all the trouble—be restored along with the queen? If so, could they not be ordered to resign immediately after the happy event had occurred? Had the queen any thought

Queen Lili'uokalani with Sam Nowlein in the gardens of
Washington Place; summer 1894.

of appointing J. O. Carter, whose wrong-headed advice she had followed in yielding to Willis' demands in December? Indeed, she must not; he was a treacherous man, likely to "sell the country." Granted that Bush and Nawahī had great influence with the commoners, were they not impractical fanatics—Bush a Seventh Day Adventist and Nawahī a painter of landscapes in oils? Did Her Majesty not know that her old favorite Charlie Wilson was dangerously friendly with certain P.G.s, that he and his wife were probably both in the pay of the P.G. marshal? Let the queen beware of Robert Wilcox, who was said to be worming his way back into her favor; he had twice failed in attempts at revolution, and he had once sided openly with Reformers and annexationists. So her friends admonished her; so they jockeyed for position in the government that was to be.

But there was much going on in royalist circles that spring of 1894 of which Lili'uokalani was not aware. The failure of the United States to use force against the Provisional Government in December had convinced many persons that restoration, if it were to come, must be effected by Islanders. At Camarinos' fruit store on King Street, at Bush's shop in Printer's Lane, in the saloons along Hotel Street, at the Sans Souci beach resort beyond Waikīkī, in the very shadow of Washington Place where Captain Sam Nowlein's guards held sway, at the *Holomua* office, and at the residences of Cummins, Gulick, and Widemann, small groups— often but two or three haoles or *hapa haoles* (part haole, part Hawaiian)—began to meet for talk of ways and means.

There were those who favored sending abroad immediately for arms and ammunition, and those who thought that fighting men with military experience must be brought from the Coast; there were those who wanted to use explosives to blow the palace into rubble and those who counted heavily on the subversion of soldiers in the P.G. army. There were successful opium smugglers who guaranteed that they could get guns past the customs officials, businessmen willing to take trips to buy munitions (with other people's money), and optimists who vowed there were arms enough already in the Islands, could they but lay their hands on them. There were some who thought that Maui, where royalist sentiment was strong and government defenses weak, should "open up the ball," and others who dreamed of seizing interisland steamers, loading them with armed natives from the outer islands and bringing them into Honolulu for a surprise attack on the capital. Some, as they vehemently denounced the "missionary" oligarchy, seemed scarcely to remember that there were natives to be considered; others spoke loud and long about the wrongs that had been done the Hawaiians. But almost nobody trusted the commoners or thought they should have any part in the planning.

As to money, the few who had any were slow to risk it in such madcap exploits as were proposed. But talk was cheap, and so were paper and postage.

"Can you procure 2000 Rifles & 20,000 rounds of ammunition?" one inquirer wrote a San Francisco friend in April; "also if 500 men can be enlisted . . . at a salary of say $40.00 per mo. & found? I know there would be no difficulty in chartering a steamer to bring them here, also the landing them would be very easy."

And in May, Robert Wilcox warned his old patron from Kalākaua's day, C. C. Moreno—now in Washington, lobbying for the royalists—that "a bloody revolution will follow if the Senate fails to do justice to Hawaii." "Many plans are under consideration by our people," he wrote. "Some of the hot-headed ones are talking of plans of the dark ages for the destruction of life. I do not believe in destroying life except in open war, but you cannot restrain these people forever." Wilcox thought all of this ought to be "an important consideration to the Congress of the United States."

The Congress of the United States, however, seemed remarkably impervious to such warnings. In its own good time it conducted inquiries and put forth reports and resolutions, all recommending noninterference in the domestic affairs of Hawai'i. Of these Lili'uokalani, her faith in the president as strong as ever, made her own wishful interpretations.

"When a crown falls, . . . it is pulverized, and when a scepter departs, it departs forever; and American opinion can not sustain any American ruler in the attempt to restore them, no matter how virtuous and sincere the reasons may be that seem to justify him."

In these plain words the Senate Committee on Foreign Relations, John T. Morgan of Alabama, chairman, condemned the administration policy of restoration in Hawai'i. Embodied in a report that summarized weeks of hearings on the same questions that Commissioner Blount had investigated, the ringing statement set the tone for the Senate's resolution, passed unanimously, which declared that "of right it belongs wholly to the people of the Hawaiian Islands to establish and maintain their own form of government . . . ;" and that "the United States ought in no wise to interfere therewith."

"Wholly to the people of the Hawaiian Islands," the resolution read. But who were the people of Hawai'i?

Lili'uokalani, told by her faithful partisans of the Senate's action, wrote in her diary, " . . . it is not for the Chinese [and] Portuguese but for the Hawaiians . . . " But no supporter of the Provisional Government quite agreed with her. Haoles as well as Polynesians, they maintained, were "the people"; and, though they thought a great deal that spring of 1894 about how to win the common natives away from the defunct monarchy, they did not doubt for one moment that white Hawaiians must take the lead in establishing a government that would hold on until Mr. Cleveland left the presidency.

Mainlanders tended to think of Island problems as those of natives versus "missionaries," or perhaps of natives versus sugar planters. But in 1894 the population of Hawai'i was already varied and complex. Men like Sanford Dole who looked forward to establishing a Republic of Hawai'i, now that interference from abroad no longer threatened, were well aware of this fact and sorely perplexed about how to deal with it.

First of all, there were the mechanics and laborers, the *malihini*s or Johnny-come-latelys of the haole community. In all sorts of ways they were as different from the "missionaries" as a jerky, clattering tramcar from a well-groomed horse and carriage. The lush years of the sugar industry had brought them to Hawai'i. In those days it was hard to get enough machinists, foundry workers, wagon builders, pipefitters, and plumbers to keep the great industry moving, to say nothing of enough barbers, bartenders, and boardinghouse keepers to serve the newcomers. Every arriving vessel had deposited on the Honolulu wharves its motley company of the skilled, the brawny, and the merely adventurous. They came from Boston, Chicago, San Francisco, and Vancouver. They came from Europe, too—many of them from Germany, others from Sweden, Austria, or Greece, sometimes directly and sometimes after a short interval in the United States—until the grimy, crowded lodging places in Fowler's Yard and along Hotel Street resounded to tongues as diverse as Babel's.

A few of them saved their wages, went to church on Sunday, took out denization papers as soon as they were eligible, and rose rapidly in the regard of the community. When depression struck, they were no worse off than the next man. But the rootless ones, who had spent their substance riotously at the Central House bar or in one of Chinatown's illicit *che fa* dens, were in trouble when the jobs stopped. They could not leave—they had no money for passage, and there was no place where they could expect to fare better. The mainland, particularly the West, was deep in its own economic troubles. They survived, full of discontent, as the unemployed did in those days of rugged individualism, by scheming, begging, borrowing, competing fiercely for tag ends of work and exhorting their fellows who had jobs and votes to get things set right again.

In politics the mechanics had tended to be anti-"missionary"; they resented the blue laws that prohibited Sunday amusements, strictly regulated the sale of liquor, and made a felony of craps and penny ante; and when collapsing sugar prices forced down their wages or threw them out of work, they loudly blamed the planters for their plight. Yet in January 1893, many of them rushed to join the Provisional Government's army, partly because they welcomed employment of any sort, and partly because annexation sounded like a cure for their woes.

Now, a year later, they were still without the plush government jobs they had coveted, and still ruled by an oligarchy they had helped to create, by men who, in filling posts and offices, stubbornly refused to rate services rendered in the overthrow above competence and experience. The disgruntled ones hurled the taunt of "family compact" (and indeed, when a fit and able person was found for an assignment, he seemed invariably to be a relative by

92

blood or marriage, a near neighbor, or a close business associate of someone on the councils). Some of them formed secret societies, such as the American League or the Schuetzen Club, to further their political aims.

As the hope of annexation faded and the prospects of restoration remained alive, it was predicted in government circles that this whole body of supporters might make a bargain with the royalists and go over to the queen's side. But turncoats were reputed to be coolly received in the monarchist camp, and a leader like Tim Murray, who had been with the Reformers since '87 and had proved especially staunch during the Black Week crisis, had a good chance of keeping his fellows in line.

There were still others who aspired to be "people" in Hawai'i. Since January of 1893, seizing quickly an unexpected opportunity, the Japanese government had been clamoring, through its minister, Saburo Fujii, for civil rights, the privilege of naturalization, and an end to discrimination because of race. There were some twenty-five thousand Japanese in the Islands then. Most of them were field hands, but some hundreds had fulfilled their contracts, left the plantations, descended on Honolulu—their small savings in hand —and gone into business. They sold fish, cut wood, hired out as caretakers and yardmen, tended store, and frequently opened their own shops. Sober, thrifty, ambitious, shrewd, they prospered; and every man of them was a thorn in the side of the restless haole tradesmen, who wailed that there ought to be a law to keep Orientals on the farms. But with Japan's big warship *Naniwa* in the harbor to back him up, Minister Fujii went on insisting that the right to naturalization and Island citizenship must be granted to his people.

The Chinese, too, had their case. Before 1887 a few educated and well-to-do Chinese had held citizenship in Hawai'i. The hastily drafted consitution of that year barred all Orientals from voting. Intent on curbing the arbitrary power of a king, the Reformers had given little thought to the Asians in their midst, and when the matter was drawn to their attention, they protested that they dared not open any rift through which thousands of illiterate cane-field workers of alien culture and strange creeds could force their way into dominance. Yet the haoles had not been able to wall off this Asia-in-Hawai'i. Long before the Japanese came on the scene, many Chinese, abandoning agriculture, had claimed their corner of Honolulu, sold food and curios, run laundries, built shrines and temples and a theater, and celebrated their New Year with firecrackers and handsome paper dragons. And, unlike the Japanese who sent home for picture brides and stubbornly kept to their own culture, the Chinese often had married Hawaiian girls. Sons of such unions, possessing the citizenship denied their fathers, had begun by the 1890s to take part in politics. They looked to the new government to redress the error of 1887; and when instead, the councils resurrected an old bill, buried since the last days of the 1892 legislature, and discussed its passage as a step toward restricting Orientals to agriculture, Chinatown seethed.

"By what right do our white-skinned brothers assume to lord it over us, and to say that we shall do business, and trade, and live and breathe, only by their consent?" cried Chang Kim at the mass meeting of February 14, 1894, when two thousand persons had pressed into the Chinese theater and a thousand more stood round about in mud and rain.

W. C. Achi, a Chinese-Hawaiian who had learned his mother's tongue but not his father's, declaimed through an interpreter: "I tell you, countrymen of my father, that there has never such . . . [an evil] law as this one been passed or even thought of." Resolutions of protest were sent to the executive building, and the new Chinese political society enrolled nine hundred members within a week.

Nor were the Portuguese backward in asserting their claim as people of the Islands. Most of them were already voters, blanketed into citizenship in 1887 by swearing to uphold the new constitution of that year. They too had come to Hawai'i as contract laborers; and once they had served their time, they had gravitated to the capital, where they clustered together in their own neighborhoods—on the slope of Punchbowl and near Punahou—raised grapes, figs, and alligator pears in their dooryards, and, being for the most part unschooled, followed the dictates of their political leaders. In January of '93 they had turned out whole-heartedly for the new government, and when its forces were permanently organized became volunteer Company C, with Portuguese officers.

Their mass meeting on February 18, 1894, passed resolutions against further immigration of either Chinese or Japanese,. and declared their colony unanimously in favor of annexation and ever ready to defend the Provisional Government, should there be need. A month earlier, at the January 17 celebration, this group had almost stolen the show, parading through Union Square just before the anniversary speeches, with torches and banners that read: "Progresso Uniao Liberdada," and "America Is Our Goal." It was no wonder that the P.G.s loved the Portuguese.

6. REPUBLIC OF HAWAI'I

The sandbags of Black Week had scarcely disappeared from the executive building verandas when the councils of the Provisional Government began to plan for a more permanent organization. In February they voted to recommend a constitutional convention. The bill they passed, after three readings and much discussion, provided that the nineteen men who made up the executive and advisory councils should become the convention's nucleus, and that eighteen other delegates should be elected by districts through the Islands.

Critics rose on all sides to say: Not enough! Elected delegates should be in the majority; let the council members run for their places if they want to be constitution makers. The *Advertiser* urged "a bold and radical move in the direction of full popular government." But the men of the councils felt they had to be safe as well as right. They had read history and knew that moderate makers of revolutions all too often had lost control to wild-eyed extremists; they did not propose to relinquish this one to the American League or the Schuetzen Club.

To vote in the election, which was set for May 2, a haole or Hawaiian had only to swear allegiance to the Provisional Government and pledge himself to oppose monarchy. For a month registration boards sat in all districts from ten to two daily, and Tuesday and Saturday evenings from six to eight. And in sober truth there was more rejoicing among the government people over every native who signed up than over ninety and nine haoles who did so.

No doubt a few Hawaiians registered under pressure from their employers, just as some had signed annexation petitions unwillingly the year before. Certainly, on the other hand, a good many refrained only through fear of reprisals "when the queen goes back." Especially in the rural districts they treated the boards with a kind of wistful respect that said, more plainly than words, "We wish we could enter into this fine game with you, but our love of our country forbids." Some spoke out frankly: "President Cleveland has sent us word that we must wait." Or "All who register will be hanged when the queen is restored." Occasionally a man put down his name one day and came back the next to have it expunged. Hawaiian women, it was said, stiffened the will of their spouses by refusing to be wives to their mates if they signed.

In all, slightly more than four thousand persons registered. At the last election under the monarchy there had been more than ten thousand voters. The government was disappointed. The queen was jubilant.

A languid campaign led up to an undramatic election day. In districts where there was no contest some haoles did not bother to vote, and some of the Hawaiians who had been brave enough to enroll lost their courage when the day came. In one Honolulu precinct a queen's man stood near the polling place to cry, "*Kāhāhā*!" (the Hawaiian's exclamation of surprise and displeasure) and turn back any native who approached. Yet five Hawaiians had been audacious enough to run, and all of them won seats. One of them was Albert Kūnui'ākea, an unacknowledged son of Kamehameha III, a man in his forties. Having gained little from monarchy in all his years, he now threw in his lot with the P.G.s— an act Hawai'i's royalty scarcely noticed.

In Ali'iōlani Hale, in the chamber that had resounded to the mirth and anger of the long 1892 legislative session, seats were so arranged for the thirty-five constitution makers that the elected alternated with the self-appointed. They assembled on May 30—six native Hawaiians (John 'Ena of the advisory council was Chinese-Hawaiian), fourteen Hawaiians of foreign parentage (half of them missionary sons), nine Americans, three British, three Portuguese, and two Germans. "Aliens and foreign adventurers," an angry royalist proclaimed them. "Men who were either born here or have resided here a long time—all fully identified with the country," W. O. Smith retorted.

They were deadly serious and confident as they faced what the *Advertiser* described as the "delicate and difficult task of framing an organic law which shall be just to all classes and all races, while it secures as far as law can, the future welfare of Hawaii." Perhaps a more honest appraisal was that which a Columbia University professor of political science made in a letter to Sanford Dole: "I understand your problem to be the construction of a consitution which will place the government in the hands of the Teutons, and preserve it there, at least for the present."

Discussion was lively but remarkably amicable. There was quick agreement on the guarantee of basic rights, on the establishment of a bicameral legislature, and the vesting of executive power in a president and cabinet. There was not such quick agreement to retain the franchise limitations of the 1887 constitution, but the advocates of a "one-man-one-vote" policy soon found themselves a helpless minority. Those in control were afraid to let go. Until they could shift their burden to the United States, they would continue to walk cautiously, to take no risks, lest they be overwhelmed and destroyed.

Particularly perplexing was the problem of the Orientals. Since 1887 both Chinese and Japanese residents had protested the racial barrier to citizenship—especially the Japanese, who were strongly supported by their government in Tokyo. Here was a dilemma—how to make concessions that would really concede nothing; how to grant face-saving privileges without undermining the strength of the so-called republic. The answer was ingenious: language was substituted for race and nationality. An Oriental who could read and write English well enough to explain a chosen passage from the constitution might gain citizenship. One who could not, might still qualify under the proviso set up especially for the illiterate Portuguese—granting special rights to those who "took active part . . . in the formation of, and have since supported the Provisional Government." That only one Japanese ever claimed naturalization under this clause was quite in line with the expectations of those who drafted it. Still, the problem was evaded. Japanese Consul General Fujii said he was pleased that race was no longer designated as a bar to citizenship.

That Sanford Dole should become the first president, his six-year term extending well beyond the time when annexation could be hoped for, was an almost unanimous wish. The convention so ruled.

At the outset there had been some talk of submitting the new constitution, once it was made, to the voters for approval. But the desire to proclaim the republic on so auspicious a day as July Fourth led to a compromise—a ratification mass meeting on the evening of July 2. Among the ten speakers (no self-respecting mass meeting would have had fewer) was Judge John Kalua, who said, "I will stand before all Hawaii and show my people what I have done to give them a new start in this country." A little band of Hawaiians cheered him, but most of his countrymen had met an hour earlier in a huge rally in Palace Square, where Bush, Nawahī, Herman Widemann, and J. O. Carter had lifted their spirits by predicting that the new government was doomed to early death; it would have neither support from the people nor recognition by the Great Powers.

Undismayed, the Provisional Government proclaimed the Republic of Hawai'i at eight o'clock on the morning of the Fourth (with no military display but with plenty of regular troops in the palace basement, sharpshooters on the veranda, armed citizen guards in the yard, and police everywhere). Two days later the entire diplomatic corps, including United States Minister Willis, recognized the new regime.

By then the city had gone back to its workaday affairs—government partisans full of quiet exultation, royalist leaders a bit downcast, dissident American Leaguers already beating the drums for amendments to the two-day-old constitution.

Crown lands, almost a million acres of fertile farmland, rolling pasture, forest tracts, and lava-strewn wastes, had come into the hands of the Provisional Government in January 1893.

The Republic of Hawai'i proclaimed from the steps of 'Iolani Palace, July 4, 1894.

There were 650,000 acres on Hawai'i, 66,000 on Maui, 22,000 on Moloka'i, 23,000 on Lāna'i, and 70,000 on O'ahu. Inalienable from the reigning sovereign, to whom they brought revenue through long-term leases, they were lost to Lili'uokalani on the day when she surrendered, and she could regain them only by regaining the throne.

It was one of the griefs of the commoners that ridges and valleys that once had belonged to their *ali'i* had now fallen to the "greedy" haoles. Though the overthrow had not impoverished them personally, and restoration would make them no richer, they counted themselves plundered and the life of the land extinguished.

The men of the Provisional Government and the republic did not see it so. They believed that the former Crown lands, at least the arable parts, should be broken up and granted or sold as small homesteads, either to heretofore landless Hawaiians or to immigrants.

All his adult life Sanford Dole had studied the land question and written about it, saying that land without people on it is worth little, that "homesteads rather than field-gangs" should be the basis of Hawai'i's social and civil progress, and that the way to solve the problem of the Islands' declining population was to revise the land laws. The first step toward such revision was taken by the legislature in 1884, but the Homestead Act of that year lay unused for some time.* In 1890 a modest tract at 'Ola'a on Hawai'i, considered suitable for coffee culture, was opened to settlers. Now in late September of 1894, the republic being well launched and under full sail, the executive and advisory councils talked earnestly of enlarging the homestead movement but of setting safeguards to prevent speculation and to conserve timber and the water supply.

As a part of the plan for making small holdings productive, Joseph Marsden, the republic's commissioner of agriculture, "with great intelligence and with enthusiasm that knows no limit" (so said the *Advertiser*) tested trees, grasses, fruits, and grains with an

---

*The Homestead Act of 1884 should not be confused with the Hawaiian Homes Commission Act, passed by the United States Congress in 1920, which was designed to benefit only those of Hawaiian blood.

eye to their cultivation in Hawai'i and appraised the capacity and value of various soils. In the editor's judgment Mr. Marsden was "a true missionary" and deserved a place "well ahead in the list of Hawai'i's benefactors."

But the republic's homestead plan failed. Only a few parcels ever were applied for, and with annexation all government lands became the property of the United States, to be used for military installations or leased for large-scale production.*

---

*Even after annexation Lili'uokalani continued her efforts to regain the Crown lands, that she might add them to her private estate and eventually bequeath them for the benefit of the Hawaiian people. But she was unsuccessful. Presumably the final answer came when, on May 16, 1910, Judge Fenton W. Booth of the United States Court of Claims delivered the decision that the Crown lands had "belonged to the office and not to the individual."

7. RUMBLINGS OF REBELLION

Lili'uokalani still had faith in America's Grover Cleveland. "What matters it if they do set up their Constitution & establish a Republic," she wrote on July 4, 1894. "When the U.S. is ready, she will undo all that her Minister has done."

But most of her supporters were beginning to doubt. It was time, they said, to send a commission to Washington to learn from the president himself his intentions toward the Islands. On July 8 the queen yielded; sending for John Cummins, Samuel Parker, and Judge H. A. Widemann, she instructed them to sail by the next steamer—on July 13. They were to ask the president whether there was "any hope for his doing anything for the restoration of the Constitutional Government of these Islands." Not officially a member of the commission, Major William T. Seward—G.A.R. veteran, a wanderer from his American family, hard up, belligerent about restoring the monarchy—traveled as Cummins' "secretary" at Cummins' expense.

For Whom Are the Stars?

On August 1, after various delays, the four men registered at the Arlington Hotel in Washington. Two weeks later they had not yet seen the president, who at first was away, and then unwell. But on August 15 they received Mr. Cleveland's letter, enclosing the statement he had intended to make to them in person.

Quite lately [it concluded], a Government has been established in Hawaii which is in full force and operation in all parts of the Islands. It is maintaining its authority and discharging all ordinary governmental functions . . . and is clearly entitled to our recognition without regard to any of the incidents which accompanied or preceded its inauguration.

This recognition and the attitude of the Congress concerning Hawaiian affairs of course leads to an absolute denial of the least present or future aid or encouragement on my part to an effort to restore any government heretofore existing in the Hawaiian Islands.

Here, then, was the answer—inescapably, almost brutally, clear. The most wishful heart could not misunderstand. There was nothing left to do but go home, encourage the queen to accept an annuity from the republic, and urge the Hawaiians to register and vote. Or was there something else?

The commissioners, homeward bound, agreed that there was. While they waited for the president, they had conferred, informally and unofficially, with Secretary Gresham. On August 4, according to a State Department memo, Judge Widemann, hinting that there might well be an uprising on the queen's behalf, had said, "The Hawaiian people would like to know precisely the attitude of the United States towards them. They do not wish to encounter the opposition of your Government." The secretary had answered, "You will encounter no opposition from this Government. We claim no right to meddle in the domestic affairs of your country." And on August 5 Samuel Parker had said, "All our people desire to know is that the government of the U.S. is not on the side of the existing government against them." In reply the secretary had confirmed the rumor that the American warship *Philadelphia* had been ordered away from Honolulu and would not be replaced. Later Parker, paraphrasing Gresham, put it this way to royalists in the Islands: "If you are prepared to act, go ahead, chew those fellows up; there are only two Americans in Honolulu—Willis and Mills—we won't interfere."

So the commissioners came home believing that they brought a mandate, though strictly an unofficial one, to "chew those [P.G.] fellows up."

The emissaries reached Honolulu on Thursday, August 30, eluded those who crowded around the *Alameda*'s gangplank with eager questions, and got away in carriages to their own houses or those of royalist leaders. "Everything is all right," Sam Parker called out to the boys who tried to block his vehicle; he drove straight to Washington Place. Judge Widemann took home his traveling bags, in one of which "among his other little things," he had placed Cleveland's letter. Without bothering to unpack it—so trifling was its importance, apparently—he called on Lili'uokalani to tell "the story of the journey." The three commissioners would come on Saturday, he said, to open the letter in Her Majesty's presence.

If Lili'uokalani passed a restless night on August 30, it was not because of uncertainty about the Cleveland letter, but because, knowing its gist as well as the import of the commissioners' talks with Secretary Gresham, she had to make a vital decision. Would she, or would she not, sanction a counterrevolution in Hawai'i?

On the next morning she sent for Major Wodehouse. He had retired from his diplomatic post on August 6 and had been succeeded by A. G. S. Hawes, but he still was the queen's friend and counselor.

I have the honor to report [Hawes wrote to the London Foreign Office in a dispatch of August 31], that the deputation sent to Washington by the Queen of Hawaii returned here yesterday, having failed to gain access to the President of the United States.

The Queen informed Major Wodehouse at a private audience this morning that she would not yield to the new Republican Govt. notwithstanding its having now been recognized by the United States. Her plans were made; she had selected her leaders; her people were well prepared, and she had determined to fight. The rising would take place in a few days' time, but Her Majesty would give me ample warning.

If the outbreak occurs and protection is required for the lives and property of British subjects, I shall request the captain of the "Hyacinth" to land some men for the purpose.

The U. S. S. *Philadelphia* had been gone for two weeks.

Royalists and republicans alike knew that on September 1 the queen had opened President Cleveland's letter in the presence of the commissioners and Samuel Nowlein, and had sworn them all to secrecy about its contents "until the time comes." At once the rumormongers fell to their work. Sealed dispatches, they said, were in the hands of someone—perhaps Commissioner Hawes, perhaps the captain of H. M. S. *Hyacinth*—and when a certain day arrived, Lili'uokalani would place herself under British protection and, declaring the republicans rebels, would call on them to surrender the government. The thing would be done without bloodshed if possible, but she would use force if necessary.

The purpose of this baseless romancing was to keep the Hawaiians from swearing allegiance to the republic and qualifying to vote in November, when a legislature was to be chosen. The scheme worked. The band boys still sang, "We will be true to Liliuokalani / Until the crown is restored," and the natives in general looked the other way when they passed the registration centers.

But the royalist leaders knew there was work to do. The furtive planning sessions that had lapsed when the queen's commission left for Washington began again—a meeting at Sans Souci on the Waikīkī shore, an informal dropping-in at Charles T. Gulick's house on King Street, hushed talk at Bertelmann's shop or at Cunha's saloon. Samuel Nowlein seemed to be everywhere at once, drawing together the threads of the plot, acting in the name of Lili'uokalani, whose volunteer guards he commanded. Robert Wilcox seemed to be nowhere. Never greatly trusted by Nowlein, Wilcox had quarreled lately with Bush and Nawahī, who rebuked him for bragging, and now he talked of going off to fight for Japan in the war against China, or for China in the war against Japan.

It was the decision to send to the Coast for arms that ended talk of immediate action. On September 12 Nowlein reported to a group at Sans Souci. He had located about three hundred fifty guns—fifty at Washington Place, a dozen at Cummins', a dozen more at his own house, forty or so at the Halfway House in Nu'uanu Valley, others in the homes of various royalists. But they would need to arm a thousand men. Clearly it was inadvisable to proceed with what they now had.

They sent Billy Cornwell to ask Judge Widemann for $25,000 to buy guns abroad. So sure were they that the judge would oblige them that they joyfully named Cornwell to go to the Coast, purchase munitions, hire men, charter a ship and bring her in at Sans Souci, where her deck-pieces could, if need be, cover the landing. They even got down to discussing signals between ship and shore, before Widemann sent word that he had decided to go to the Coast himself. That was at five o'clock on the afternoon of Friday, September 14. The judge sailed next day on the *Australia*.

Herman Widemann's final effort to forestall armed revolt by diplomacy seems to have been wholly his own idea, but he had asked John E. Bush for help in persuading the queen. Accordingly, Bush had gathered a few native signatures to a petition, asking Her Majesty to send an envoy to the great powers of Europe. When he presented the plea, on September 13, Widemann, opportunely present, offered to go, bearing all the expense himself. Papers were hurriedly signed, the diplomatic corps apprised, the judge's bags packed, his still-valid passport presented; and suddenly, with his departure, royalist planning found itself back in the doldrums where it had languished all summer. For three months the queen would counsel peace and patience; the natives would be cajoled with groundless optimism; and little coteries of schemers would continue to diagram surprise attacks and debate the relative merits of bombs and bullets.

"For four or five months," *Holomua* expostulated, "we are to wait for Mr. Widemann to return from his little mission to Paris, Siberia, or somewhere else. When he returns we presume that somebody else will proceed to Alaska or Tasmania . . . and in the meantime the kanaka [native Hawaiian man] sits on his 'soil' and waits."

Ka Leo, in these days of waiting, proved adept at inventing cheerful tidings. Thus on November 16 it reported: "The three great powers, England, France and Germany, have recently considered the question laid before them by the Queen and Hawaiian people . . . and after mature consultation have ordered the United States of America to . . . bring about restoration." And a few days later: "Mr. Widemann, we understand, sends back hopeful news of his visit to the several governments with whose officials he has held intercourse on the Hawaiian question."

But Mr. Widemann had no hopeful news to send. In London he had addressed to Lord Kimberley of the Foreign Office a request for an appointment, and on November 1 had received a courteous refusal. On the back of Widemann's letter, now filed in the Public Record Office, is a note, doubtless written by Sir Percy Anderson, who signed the refusal: "More than one hint has been conveyed to him that he cannot be officially received, but he means to try. If he is allowed to call he could only be told that his protest cannot be received as the Govt have no intention of interfering into the domestic affairs of the Hawaiians with whom the Republic is at present the established form of government.

"Would it be best to write this to him and decline the interview?"

At the bottom of the page in red ink is Lord Kimberley's reply, signed "K": "Write and decline as you suggest."

So the judge moved on, only to find that France and Germany, too, had recognized the Republic of Hawai'i and were not disposed to discuss the matter further.

For weeks after Judge Widemann's departure, the men who had asked him for $25,000 believed that, on his way to Europe, he would buy arms in California and pay for them with his own money. But at last they saw that nothing of the sort had happened. Funds must be raised in Honolulu and another man must go to make the purchase.

Someone suggested that the natives be taxed a dollar apiece each month until restoration was accomplished. On O'ahu the royalists were too hopelessly divided to join in such an appeal, and on Maui two weeks of pressing effort brought in just $37. The cheerful make-believe of earlier months had backfired. Natives who had been told again and again that help from abroad was certain, who had been assured that guns and men were already on the way, grew sullen when they heard that only through their

sacrifices could the great cause prosper. A *hapa haole* at 'Ulupalakua
said he would not pay a cent until the queen was actually restored;
then he would not mind giving a bullock or two for a *lūʻau* to
celebrate the event. Let the leaders at Honolulu find the coin,
others said. They could pay themselves back from the Treasury
when the deed was accomplished.

It was much the same with the Hui Aloha ʻĀina. The women's
branch had accumulated $475 but would not hear to spending it
on arms. The ladies were saving the sum, they said, for a feast
when the time came for rejoicing.

In the end wealthy royalists chipped in, and Major Seward
left for the Coast, so quietly that most of Honolulu took no note.

In the marshal's office at the station house E. G. Hitchcock—
the squint-eyed, red-haired "Old Man" who had come down
from Hilo in the late spring of '93 to deal with gamblers and
smugglers—read the reports of his secret agents and pieced
together a picture of royalist activity. The letters, which came to
him usually through the post office, were as unlike as the men who
sent them, and the marshal scarcely needed to glance at the false
name or initials at the bottom of a page to know who had written
it. He had learned to recognize the eccentric spelling of "Hickey";
the brief penciled notes of "C. W. J." and "J. L. X.," who worked
as a team; the terse, fact-packed bulletins from "Blaine"; the
clumsy, tortured syntax of "Buffalo"; the self-conscious sneer and
elegant literary allusions of "J. B. Adams"; the neat item headings
and comprehensive reporting of "Washington."

For a maximum of $75 a month each, the department hired
an ex-policeman, a dismissed turnkey, a sometime schoolteacher,
a former band boy—all of whom could damn the Provisional
government convincingly in the presence of royalists—and
newcomers to Honolulu, whose loyalties the public had not yet
discovered and whose affiliations were unsuspected.

The marshal had a man in Bush's employ—one who could
set type while he listened to the royalist talk that eddied around
him, and who then could go evenings after work to mingle with
the guards at Washington Place, where he chatted with Nowlein.
He had a man in the old band who went with Trumpeter Jim

Brown to secret meetings. He had several agents who hung around the business district, in and out of the saloons and stores and shops where royalists gathered. He had a spy in the Schuetzen Verein; and that was well, for in the summer of '94 the club that once had practiced shooting to defend the government turned rabidly antirepublican.

There were memos in the marshal's mail about everything from monarchists' quarrels to dynamite plots. Certain names began to appear again and again in the chits: Samuel Nowlein, commander of the volunteer guard at Washington Place; William H. Rickard, British-born sugar planter, whose home was on Hawai'i; Thomas Beresford Walker, son-in-law of John Cummins; Charles T. Gulick, cousin on both sides to missionary families, but since the middle of Kalākaua's reign, when he took a cabinet post under Gibson, at odds with Reformers and republicans; Carl Widemann, son of the judge who by his trip abroad was trying to stave off revolt; Henry Bertelmann, the back part of whose carpentry shop was a consulting room for would-be rebels; John E. Bush and Joseph Nawahī, leaders of the Hui Aloha 'Āina; and E. C. Crick, a chemist lately come to the Islands. But not Robert Wilcox. The "professional revolutionist" still was holding himself aloof from the movement.

So the Old Man—son of a missionary, a devoted friend of the Hawaiian people and greatly loved on the Big Island, where he had lived most of his life, but tough as *kauila* wood when it came to combatting crooks and conspirators—sorted the scraps of paper, discounted the extravagant yarns of the gullible, ignored the intricate falsehoods of a known counterspy, encouraged the wiliest of his agents to adopt new ruses, and warned the republic, early and late, that an armed uprising was in the making.

As for the government, not since Black Week in '93 had the councils spent so much time discussing military matters. In June, Colonel Soper had resigned the active command of the National Guard to become an officer on the staff of Commander-in-Chief Dole. Now Lieutenant Colonel Fisher, who had replaced him, overhauled the defenses of the executive building, rearranged the artillery, added more Gatling guns, and intensified the training of the regulars who manned them. In new uniforms, identical with those of the United States Army, the battalion drilled impressively on Thanksgiving Day of '94. Ankle-deep mud on Union Square (the season had been unusually rainy) did not keep the handsomely outfitted soldiers from marching smartly, and in signal skirmish Company E moved with machine precision as it responded to the whistle or the sword gestures of its officer. San Francisco's chief of police, a visitor, pronounced the regiment equal to California's best.

Major Seward came by the *Australia* on December 1. He looked worn and tired, and was glad, he said, that he could leave to others the arrangements for landing the arms he had purchased. Three days before his ship sailed from the Coast, he had seen a vessel loaded at Sausalito. Some six or seven sacks of "potatoes" and "onions" had gone on board, one large case about three and a half or four feet square by about four feet long, and several cases "similar to potato crates but tightly boxed." That same evening at a little past ten, he had seen the schooner towed to sea and watched her disappear into the night. If winds were fair she would be in the Moloka'i channel, off Waimānalo, in two or three weeks. There she would signal and await further orders.

How much of all this Lili'uokalani's friends told her has never been revealed, but on December 3 she wrote in her diary, "Heard good news for our side. . . ." She had had word from Judge Widemann, too, by the *Australia*, but it was not good. The last excuse for delay had vanished. Once more the queen sent for Major Wodehouse. He said he would ask Commissioner Hawes to detain H. M. S. *Hyacinth.*

"I have been partly guided," Hawes wrote on December 7 to the British Foreign Office, "by very confidential information I have received with regard to the intended rising of the Royalists. The failure of Mr. Widemann's mission to Europe having exhausted all peaceful efforts to obtain the restoration of the Queen, she has determined to carry into effect the wishes of her people, and a desperate effort by force to overthrow the Republican Government has now been fully decided on. . . . the rising is . . . expected to take place this month."

Lord Kimberley wrote on the back of this letter for the

guidance of the undersecretary who would answer it, ". . . it is very strange that an outbreak is always 'imminent'—never happens. We can't keep a ship there permanently."

The arrest, on December 8, of John E. Bush, Joseph Nawahī, and E. C. Crick on charges of conspiracy shocked royalist Honolulu. Search parties equipped with warrants, prowling through their premises for arms, they had come to expect. In spite of wet weather they had dug holes, improvised boxes, and stowed their arms by threes and fours and eights under their shrubbery and beneath their privies; and in general they had been successful in concealment. But even if weapons were found, the fine was only $50 for possessing them illegally. Conspiracy was something different.

Bush and Crick had been taken at Bush's in Printer's Lane. Nawahī, hurrying to the station house to offer condolence and help, had found that there was a warrant out for him too. He had saved Captain Robert Parker the trouble of looking for him. Locked in separate cells, the three were allowed to send for C. W. Ashford to act as their counsel in the preliminary examination ten days hence.

All the night of December 8, hacks rumbled here and there, moving arms to new and, it was hoped, safer caches. Tempers grew touchy as every queen's man wondered who had betrayed the cause. Talkative royalists began predicting that certain men whom they claimed to know as spies would "be in their graves before New Year's."

On Sunday, natives met in various parts of the city to organize a jail delivery. One group, back of Kaumakapili Church, heard a letter from Robert Wilcox. He would not lead a raid, Wilcox said, but he would help if the natives started one. Tonight at twelve was the time. But before midnight, white royalists sent scouts around, telling the Hawaiians to lie low, because the P.G.s were "on to them."

Christmas in 1894 came to a Honolulu where peace was fragile and goodwill scarce. On the holiday itself there were no royalist meetings—at least Marshal Hitchcock's spies reported none. But with the next dawn, dread and discord returned. On

December 26, Bush, Nawahī, and Crick, their preliminary hearing ended, were bound over to circuit court to be tried at the February term; the government refused bail and consigned them to Oʻahu prison—known, from its waterfront location, as the Reef.

On the twenty-eighth, the little steamer *Waimanalo*, with a royalist as skipper, puffed out of Honolulu harbor on a secret mission that even the ablest of the marshal's men could not discover.

On the twenty-ninth, Samuel Nowlein summoned Robert Wilcox to Bertelmann's shop and invited him to act at least a minor role in the forthcoming drama of restoration.

"With what are you going to start this thing?" Wilcox asked warily. Sam told him about a schooner lying somewhere off Molokaʻi with rifles and revolvers aplenty.

Robert asked about cannon. Sam said there were none; he didn't think they were going to need any big guns.

The same old thing, Wilcox told himself in disgust when Nowlein had finished; a plan that would succeed only if the other side did not do anything. He stood silent, looking at Nowlein and Bertelmann, whose hands were full of lists and maps, as one would look at a child with foolish notions.

"Well, what is it?" Sam asked impatiently. "If you have anything against it, speak out." But since there was everything against it and nothing for it, Robert only shrugged and went his way.

Meanwhile the government's secret agents poured in their reports, some neatly written, some almost illegible. On January 2 the one who signed himself "J. B. Adams" reviewed the record for the past several months and came to the conclusion that no trouble was brewing. He wrote:

The royalists have no intention of rising! They know your detectives. They say to them: such and such will happen; and the detectives report the same, not having sense enough to understand that they are being fooled to the top of their bent. . . . There is not even a shadow of an uprising. I have said so all along. This has justified my statements. . . .

Taken at face value, this would have been comforting. But the Old Man had received other reports, not so well composed but more convincing. Washington, it is true, was lying low; he had exposed his identity when he testified for the government in the Bush-Nawahī-Crick hearings. No royalist would trust him now. But "Blaine" and "J. R. Munn," "H. John" and "O. Henry" still dropped their messages into the post office for Marshal Hitchcock.

December 27, 1894. . . . I was talking to . . . Rickard today on Merchant street he is as close as a clam, but he said it was a sure thing and would be put through, but could not say exactly when only in the near future. . . . he told me he was watched and had to be careful for the present. They are all very careful just now. . . .

December 29, 1894. . . . if the Schooner arrived tonight or tomorrow night they intend making the attempt but she will not come into the Harbour I think it will be some place at Waikiki.

January 2, 1895. Brown told me tonight that the leader of the band has got the band boys guns . . . no big guns has come they say. . . .

I was at a luau & there was over 100 there the whites told the natives to be on their guard & not talk at all. . . .

January 3, 1895. That schooner that I informed you of last Saturday was lying off and on all day on Friday on the Molokai Coast she is a small Black Schr. about 45 or 50 tons burthen. I have not been able to find out the last two days it is very hard as only a few are in the Secret and they guard it closely.

January 6, 1895. . . . They will act tonight on the old plan that is if they can get the natives to act as this is Sunday night and the natives will not be missed from around town.

I think that if you search Queen Kapiolani's yard on Punchbowl Street—there is arms there because there is where the native band boys are to congregate at—if there be any action. I am to be there at 8 with them and they are to furnish me with a rifle and I shall discharge it premature say an hour before time accidentaly and that will be a notice to you of business.

[*And then without date or hour*]. . . . rifles at H. Bertelmans Overthrow to take place tonight—2000 men. . . . Will start in from Dimond Head between one & 2 A.M. Bipikane told me. . . .

8. SCHOONER FROM THE EAST

On Rabbit Island off Waimānalo the royalist watchers whiled away the days fishing for *humuhumu* or gathering *'opihi* from the rocks. Sometimes they went back to the O'ahu mainland for fresh water or poi. At night they camped on the matted grass in the island's crater and stood guard, turn about, on the seaward rim, searching the black ocean for the schooner that would come from the east.

When she flashed a blue light, they were to answer with a red one. Then she would show a strong white light and stand in toward shore. They would row out in the four-oared gig to meet her, hand a letter to her captain, and be told what to do about the guns she was bringing. Thus George Townsend and Charles Warren, both *hapa haole*, and the four Hawaiian boat boys would play their part in the queen's restoration.

Samuel Nowlein knew well the two men he had chosen to manage the ticklish business at Rabbit Island. With red-headed George Townsend he had fought many a blaze in the days of the volunteer fire department. Clanging through Honolulu's streets on Engine No. 2 or hand-pumping its little stream of water to quench flames no brighter than his hair and whiskers, Townsend had been one of the most nimble and doughty members of the crew. Between alarms he had worked as a carpenter, and, since under the monarchy fire-fighters were exempted from taxes, he had made out well enough, though his family was large. When the Provisional Government created the new, smaller, more efficient department and began to pay the men, Red George was retained. But by 1894 serving the haole government for pay had become disreputable in the eyes of royalists, and Samuel Nowlein had little trouble in persuading George to resign and work with him for the queen's cause. For a man in the royalists' employ there were no stated wages. When he could, Nowlein handed George five or ten dollars; when there was no food in the house and no money to buy any, Mrs. Townsend called on Nowlein and came away with enough to meet the crisis. Plenty of Hawaiian and *hapa haole* households in those days lived largely on the hope of restoration and the wealth they believed it would bring them.

When, on the afternoon of December 10, Nowlein called George into the back room at Henry Bertelmann's and ordered him to set out that very evening for Waimānalo, George did not demur. He only asked who were the white men that were backing the movement. He had heard that there were hundreds of them, ready to help if only the Hawaiians got things started. Nowlein would name no names. "Men that have money are backing this thing, George," he said. "Don't you be scared. You will know in time."

Curly-haired Charles Warren had been a soldier of the monarchy. For eight years, under both Kalākaua and Liliʻuokalani, he had served as quartermaster sergeant. Nowlein had been his superior. Since the overthrow, scores of devoted Hawaiians had taken their turns, some by night and some by day, patrolling the tree-shaded grounds of Washington Place that the queen might feel secure. They were not allowed arms; they carried policemen's clubs. And they were paid only in promises of preferment and reward when Liliʻuokalani returned to her throne. Warren was one of these.

In the spring of 1894, however, restless and disillusioned at the failure of the United States to restore the queen, Warren had gone to Kaua'i to look for a paying job. Early in September, Nowlein wrote him to come back to Honolulu. Warren came up at once, resumed his role as daytime guard, listened to Nowlein's stories of the hundreds who stood ready to rise against the republic, and at night sewed cartridge belts from the canvas Nowlein furnished him.

To each of them—Townsend and Warren—Nowlein gave the same directions: to join the other at the Empire saloon on the afternoon of December 10, take the five o'clock tram up Nu'uanu Avenue to the end of the line, meet a man leading two horses, mount and ride over the Pali to Waimānalo. There John Li'ili'i, John Cummins' lad, would have ready a boat, boys to row it, food, and further directions.

As the mule-drawn tram jolted up the valley, the two men sat apart like strangers, staring at the pleasant grounds and comfortable houses of those who supported the republic—those against whom they felt no personal enmity, but whose government they hated for the queen's sake. At the terminus they fell into step and walked slowly along the rutted road, uncertain from which direction the horses would come. It was fully dark by the time a young Hawaiian rode up on a mule, leading two saddled bays. Townsend and Warren forgot to use the password they had been given; but Kaulī, worn out with urging the reluctant horses from Pāwa'a by way of Punchbowl, asked no questions. Who but the appointed men would be there in the dark, sauntering toward the Halfway House?

From the gusty Pali the descent into Ko'olau Poko was by the rugged, treacherous trail that zigzagged down the windward side of the precipice, then veered off to the east across the wooded spurs at the base of mighty Kōnāhuanui, *mauka* of jagged Olomana and the Kailua marshland. By ten o'clock their mounts had brought them to the John Cummins establishment at Waimānalo. Mauna Loke, the mansion, was dark, but in one of the small houses a lamp burned. John Li'ili'i was expecting them.

Li'ili'i was a nickname; it meant "little," and had been bestowed on John Kahoeka as a child. Like the haole diminutive "Johnny," it clung to him in manhood. The Hawaiians, who have a bent for irony, delighted to call this strapping stalwart Keoni Li'ili'i—Little John. They rarely used his last name.

Nuʻuanu Pali road in the 1890s.

Who he was or just how many years he had been on earth John Li'ili'i did not know, but as long as he could remember, he had been John Cummins' "boy," living at the Cummins place; working desultorily as farmhand, fisherman, and *paniolo* (cowboy); training racehorses; waiting on distinguished visitors. For a quarter of a century before the overthrow, Cummins, whose mother had been a Hawaiian chiefess, had expressed his native aloha in lavish hospitality.

Li'ili'i had been full-grown when Queen Emma came to Mauna Loke, in '75. It was said that Cummins had set the visit for November 5, Guy Fawkes Day, to honor his English father; and tradition held it the most splendid of all John Cummins' entertainments—knights dressed in red, great arches bearing Hawaiian mottoes in letters of flame, trumpeters blowing lustily on *lauhala* (pandanus leaf) horns, adoring subjects prone on the ground in deference to the dowager, widow of Kamehameha IV. There were leis, gifts, a *lū'au* that lasted for hours, fireworks, three hundred torches burning through the night, and hulas that throbbed till dawn.

Other *ali'i* had been feted there, and innumerable guests of lesser rank, both haole and Hawaiian. Even when there were no outsiders, the place was lively. In the dining room, after a meal had been cleared away, family, neighbors, household servants, ranch hands gathered for an evening of fun. Fiddle, accordian, tambourine soon set feet dancing. John Cummins himself joined the music makers with, as one guest wrote, "the very artistic instrument called the bones." Later a recreation hall, long and lofty, was built—stocked with books, an automatic organ, and chirping canaries; decorated with Chinese fans and portraits of Hawaiian royalty. These were the times that had made a legend of Mauna Loke and its open-hearted master. These were the times that John Li'ili'i Kahoeka could have recalled, but seldom did, in the black days of 1894.

Marked, and in some measure mournful, changes had come to Waimānalo in the twenty years since Queen Emma's visit. The famous ranch, with its blooded stock and its busy racetrack, had given way to the sugar plantation, with its whispering cane fields, its grinding-mill, its snorting locomotives, and its Chinese laborers. When capital was needed—more than free-spending John

Cummins possessed—haole dollars flooded in, and haole judgment governed the business decisions, even though Cummins was still the manager. After the overthrow, having no more heart for entertaining, and needing money, Cummins offered his shares in the sugar company for sale, committed Mauna Loke to caretakers, and turned his back on Waimānalo. He had lived since then at Pāwaʻa, east of Honolulu, where the road to Waikīkī bore sharply *makai*. Here, in an ample, shady enclosure with comfortable houses and commodious stables, John Cummins lived quietly, surrounded by children, grandchildren, friends, and retainers.

John Liʻiliʻi stayed on at Waimānalo, raised a little taro, fished in the bay, tended Cummins' mares and raised Cummins' colts. Once a year, at Christmas, he rode his own horse to Waialua to the races. It was a good enough life, whoever ran the government at Honolulu; but when he went to Pāwaʻa on business early in December and learned from Major Seward about the schooner that was coming, he said yes, he would do whatever was wanted—except that he would not forego the trip to Waialua.

Three miles beyond the Cummins place, Townsend and Warren, with Kaulī as guide, came to the landing, where John Liʻiliʻi waited with the boat—an old clinker-built dinghy, a trifle leaky but still seaworthy. At Pāwaʻa Major Seward had given him fifty dollars to buy a gig; he had found this one for thirty-six and had spent the rest of the money on food and wool shirts, for nights could be cold in December. The *J. A. Cummins*, one of the coastwise steamers built in Cummins' heyday, had brought the boat around from Honolulu, and Johnny had engaged Maulia and Kamaka, as well as his young brother Kaulī, to man it. He had the equipment for signaling and a letter from the major to the schooner's captain. To make sure of the boys, he had sworn them to secrecy and loyalty, using a wordy and horrendous oath he had invented.

The final stage of the journey brought Warren and Townsend to John Liʻiliʻi's fishing shack, a mile along the beach. There, directly before them, lay Rabbit Island, grim under a waning moon, looking like the head of a mammoth dog whose half-submerged nose pointed toward Makapuʻu. But they did not go off to it now, for it was past midnight. Tomorrow, Johnny said,

Rabbit Island from near Waimānalo.

they could fish a little to add to their food, and in the afternoon they would see how the gig did in the choppy channel.

Nights on Rabbit Island proved cold and cheerless at best, rainy and downright miserable at worst. At the northeastern lookout the wind was savage. Trips across the boisterous channel to the mainland were wet and arduous. John Liʻiliʻi, when he set off on Saturday, December 15, to go to Waialua, left a fretful and dispirited company. But Johnny sent Kawelo to take his place, and Kawelo brought a tent. After that, with a boatload of wood, water, and food, they made reasonably cheerful camp on the island and held out until December 20. That night George and Charley said they would take the first watch together. In the twilight they climbed to the high point, and before it was quite dark they saw a blue light on the horizon. With a red rocket they flashed their answer.

In a little more than two hours of rowing and sailing they were alongside the *Wahlberg*. Townsend gave the password, "missionary," climbed aboard, and presented the letter—a good deal soiled now and twisted up in a roll. Captain Martin went below to read it. When he came on deck again, he ordered the mate to open the hatch and pass up two cases of revolvers.

It was long past midnight when the oarsmen beached the loaded gig on Rabbit Island. With the help of the boys, Townsend began at once to open and burn the wooden boxes and to wrap the revolvers in grain sacks and bury them in the sand on the lee side, facing Waimānalo. At dawn he took Kaulī ashore and dispatched him to Honolulu with word of the landing. Next day he rode into town, found Samuel Nowlein, and supplemented Kaulī's report with his own.

Charley Warren had stayed on board the *Wahlberg*. The main part of the arms, the major's letter had directed, were to be transferred to the steamer *Waimanalo*, which would put out from Honolulu as soon as she had word of the schooner's arrival. Captain Martin had asked for a man to help get things ready—to bring the freight from the hold, break open the white pine boxes, lay out the rifles on deck, and load up the belts with cartridges, that all might be in readiness for the *Waimanalo* when she came.

Tall, stooped Captain Martin, whose bronzed skin set off his yellow hair and mustache, asked one day as Warren plied his chisel, "Do you fellows think you're going to win this thing?"

Charley Warren hoped so.

Martin quizzed him about this and that royalist leader—Nowlein, Seward, W. H. Rickard—and about Rudolph Spreckels, the Maui planter, son of the famous Claus.

Warren's laconic answers did not add much to the captain's information.

In all, there were 291 Winchester rifles, of which Martin claimed 6 to use on his sealing voyage to Japan. As the year ended, the *Wahlberg*, keeping well off the regular ship lanes, was still looking for the little steamer that bore the name of the Cummins ranch.

George Townsend by now had received new orders. Nowlein had found him in Molteno's barbershop, beckoned him again into Bertelmann's back room, and told him he was to go to sea in the *Waimanalo*. With a letter to Captain Davis, Townsend sought out the dock where the steamer was loading. There was a delay in getting extra coal for the secret voyage, but at last about seven o'clock on the evening of December 28 the little vessel cleared port and steamed into heavy seas around the eastern end of O'ahu.

Once the paddy and lumber had been discharged at Kāne'ohe, the *Waimanalo* crew began looking for the *Wahlberg*. It was early New Year's Day before they sighted her, about forty-five miles off Kahuku Point, lying to their leeward. At noon Townsend was on her deck, where Warren had the arms ready to come off. It took two trips with the gig to transfer them. Then the captains exchanged visits, finishing up the amenities with a round of drinks in the steamer's cabin; and soon the schooner stood off to the northwest—a trim, fore-and-aft rigged, single-masted craft, black with white railings—taking final leave of Hawai'i and its turmoil.

Not so the *Waimanalo*. She now headed for Honolulu and trouble—trouble that eventually brought her master before a military court. But first she paused at Rabbit Island, where Townsend roused the sleeping Kaulī and sent him to Nowlein with a message: At eleven the next night, January 2, the steamer would be off Bertelmann's place at Diamond Head. Final instructions must be sent to it there.

On Wednesday, January 2, Samuel Nowlein faced two of his colleagues—members of what might have been called the royalist high command if the movement had not been so haphazardly organized. He told them that, though the guns on board the *Waimanalo* were due in Honolulu that night, he was not ready. The revolvers that had been deposited at Rabbit Island had been brought, after outrageous delay, as far as the Halfway House in Nuʻuanu Valley. He still had to get them safely into the city and distribute them. As to the rifles, he had thought to have part of them landed by a small boat at Kakaʻako while the steamer docked with the rest at the fish market. His men, he said, were all right for Kakaʻako; the captains of the squads had been appointed and instructed; they knew what buildings they were to seize and what government officials they were to take prisoner. It was the action based on the fish market that was dubious. He had asked a certain haole to map that part of the strategy, and now the haole told him that he had been too busy to do anything about it.

The rifles, Nowlein urged, must not be landed until the attack was completely prepared. Revolvers, yes; they could be concealed. But three hundred rifles or more, especially in the hands of natives—"You just can't keep natives from talking to each other and exposing the whole thing!"

The gentlemen listened impatiently. They reminded him that, together with Major Seward, they had raised the money, bought the arms and shipped them, and engaged the *Waimanalo* to land them. To Nowlein they had left only the mustering of the Hawaiians and the planning of the assault, and for weeks he had been assuring them that everything was in a fine state of forwardness. But after they had expostulated, there was nothing to do but agree to a postponment—for twenty-four hours. Could Nowlein be ready by Thursday midnight? Nowlein was certain that he could.

Food and coal on the *Waimanalo* were running low by Wednesday evening, but there was still plenty of whiskey. A haole royalist had paid for a case and sent it on board the day of the sailing; the captain, the mate, the two Chinese crewmen, and George and Charley had all the liquor they wanted. With every swallow the prospects grew brighter; the men talked of little else than the impending downfall of the "missionary" government and the golden age that would begin when Lili'uokalani reigned again. Captain Davis had been promised $10,000 if he brought off his part successfully.

Exactly as George had predicted, they were opposite Diamond Head at eleven o'clock on January 2, standing head in and showing their lights. A small boat put out to them, signaling with a lantern, and a tall, thin-faced haole came on board. Most of them recognized W. H. Rickard. He shook hands all around, and then with the captain went into the cabin. In a moment, Charley, lingering near the open door, heard himself addressed. Rickard was asking the exact number of rifles and cartridges. When he had written down the figures Charley gave him, Rickard turned back to the captain. "You can't run into the fish market," Captain Davis told him impatiently. "The dredger is there. You'll have to get two boats to land it in, one at each place."

Rickard added this information to the letter and sent off the missive in the whaleboat. Captain Davis sent George to tell the helmsman to take the *Waimanalo* to sea again. They steamed south-southwest, far out of sight of O'ahu. Next morning they broke freight to get food and began tearing up the floor for fuel. And to pass the time, they threw chunks of wood overboard and shot at them, testing their marksmanship.

In Honolulu the word passed among the Hawaiians: "Tonight we turn out."

"Meet near the old kerosene warehouse at Kaka'ako."

"Go there where the *kiawe* trees are thick near the immigrant station."

"There will be a *lū'au* at Alex Smith's house near the market."

"Sam Nowlein and some of the boys are going fishing tonight down by the harbor, and Sam wants you to come along."

Everybody knew what was meant.

The time set for gathering was midnight—the arms were to

come at one—but the Hawaiians, usually so deliberate, could not wait. By eight-thirty the trend toward the waterfront was noticeable; by nine o'clock Kaka'ako teemed with natives. When government "specials" tried to break up the crowds, a group of bold young *hapa haole* royalists fell upon them, took their guns and isolated them under guard on the beach. Regular police soon marched briskly from the station house, swinging their billies. They scattered the crowd and rescued their unfortunate colleagues. Long before midnight, harassed Sam Nowlein saw that the action was a failure. Boatloads of guns from the *Waimanalo* could not be landed in this melee, and the town that was to have been surprised in its sleep was on guard from end to end. Quickly the word spread: "Not tonight! Go home and wait. Your leaders will send you word—soon."

At ten o'clock Nowlein met his lieutenant, Henry Bertelmann, by appointment at the Hawaiian Hotel, told him about the fiasco and begged him to do something to stop the *Waimanalo*. It was from Bertelmann's seaside home near Diamond Head that a boat had taken Rickard out to the steamer the evening before. Bertelmann's houseboy, long-haired Pua (who had vowed not to cut his heavy black locks until Lili'uokalani was restored) had been coxswain then and was prepared to fill the same role tonight if Bertelmann's whaleboat went off to help unload the arms. A second boat, sent from town by Nowlein in response to last night's message from Rickard, must by this time be lying on Bertelmann's beach, waiting for its crew. Clearly, Henry Bertelmann was the man to save the day. Bertelmann gestured his hopelessness. He would go home, he said, as fast as a hack could carry him, but certainly the boats would have gone to sea before he could arrive. The *Waimanalo* would have to take her chances.

Quite beside himself, Nowlein walked *waikīkī* along King Street, dispersing little bands of Hawaiians and praying to heaven to send him a man to turn back the *Waimanalo*. Heaven did. Not far beyond Punchbowl Street he encountered Robert Wilcox.

Not until that afternoon had Robert Wilcox made a final decision to join the movement. He regarded Nowlein as muddle-headed and incompetent, and resented with all his heart Nowlein's ignoring him until the uprising was about to come off and then offering him a distasteful assignment—to arrest President Dole at his home.

For several days after Nowlein first spoke to him, Wilcox had gone about town conferring with this person and that. Should he hold to his plan to go to Peking, where his Chinese friends assured him there would be a commission for him? Or should he swallow his pride and try once more to restore Hawai'i to the Hawaiians? Most of his advisers, Wilcox said afterward, urged him to stay clear of Nowlein's ill-designed undertaking. But the more he thought about it, the more he saw that his duty was to his own country and to Lili'uokalani, however little he liked the leadership of the present enterprise. So, in the end, he told Nowlein that he would help him. But he seems not to have given a plain answer about arresting Dole. Apparently Robert had thought up an activity much more to his liking—to gather a crew of rowers and man the second boat, the one Nowlein had sent from Honolulu Harbor to Diamond Head a few hours earlier. Perhaps he told Nowlein that he would send a substitute to make the arrest. Perhaps the two men left all the details in a mist of half-promises and ambiguity. It would have been like Sam Nowlein to do so. At any rate, Robert Wilcox went straight to see Lot Lane.

The Lane boys, Irish-Hawaiians, had their fighting blood up. At the Lane ranch in Ko'olau their father, William Carey Lane, had reminded his sons that the blood of the best families of County Cork flowed in their veins. "With these great spirited ancestors behind you," he had exhorted them, "you will go and if need be give up your lives in the fight . . . to protect the homeland of your mother and her people."

While the excitement lasted, the Lanes were living with their sister Jessie, Mrs. Junius Ka'ae, on Beretania Street near Washington Place. Here were assembled on the evening of January 3 the brothers Lot, James, and John; a nephew, William; and a friend, Robert Haku'ole Sylva, ready to do anything that needed doing in the queen's behalf.

Robert Wilcox arrived at nine and, taking Lot aside, discussed the Dole arrest. Robert suggested that Lot might go.

"You must go quietly," he warned. "Remember that such a man as Mr. Dole has a guard there, and of course he has a right to shoot you down—"

Lot said that if Robert would not go, neither would he.

Then, said Robert, Lot would have to find Sam Nowlein and tell him of their decision.

And so it was that, when Robert Wilcox with his volunteer boat crew sallied out of the Kaʻae house about ten o'clock on January 3, bound for Waikīkī and adventure, Lot Lane was not with them. After he had seen Nowlein, it was agreed, Lot would ride his hourse to the beach and join the others—if he could find them.

By twos and threes, not wanting to attract attention, Wilcox' little company sauntered down Punchbowl Street to King Street and started along King toward the tramcar stop at Alapaʻi. John Lane and Hakuʻole Sylva took the lead, singing. It would be hard to imagine a procession less martial.

Near Kawaiahaʻo Church, Nowlein overtook them. Ignoring the others, who drifted into the shadows, he told Wilcox that all action was now postponed, and ordered him to Diamond Head to convey this word to the *Waimanalo*. Then, needing to be everywhere at once, Nowlein turned back into town.

Wilcox dismissed the now useless party, and asked a passing Hawaiian to summon him a hack from Stand 290—a good royalist hack stand, whose drivers did not tell tales. But Hakuʻole Sylva refused to be sent home without an adventure of some sort, and soon the two of them were riding fast toward Bertelmann's at Diamond Head.

When Wilcox came on board the *Waimanalo* and told his news, the captain was profane. The landing already had been postponed a whole day beyond the original agreement. He had not bargained for a long voyage; he was out of coal and out of food. The arms would have to be delivered that night or not at all. The steamer was dark, but when the moon broke through the clouds, Wilcox could see the two whaleboats alongside, one of them already loaded with guns. It was evident that the second boat had not waited to be rowed by the Lane boys.

W. H. Rickard, ordering the captain to make no move until they had further word from Honolulu, stepped into the canoe that had brought Wilcox and had himself paddled ashore. A long two hours later the canoe came back, bringing the written message: "Either go to sea or find some good place to land the stuff."

Captain Davis was for dumping everything overboard.

"Never!" said Robert Wilcox, taking command. In a little while two heavily loaded boats put off, heading upshore toward Kāhala, where presumably there was the best chance of getting over the reef.

It was high tide and calm until they came to the surf at the shoreline. One boat—the one bearing Wilcox, Haku'ole, and Townsend—scraped the coral, but the oarsmen jumped overboard to lighten it and pull it off. Pua, the long-haired coxswain, then guided it west almost to Kūpikipiki'o (Black Point). There in a small, dry gulch they hid the guns under the thorny lantana.

Charley Warren directed the other boat east to a place well toward Wai'alae and buried his load in the sand. When he had rejoined Townsend and Wilcox, they roused old Ka'ili, who leased the fishing rights at Kāhala, and told him they had cached some stuff—*ukana*, baggage, was the word they used—in two places and that he should go in the morning and obliterate the footprints on the beach. Ka'ili said he would. He did not ask what sort of *ukana*.

At five o'clock on the morning of January 4, the *Waimanalo*, still burning floor wood, was crossing the harbor bar at Honolulu. Just inside the reef a coast guard launch hailed her and put a man aboard to inspect her cargo. Charlie Peterson, the lookout, had reported to the collector general of customs that on Wednesday evening a caller had asked him not to telephone word of the *Waimanalo* if he should see her that night or the next. To the collector that sounded like opium.

But the inspector found nothing illicit, and soon gave the little steamer a clean bill. Captain Davis, feeling carefree and valiant, told himself that what the royalists did from here on was not his worry. He was *pau*, finished, with the affair—except to collect $10,000.

That was Friday. Three days of freedom lay before him. On Monday he was arrested and charged with treason.

9. AT DIAMOND HEAD

Almost three hundred Winchester rifles lay rusting in a gully at Black Point and in a shallow pit in the sand at Kāhala. Someone, Sam Nowlein knew, would have to dig them up and clean them, and the men who were to use them would have to be mustered at Diamond Head. On Saturday, January 5, Nowlein summoned Charley Warren to Washington Place and ordered him to Kāhala; then he drove in his buggy to Pālama to deliver a similar message to George Townsend. "You'd better go along with us tonight," he said. "We're going to have a fishing party and stay until tomorrow evening and then come home."

"I'm tired," George demurred. But he asked who else would be there.

"A good many of the boys," Nowlein answered. "Come out before dark."

It was a command. "All right," George said.

Lot Lane, too, took steps to get the work done. "Come up to the house this evening," Jessie Ka'ae said to her cousin Keli'ikuewa on Saturday afternoon. "Lot wants to see you." Lot himself invited Charlie Bartow and Robert Haku'ole Sylva. Four or five Lanes— nephew William as well as brothers Jim, John, and Pat—could be counted on.

But to get other boys to go, Lot said, he would have to pay their tram fare—or even better send them out in hacks—for many a good royalist did not have the dime to buy a ride on the horsecars. Assembling an army three miles or more from town was going to be much harder than gathering one at Kaka'ako and the fish market.

To get money for the fares, Lot had decided to mortgage his horse to his sister Maria, Mrs. John 'Ena. The 'Enas had plenty; they were also supporters of the republic—at least John 'Ena was. But Maria need not know why Lot wanted a loan.

"But your horse—" Haku'ole protested. He knew that the fine animal meant more to Lot than any other possession.

Lot spoke with spirit. They were going to war, he reminded Haku'ole, and might be killed, and then the horse would not be of any use to them. But if they could raise twenty-five or thirty dollars, he and Haku'ole between them could recruit scores of good men. Not for nothing did the blood of the Careys and the Lanes of Ireland run in his veins. Not for nothing had he been named for Lot Kamehameha, fifth king of Hawai'i.

Jessie, no mean patriot herself, consented to transact the business. Let Haku'ole summon a 290 hack and go with her, and she would talk her sister into the bargain.

When Jessie Ka'ae and Robert Haku'ole Sylva came back in a little more than an hour, they brought two ten-dollar gold pieces, $7.50 in change, and a bottle of brandy. Maria 'Ena had given them thirty dollars, and they had driven around by the Bay Horse saloon to pick up a little cheer for the boys who were going into danger.

Often in a Hawaiian household there was no set time for supper; poi and fish or meat were laid out, and each comer ate when he felt inclined. Now they all gathered around the Ka'aes' long table, where the food still stood in plates and bowls, to drink a toast to the undertaking. There was Junius Ka'ae, silent in the midst of the bubbling talk. There was Jessie, with her pretty face and her sparkling eyes. She called the first toast: "To the queen."

There was thirty-year-old Lot, tall and solid and defiant, all dressed up in white pants and a dark cutaway coat. There was twenty-two-year-old John, who loved dancing and was "learning the salesman's life" down at the B. F. Ehlers department store, and twenty-year-old Jim, a husky but moody and unpredictable fellow. There was seventeen-year-old William, a smooth-shaven, cherub-faced lad, who adored his uncles and eagerly followed their lead in all things. Robert Haku'ole Sylva, educated, thoughtful, and grave; Keli'ikuewa, immature and a bit tipsy; and Charles Bartow, Lot's quick-tempered haole friend, completed the circle. Pat Lane, a fourth brother, was not there. He would turn up later, Lot said, at the place where the work was to be done.

Scarcely had they lifted their glasses to toast the queen when someone—was it Junius?—cried, "Forward to victory!" and all the soldiers-to-be shouted, "*Mahalo!*"

Afterward at the trials, some of them said that they had drunk only to Jessie Ka'ae's health that night, that they did not remember that anyone mentioned victory. But Haku'ole told the story simply and convincingly. All their thoughts were turned toward Lili'uokalani, he said, and all their hearts were filled with hope and confidence.

John Lane took only a sip; he did not believe in liquor. Haku'ole refused a second glass; he knew the importance of keeping sober. Keli'ikuewa drank too much.

Junius Ka'ae grew talkative. "When you get to the Waikīkī bridge," he said, "then go singly; don't go together in a bunch. . . . if you do somebody will see you there and follow you and watch you and the thing may be discovered." Around the room the boys nodded in agreement. This was good advice, though afterward when he was asked about it in court, Ka'ae was sure he could not have said any such thing.

The bottle was empty, and it was time to go. Lot told the others to start on by tramcar; he and Haku'ole would follow when they had done their recruiting. John said he had dancing school at eight; he would take a hack out later, if Lot would give him the fare. Lot gave him something—a part of the change from the gold piece that had bought the brandy—and debonair John, polkas and gavottes already singing in his blood, hurried away. Befuddled Keli'ikuewa walked a few steps with Bill and Jim, then fell behind. Both he and John turned up for breakfast next morning without having been to Diamond Head, still intending to go.

Lot gave Haku'ole one of the two unbroken gold pieces and parted from him at E. O. Hall's corner, Fort and King. Hotel Street, a block *mauka*, was full of idlers, especially at the merry-go-round. In the saloons white men and brown tippled, and bragged of what they would do to the P.G.s when the time came. Haku'ole changed his eagle at a Chinese clothing store and, remembering how dressed up all the Lanes had been, bought himself a pair of shoes. Then he strolled about, looking for Lili'uokalani men and dealing out ten-cent tram fares to those who said they would go out to Bertelmann's. It was nearly ten o'clock when Haku'ole, alone in a 290 hack, reached Kāhala. Lot Lane, Charley Warren, George Townsend, and perhaps thirty others were already working at the guns.

The way the ocean foams and splashes around Black Point, spurting high against the dark rocks, has given the little headland the Hawaiian name of Kūpikipiki'ō, raging sea. Just east of here Princess Ruth Ke'elikōlani, one of the last of the Kamehameha family, had had a beach house, a rambling frame structure with wide lanais. The place now belonged to Lili'uokalani, who, because she had her beloved cottage, Hamohamo, in Waikīkī, leased Kāhala to others. Ka'ili, retired from preaching, held the fishing rights and acted as caretaker. Some Japanese had the franchise to cut wood in the *kiawe* grove and sell it in town, remitting Lili'uokalani's share through Ka'ili. A hundred yards or so 'ewa of the beach house, Townsend and Wilcox had hidden their guns early Friday morning. Two or three hundred yards toward Koko Head, near the fence that divided the Kāhala land from Paul Isenberg's dairy ranch at Wai'alae, Warren had cached his boatload of weapons.

On Saturday evening Warren, first to arrive at the scene, sat on the veranda in the dusk, eating the lunch he had carried with him. Just as he was finishing, Townsend came in, followed by the small band of Hawaiians he had rounded up on the other side of the point. He had already showed them the guns in the gully and allowed each to arm himself with a carbine and a cartridge belt.

"Now that all of you have seen these things," he had said

Sketch of Diamond Head in Notebook I of Dr. N. B. Emerson's record of the counterrevolution. Ka'alāwai and Kūpikipiki'ō are in center foreground; Bertelmann's house was just around the point of Diamond Head, out of the picture to the left.

cheerfully as he dealt out the weapons, "you've got to stay. If you try to go, I'll shoot you." No one had seemed much alarmed.

Warren and Townsend conferred, then united their forces and marched them up the shore to the easternmost cache.

"Dig here," said Charley Warren.

The men dug in the sand up to their elbows and pulled out the guns, more than two hundred of them, filled with sand and already somewhat rusted. Warren had half of them taken into the house, the rest to the gully where the other arms lay. Carrying six or seven guns apiece, the men staggered along the shore. It was a perfect night for stealth—intermittent rain and no moon. But the gully did not satisfy Townsend. He straightway ordered the bulk of arms carried *'ewa* across the Kūpikipiki'ō ridge and deposited in a fissure in the coral on the western side, where the shore was so steep that the bearers had to find footholds in the rocks at various levels and hand the weapons down one by one to the man who stood at the mouth of the cave. Lot Lane protested that the new place was not in the least a good one, that at high tide the salt water would spray in and wet the guns; and presently Townsend saw that Lane was right and shouted that they would have to take the arms to the nearest house. At this, half of the men rebelled. They had toted enough Winchesters for one night. Trooping back across the point to Ka'ili's at Kāhala, they became the nucleus of the force that Nowlein eventually commanded. In charge there, Warren announced genially that he had purchased poi and squid from Hawaiians in the neighborhood and that every man who was hungry could help himself. At four o'clock they had public prayers; then they snatched two hours of sleep, were up at six for more squid and poi and more prayers, and began briskly cleaning the guns they had brought in the night before.

At Ka'alāwai, west of the point, Townsend had found Antone Rosa's caretaker, who, cowed by the sight of George's nickel-plated revolver, unlocked the house that became the second headquarters for the rebels. Here, because they had to bring in the guns from the cave—as difficult a feat as putting them there in the first place—there was no sleep at all. There were also no prayers and more drinking than at Kāhala.

There would have been nothing for breakfast at Ka'alāwai if someone had not shot a bullock, one that strayed from the Isenberg ranch; the men hacked off thick steaks and barbecued them in the yard. About ten o'clock long-haired Pua drove up with a barrel of poi and some chicken and salmon. Manuel Rosa and Pat Lane brought in a fresh supply of gin. At both camps there was now food enough and to spare.

Sunday at Diamond Head was a day of mounting hope and exuberance. The morning sun blued the sea and warmed men's courage; the breeze rolled white breakers shoreward and cooled men's tempers. After the arduous work of the night, the cleaning of guns was a pleasant, leisurely task, carried on to the accompaniment of sanguine chatter. And all day long more patriots (*po'e aloha 'āina*) came to join them.

They came from Kaumakapili, from Leleo and Kīkīhale and Smith's Bridge, from Kaka'ako and the *mauka* slopes of Punchbowl, from Kalihi and Moanalua, from Iwilei, Mō'ili'ili, and the little settlement near Punahou. By twos and threes and fours they came, along Beretania Street and Wai'alae Road, a route that brought them straight to Kāhala, or by tram or bus to Waikīkī and thence on the beach to Ka'alāwai. Barefooted and without hats

The Waikīkī Road in the 1890s.

or jackets, some of them looked dressed for a fishing expedition; others wore their Sunday best.

They were as old as Sam Kia (fifty-two) and Koia Kapena ("What's that ancient fellow doing here?" some of the boys shouted when they saw him at Kāhala) and as young as Tommy ʻAi (fourteen) and Kolomona (fifteen).

They were as well-heeled as Carl Widemann, scion of one of Hawaiʻi's richest families, and as hard up as Kaneuu, who accepted twenty-five cents from John Lane for bus fare and then walked the seven miles to Kaʻalāwai to save it.

They were as robust and noisy as old Bipikāne, who flexed his biceps and bellowed like a bull, and as frail and gentle as Buff Moepali, who walked "slow on account of . . . not being very strong," and Hāhā, who gasped with asthma.

They were as experienced and confident as Pālau and Pūkila, former soldiers and policemen, and as green and uncertain as John James Matthews, who had scarcely looked at a gun in his short life, let alone handled one.

They were as full of ʻawa and gin as William Pua and Billy Widdifield, who could hardly tell how they got to the rendezvous, and as sober as Sam Koloa, the Salvation Army man, who led the prayers at Kāhala.

They were carpenters, house painters, blacksmiths, tram drivers, draymen, stevedores, and former band boys and clerks who had thrown up their jobs rather than sign the P.G. oath. Almost to a man they boasted Hawaiian blood; a few were part Portuguese or part haole. Some of them spoke and read and wrote two languages, having been educated in church schools; others knew only their native tongue. Many had children, whose future they meant to secure by restoring the monarchy.

The call to gather beyond Diamond Head had gone the rounds within a few hours, chiefly by word of mouth—though Joe Clark, waking from a noonday nap, had found on his table a note, formally worded in Hawaiian, requesting his presence at Kaʻalāwai "at a lūʻau for the aloha ʻāina."

Those who had womenfolk had made excuses before setting out. They were going for a walk in the park or a sea bath at Waikīkī. One craved "to look at the birds" at the ostrich farm, and another wanted to visit the Diamond Head signal station and examine lookout Charlie Peterson's wonderful telescope. Solomon Kūpihea and Bill Ihu had joined in convincing John Silva's wife that they were all off in search of a weed they could use to stupify fish and so enlarge their catch. A meeting—"with speaking"—was one of the easiest pretexts to offer to one's *wahine*, one's wife. But in their hearts these men knew the time had come for more than talk.

A half-mile or so beyond Bertelmann's, new arrivals by the beach encountered the sentries Townsend had posted. Some had the password, *aloha 'āina*, and some had to persuade the guards with grins and gestures that they were loyal. Directed to Antone Rosa's, they hailed their fellows, refreshed themselves with food and drink, and lounged about or set to work according to the whim of the moment. "You can't leave now," they were told. "The sentries will shoot if you try."

There was a little grumbling because no haole royalists were in sight. There were even some desertions, in spite of the threats. If all who came there on Saturday and Sunday had stayed, George Townsend testified afterward, there would scarcely have been enough guns to go around. As it was, there were rifles to spare— rifles to be hidden again or carried by wagon when it was time for the troops to move.

But for the most part the men were happy and eager. Those who were used to handling firearms instructed those who were not, cheering them up meanwhile with the promise that two thousand royalists waited in town to rise to their aid, and that the enemy, surprised and panicked, would surrender without bloodshed. And for every doubter who noted fearfully that Sam Nowlein and Robert Wilcox had not yet come, there were half a dozen bold ones to assert that in Red George and Lot Lane and Pūkila, in Charley Warren and Carl Widemann and Joe Clark they had all the leaders they needed. So they joked and sang, ate and drank, scoffed at the "missionaries," toasted the queen, and exulted that "the life of the land" was about to be restored.

A little before noon George Townsend sent Kaua'i and Apelehama eastward beyond Kāhala to recruit ranch hands and fishermen. Kaua'i was first plied with gin to make him forget a sore foot and then given the only available horse. Apelehama was armed with a pistol and advised to get himself a mount at Waiʻalae. For such reluctant emissaries they did extremely well, rounding up most of the male residents between Kūpikipikiʻo and Koko Head. "If you are *aloha ʻāina*," they said to all whom they met, "go over to Kāhala; there is work there, and you will find out what it is." Apelehama, who had had the foresight to take a blank book and pencil, would brandish the pistol and demand each fellow's signature, implying that anyone who did not subscribe would be shot on the instant, and that any signer who did not appear forthwith at camp would be sent for.

They were stern with excuse makers. When the men of one household said they must go over to Maunalua to receive and divide their fish money, Kauaʻi cried, "Oh, never mind that money. . . . Your country is of more importance than your money." And when this did not deter them, both recruiting officers followed them to the meeting place and back. Finally Nahinalu, the married one, threw some coins down before his wife, saying, "Here is some money to support you; it is better for me to go with these men than to stop here and be shot." The other four fishermen agreed, but Kauaʻi and Apelehama were too shrewd to march them off conspicuously in a company; they bade them string along one at a time, and some of them did not get to camp until dark.

Any resentment these country boys may have felt at the manner of their drafting vanished when they joined the jolly crowd at Kāhala. "They all came in laughing," Charley Warren testified. "I didn't see anyone that wanted to go home."

Carl Widemann and Louis Marshall came to Kaʻalāwai on Sunday morning, fresh from a comfortable night and a hearty breakfast at Sans Souci. They were the elite of the *poʻe aloha ʻāina*. While his distinguished father, Judge Herman Widemann, drafted diplomatic protests and went abroad on missions for Liliʻuokalani, impetuous Carl had thrown himself into plotting. His right-hand men were Marshall and William H. C. Greig.

Boyish, pink-cheeked Louis Marshall, an American still in his teens, had come to Honolulu quite on his own, seeking a job. He had found one readily at the Foster harness shop, had become the protégé of the wealthy widow, Mrs. Thomas Foster, and had made friends with the city's young blades. He had also won acclaim as a cyclist. Lili'uokalani's partisan from the first, he consorted with the princes, David and Jonah, who also rode in bicycle meets.

William H. C. Greig was from a well-to-do Tahitian family which owned a large part of Fanning's Island. Charming and popular, he had won his way into a good position at the Lewers and Cooke lumber company and into the social circle that the princes dominated.

In town these young men made the harness shop their center, just as Nowlein's crowd gathered at Molteno's and Bertelmann's. At Waikīkī they had the run of Dowager Queen Kapi'olani's place. That is where they had gone on Thursday when they fled from Kaka'ako. For they were the ones who, on the night of January 3, with a handful of less fashionable brawlers, had had hilarious fun "standing up" the special police. They had cowed the P.G.s, stripped them of their guns, and forced them to sit docilely on the beach. Then sixty regulars had come, and the rash young aristocrats had made off. They had not dared to go home since, for they knew that they had been recognized and that Marshal Hitchcock was looking for them.

Hiding out in a gentlemanly manner, they had kept themselves informed of the royalists' every move. But rain overtook them when they started for Kāhala on Saturday evening, and they put up for the night at George Lycurgus' oceanside resort. A round of drinks somewhat relieved the evening's gloom. They ordered an eight-o'clock breakfast and went early to bed. On Sunday morning Greig, who had work to do at the lumber office, turned toward town, while Widemann and Marshall set out along the beach to Ka'alāwai.

Such liaison as the two camps had through most of that day was the work of this pair. They ranged back and forth, carrying messages, making suggestions, and merely by their jaunty presence lifting spirits where any were inclined to droop. Greig joined them again at sunset.

By midafternoon they had taken some twenty prisoners at Ka'alāwai. Young Alex Isenberg was the first one. On his horse he had been headed for town from his brother's Wai'alae ranch. After that, they impounded several innocent pedestrians—two women among them—who were out for Sunday strolls; and still later William Pua and Jim Lane raided the signal station, captured Charlie Peterson and his fifteen-year-old daughter, and tore out the telephones. Under mild surveillance in the Rosa house the prisoners passed the slow hours, nervously observing the rebels. But they were treated well—greeted cheerfully by those who knew them, invited to share the roast meat and the barreled poi, and furnished with what reading matter the place afforded, mostly copies of the *Police Gazette*.

Chief guard Bipikāne relaxed in a rocking chair with a gun across his knees and delighted to order his subordinates to pass back and forth at the doors or to escort into the yard anyone who must answer a call of nature. Coming along the beach that morning, he very nearly had been turned back because he did not say, "*Aloha 'āina*." But when he shouted, "Well, I am Bipikāne, and that is all the password I have got," the sentries let him by, knowing him to be robustly loyal.

"I had hopes," Bipikāne said afterward, "that there would be about a million people out there. . . . I found that there were very few and it pained my soul. . . . But I could not go home . . . because it was death behind me. . . . So I was kept there . . . and I guarded the prisoners. . . ."

A light wagon clattered up to the Rosa house, and Bipikāne exclaimed with pleasure, "It's my *keiki*, my child!" John Wise was not really Bipikāne's son, but the older man had adopted the younger into his household at Pālama and loved him with all his sturdy heart, because Wise, though educated in the United States, had chosen the side of the queen. Now Wise came, driving Bipikāne's decrepit horse and broken-down cart, to deliver the revolvers and rifles that had long been concealed in Bipikāne's outhouse.

As soon as he had unloaded, Wise had hurried away, saying that he would return in the evening and bring more men. Near Bertelmann's as he drove toward town, he fell in with his friend Prince Kūhiō, who, on his dapple-gray horse, had been making the rounds, bestowing his smiles on those about to fight for the house of Kalākaua. Kūhiō, like Wise, when he had finished his business in town, meant to come again to Diamond Head to help lead the rebels in their midnight march on Honolulu. But it was not to be. Before either Wise or Kūhiō came that way again, government policemen were blocking the road at the Sans Souci gate.

10. SHOTS IN THE DARK

At four o'clock Robert Wilcox came to Kaʻalāwai, dressed in ordinary Sunday clothes but carrying on his arm the long, full cloak of his Italian military uniform. He was not pleased with what he found. Nobody had counted the men or drilled them. The division of the slender forces into two camps with no real communication between them appalled him. But most of all he raged at the presence of gin and tipsy recruits. He blustered through the house, smashing empty bottles, unable to find any full ones.

Learning that Nowlein had not arrived at Kāhala, Wilcox sent Carl Widemann there to take command. He ignored George Townsend, whom he blamed for the drinking, and treated Lot Lane as his adjutant. "As soon as it gets dark, so the prisoners can't see," he told Lane, "we'll muster into squads and be ready to fall in behind Nowlein when he starts for town."

But at dusk, before the squads were complete, Robert Pālau, back from town where he had gone to round up more men, dismayed the camp with his news. Over near Bertelmann's gate the republic's police captain, Robert Parker, had challenged Pālau's party.

"Going fishing," Pālau had answered when asked his business in the neighborhood, and Parker had let the group pass. But Pālau thought there were other police at Bertelmann's, and that some of the *aloha ʻāina* boys who were not glib liars would not get through.

At once Wilcox detailed six men to march to Bertelmann's, surround Parker and his aides, disarm them, and bring them captive to Antone Rosa's. When Lot Lane objected, Robert's temper flared. Instead of Lot, the natural choice to command the party, he named William Pua, who had drunk pretty steadily all day. Lot himself was not altogether sober, and the rest of the squad were what Hakuʻole Sylva called *ʻōpulepule*, somewhat crazy.

As this unimpressive company passed the Kaʻalāwai sentries, a recruit, just arriving, sang out, "Bertelmann's is full of police." Thereupon Pua went back to Wilcox, who enlarged the squad to twelve and dispatched fifteen more men under Pūkila to follow them. Quarreling broke out at once in the first squad. Bartow, the haole, objected to taking orders from a *kanaka*, especially a tipsy one. Pua pulled his pistol. Bartow in turn drew his. Lot Lane seized Pua, and Ioʻela Kiakahi restrained Bartow. When the anger had cooled and the chief contenders had shaken hands, the little band prepared to move on. But now Pūkila's men had overtaken them. While the two squads, mingling, paused at Smith's well near the end of the government road for a drink of water, a third squad came up, followed by Robert Wilcox and Joe Clark.

Wilcox's reproof was sharp. In an instant the commanders had reformed their squads and started an orderly advance. Wilcox and Clark, joined by the penitent Bartow, brought up the rear. Then suddenly Bartow darted into one of the yards *makai* of the road, pointing his gun into the air. "Come on!" he shouted. "The boys are fighting at Bertelmann's."

It was impossible to tell who had shot first that night. A moving shadow, a lurking form that might have been one of Parker's police had excited some chap whose trigger finger had been itching all day. Suddenly there were flashes in all directions and bullets singing through the bushes amid cries of "Who's there?" and answers of "*Aloha 'āina!*" And then the voices of Robert Wilcox and Joe Clark, calling to the men to cease fire and muster on the beach.

Luck was bad for the royalist rebels. In 1893 a single shot, fired at a native policeman, had so distracted the attention of the populace that the haole insurgents had been able to march unarmed up Merchant Street to Ali'iōlani Hale, where they had taken possession without a fight. But the shot that first rang through the shrubbery at Bertelmann's was the undoing of the rebels of 1895. That crazy skirmish in the dusk gave away their position, showed them undisciplined and ill led, and, when reported at Kāhala and Ka'alāwai, so disheartened the whole royalist band that from that hour the cause was lost.

Yet for the moment the rebels seemed to have the advantage; the police had emptied their guns and withdrawn, and none of Wilcox' men had been hit in the fray. Wilcox ordered a retreat to the culvert near the end of the government road below the signal station, perhaps a quarter of a mile, where he proposed to throw a line across the highway and up the side of Diamond Head to protect the camp at Ka'alāwai. But just as he had discovered that seven or eight of his men were missing, the shooting began again at Bertelmann's.

Afterward, few of the rebels could give a coherent account of that night's events. But Robert Haku'ole Sylva remembered how, when most of the Wilcox men withdrew up the road, a handful remained behind "to rest." Four of these stragglers—Jim and Bill Lane, Tom Poole, and Haku'ole himself—had sat down in the wide *mauka* doorway of Bertelmann's *hālau* (canoe shed), the floor of which was some eighteen inches below the level of the yard. Squatting there unseen, they could observe what went on in the lighted house and the moonlit yard. At the foot of the steps long-haired Pua, on guard, paced back and forth with a whip, shaking his bushy locks. Native policemen—some of Parker's men—dodged here and there about the grounds. Suddenly Pua let out a shrill whistle, and a woman's voice screamed, "Here they come!"

Back of the house, striding straight toward the *hālau*, two figures emerged from the shadows. Haku'ole and Tom Poole stood up and aimed, but waited. When the foremost invader was almost upon them, a shot rang out, and a heavy-set haole sprawled forward into the *hālau*. Haku'ole was not sure whether Tom Poole had shot the man or whether, stumbling down the foot-and-a-half drop, the haole had discharged his own gun accidentally. Tom Poole said afterward that he had paused in his flight, taken shaky aim, and pulled the trigger. "One haole is dead," he boasted then. "I killed him."

All was confusion. Haku'ole crouched behind a *hau* tree. From somewhere, Io'ela and Pūkila and a half-dozen other Wilcox men appeared, discharging their guns toward the yard. Two policemen snatched Jim and William Lane as they ran for a shed, *'ewa*, and forced them into the house. The boys on the beach recognized Captain Parker. They came around *mauka* of the *hālau* and saw that the fallen man was no longer there. Then they shot into the house, and the fire was returned, at first from the kitchen and in a moment from the west veranda. A bullet struck Io'ela in his cartridge belt, but nobody was wounded. Someone said, "Set fire to the house." But the woman who had shouted the warning had come down to them. "No, don't you do that," she shrieked, and they all regained their senses and thought how there were more of their own people inside than of the enemy.

When the shooting from the house ceased, several policemen ran out of it toward the road. Rebel bullets followed them, pelting against the cliff, *mauka*. A carriage drove up to the gate and two men tried to cross to the front steps; rebel fire drove them back.

Suddenly Henry Bertelmann's voice called from the house, "Stop shooting, boys!"

After that the retreat was on. Pell mell, through Beckley's side gate or over the rail fences, the rebels made off toward the culvert, where Wilcox was establishing a line and posting guards.

"Now is the time for us to march into town," Joe Clark kept saying. "We'll never have a better time. If we wait until midnight or until morning, we'll find the way blocked and can't get in."

But Wilcox would not agree. He was under orders, he said,

and must obey. Until Sam Nowlein said so, there would be no marching on the city.

Joe was not convinced. He did not see that they were bound by what an absent commander had said hours ago. Leaving Pūkila in charge of the men at the culvert, Joe, Lot Lane, and Wilcox went back to the camp at Rosa's. Wilcox clearly was worried. "Don't tell the men at the house," he said. "Don't tell them anything."

Joe continued to argue, but in the end he gave it up; Wilcox was inflexible. When a messenger came on horseback, asking him to go over to Kāhala for conference, Wilcox ordered Joe Clark to return to the skirmish line and take charge.

Joe said, "Perhaps you had better send George Townsend." He was miffed that his suggestion had not prevailed.

But Wilcox said, "No. Townsend is not the right man."

"Then I'll go and do the best I can," Joe said. He was to hold the place at all hazards until he was relieved or given other orders.

It was not, after all, one of Marshal Hitchcock's busy agents who had warned the government and sent Captain Parker and his policemen to Bertelmann's at Diamond Head. It was a twenty-three-year-old Hawaiian, whose identity, known at the time to only two or three officials, has remained a well-kept secret.

In June, five months after the counterrevolution was crushed, the marshal sent to a dozen prominent citizens a note which read: "I deem it advisable to remember in a pecuniary manner the services of the person (a native Hawaiian) who above all others rendered the Police Department the knowledge on Jan. 6th, 1895, whereby the Republic was enabled to take such measures as to save great bloodshed. . . . I shall be glad to receive the sum of Twenty or Twenty-five dollars each from those to whom I present this."

On file with the marshal's papers is the young man's receipt for three hundred dollars "as gift from friends to me." But the signature—Kahekili—is obviously a pseudonym.

It was Tim Murray, an officer in the Citizens' Guard and a close associate of Marshal Hitchcock, who had persuaded the youth, an employe of his, to transfer his loyalty from the queen to the republic.

"I knew he was in with Bipikane, Nowlein, Bertelmann, &c...," Murray wrote long afterward, and went on to tell how he had promised not to let the government "injure or molest" any of the lad's family, and how, about a month before the outbreak, the new spy began reporting on the royalist meetings he attended.

"On Jan. 4," Murray's narrative continues, "he told me ... that the plan was to have the guns landed between Waikiki and Koko Head & he was to be one of the party to land them. That if he could absent himself without raising suspicion he ... would call on me at my home ... if possible on Sat. night Jan 5–6 between 12 m & 2 A.M., but if not, then certainly on the following day Sunday 6th."

It was four o'clock Sunday afternoon when the marshal's telephone rang. A woman's voice with an urgent note in it asked for Mr. Murray. There was someone to see him—at his house—a *kanaka*. It seemed to be important.

It took a quarter of an hour for the marshal to find Murray, but less than five minutes for the two to agree on a course of action. Murray sped home in a hack and, taking the young spy, set out along Fort Street as if for a stroll. Within the block these two met the marshal, who had come by a separate conveyance. There, in the Sunday quiet, the informer put his story on record.

All day, he said, there had been sentries out there to stop anybody who tried to leave; but when he had complained of feeling sick and asked to go over to Isenberg's to get some milk, they had let him go. He had come in by the Wai'alae Road as fast as he could and had gone straight to Mr. Murray's house, thinking he might find his employer at home. He said there were guns at Bertelmann's, that the overthrow would take place that night, that two thousand men had gathered at Diamond Head and would start in about 1:00 A.M.

The marshal acted at once. He dispatched his deputy, Arthur M. Brown, on horseback to size up the situation while he himself sought out a judge to give him a search warrant. But he sent Brown to the wrong place. Perhaps the Hawaiian thought the country place at Ka'alāwai, where he had been cleaning guns, belonged to his royalist friend Bertelmann, about whose Diamond Head home there had been so much talk. At least, it was to Bertelmann's that

Hitchcock, when finally he had the warrant, sent Police Captain Robert Parker, with Lieutenant Holī and six other officers, to serve it.

Parker had worked for the government in one capacity and another for almost fifteen years. He had served King Kalākaua well as a lieutenant of household guards, and Lili'uokalani as a captain of police; but after the revolution of 1893 he had cast his lot with the Provisional Government and its successor, the republic, winning golden opinions for the vigor with which he searched out opium smugglers and royalist plotters. Parker was three-fourths Hawaiian; his maternal grandfather was John Palmer Parker of Massachusetts, who established the famed Parker Ranch on the Big Island, and Samuel Parker, the handsome, dashing royalist, was his cousin. His surname was really Waipā, his father being a petty chief on Hawai'i, but he had long signed himself Robert W. Parker.

At first after the overthrow, Lili'uokalani had believed him her friend in the enemy's camp. In her diary she had noted that "R. Waipa ... must not give the P.G. cause to suspect him, because being in the police he may be of service when the time comes for a change." But Parker's new employers found him faithful to the republic.

Now, at dusk on January 6, he stationed his policemen—Mo'au, Nohonoho, Chamberlain, Akina, Luahiwa, and Pe'ahi—along the line fences east and west of Bertelmann's and with Lieutenant Holī began patrolling the road *mauka* of the house. A few words with Deputy Marshal Brown had convinced Parker that he had better not serve the search warrant at present. In the hour just past Brown had seen a score of Hawaiians, singly or in small groups, saunter eastward. None of them had entered the Bertelmann premises; the house had remained quiet and, in the gathering shadows, dark. Clearly the meeting place was not here, but beyond; and this, Brown thought, called for a change of orders from the marshal. Serving the warrant now would tip off the rebels to the presence of the police, who were certainly too few to deal with such a troop as must have assembled farther up the shore. So, leaving Parker and his men on guard, Brown rode posthaste for Honolulu to confer with the marshal.

There was irony in the way things fell out at Diamond Head

that Sunday. "Don't you land any of that stuff here!" Henry Bertelmann had yelled at William Rickard when Rickard came ashore from the *Waimanalo* on January 3 at midnight. And on Saturday, because he had lost faith in the movement and wanted to be away from Honolulu when the fighting began, Bertelmann had brought his mother, his wife, and his children here from his town house. As evening closed on Sunday, he no more expected to be involved in trouble than did James Castle and Charles Carter at their beach residences nearby, or George Lycurgus, host at Sans Souci. Yet the young spy's report had brought the officers of the law to his door, and presently a white royalist who lived nearby slipped in from *makai* to warn Bertelmann that his grounds were being watched.

Bertelmann's house, a neat bungalow with slatted blinds, faced west toward Waikīkī. Steps from the front veranda led down to a curving drive that began at the gate, *mauka*, and ended at the row of small buildings—a stable, a boathouse, a shed for fishing tackle, and a caretaker's cottage—*makai*. A grove of *kiawe* trees sheltered the house from the road; ti and *kolomona* shrouded the rail fences that enclosed the place on three sides.

Policemen, watching from the shadows, saw that lamps had been lighted indoors. A little later they saw a long-haired Hawaiian, carrying a whip, go around the yard and peer into the shrubbery. Still later Henry Bertelmann with two cigar-smoking companions made a circuit. The officers stood their ground, cautious lest a twig snap or a stone crunch. Lieutenant Holī paced back and forth in the road, and Captain Parker walked a beat from road to beach, *makai* through one adjoining yard, *mauka* through the other. Time dragged.

The first shots came from the beach, *makai* of Beckley's house. In an instant that yard seemed full of rebels, firing at Nohonoho and Pe'ahi, who ran for the road. From among the *kiawe* trees bullets flew over the fence. Holī emptied his revolver and reloaded. Two men bolted eastward into Beckley's; Holī saw that his remaining adversary was Henry Bertelmann. The two shot it out until both their guns were empty. A bullet had knocked off Holī's cap, but he did not know until Bertelmann had withdrawn that he had been shot in the breast. Dizzy and reeling, he stumbled along

Bertelmann's house at the foot of Diamond Head. The cross indicates where Charles Carter stood when shot. Sketch made from a photo and published in the San Francisco *Examiner*, January 19, 1895.

the road until a passerby took him into his buggy and carried him to a doctor.

"They are too many for us," the rest of Parker's men told their captain as they gathered around him near Bowler's gate, townside of Bertelmann's. Parker consented to a retreat—to Sans Souci, where they could telephone for reinforcements. They feared Holī was dead.

The din at Bertelmann's reverberated along the beach to where James B. Castle waited anxiously for signs of an outbreak. An hour before, Deputy Marshal Brown had come to his house—an elegant, turreted mansion set where the shore juts out at the east end of Kapiʻolani Park—to telephone to Hitchcock that he was on his way in for consultation. Shortly afterward, a call from the marshal's office had warned Castle to be on his guard, since there was likely to be trouble in his neighborhood.

Jim Castle, a member of the Citizens' Guard, had loaded his rifle and his revolver and laid them where he could get them without disturbing his wife. Then he had gone next door to warn Charles Carter and Charles' cousin Alfred that the long-expected encounter might come before the night was over. While the men talked, the sputter of shooting reached them. Charles ran out of his house with a rifle for his cousin and a revolver for himself; Castle took his weapons, and the three of them hastened up the road. In front of Sans Souci they met Captain Parker with his retreating officers and Deputy Marshal Brown, just back from town with several more policemen and the promise that soldiers would follow.

Up the shore all was quiet now. It would be well, Parker and Brown agreed, to go cautiously back to Bertelmann's and see whether they could find Lieutenant Holī. Then if they encountered no resistance, they would serve the search warrant.

The party straggled up Campbell's lane, across Bowler's grounds into the road, and through Bertelmann's front gate. At the steps, long-haired Pua, swinging his whip, challenged them but did not deny entrance. Henry Bertelmann and his mother sat on the veranda. Yes, Henry said, he would hear the warrant read; Brown and Parker went with him into the dining room.

The reading of the warrant was never finished. Shooting began again almost at once in a far corner of the yard. There were men's shouts and women's screams. In a moment Alfred Carter, helped by the deputy marshal, brought in his wounded cousin Charles and laid him on the bed in the room across the hall. Alfred started for Sans Souci to get a doctor. Brown went out to quell the riot in the yard. The old woman, Bertelmann's mother, ran back and forth, pleading in Hawaiian for Henry to "stop it." Somewhere in the house, children were crying. Bullets kept pelting against a slat door at the back; feet pounded across the veranda; voices shrilled. Joe Luahiwa looked coolly at Henry Bertelmann and said, "If anybody comes in this room, you will be the first dead man. You'd better order them off."

Bertelmann did. "Stop shooting, boys," he shouted in Hawaiian, "if you don't want us all killed—"

They recognized his voice, or else their madness had spent itself.

11. DEFEAT

Samuel Nowlein was still in town when the evening church bells rang. He had called at Washington Place in time to see Lili'uokalani return in her carriage from a late afternoon drive. Back at home, he had burned some papers, eaten supper, and telephoned Stand 290 for a hack. As they rumbled eastward along King Street, the driver remarked that there seemed to be some excitement around Central Union Church. Services were letting out early. Sam Nowlein made no comment.

Along Wai'alae Road the driver cocked his ear for sounds of danger. Just before they came to the hill that haoles called Telegraph and Hawaiians, Kaimukī, the hackman pulled up his horse with a start. A babel of voices rose from the darkness ahead. Men— a dozen or so—must be coming toward them down the road. If these were part of the royalist force, what were they doing here, hours ahead of time? If they were government men, things were bad indeed.

Nowlein leaped out and dismissed his hack with a gesture. Long before the driver had turned his vehicle in the narrow roadway and started for town, Nowlein had climbed the stone wall *makai* and struck off through the matted lantana. The walk to Kāhala took almost two hours. Footsore and irritable, drenched with dew and perspiration, the leader found little at the camp to hearten him. Carl Widemann and Louis Marshall commanded— if you could use the word—thirty-two dispirited men, who, drunk or sleepy or both, lounged about the house and yard. Word had come from Kaʻalāwai of the disastrous skirmish at Bertelmann's. Later, Widemann had sent out two small detachments to guard Waiʻalae Road, so he said, and keep it open for the march into town. Nowlein thought it was one of these parties he had heard when he left the hack. If so, he was appalled at their unsoldierly behavior.

So everything was at sixes and sevens. Nowlein was hardly the man to set matters right, but he did his best. He sent for Wilcox, who came over to detail the bad news. Beyond all question, Wilcox said, Honolulu was alerted. National Guard regulars, no doubt, would soon attack his men on the Diamond Head flank, and in town the Citizens' Guard would be flocking to their posts, the sharpshooters and artillery would be thrown into the field, and all approaches to the city defended against a rebel advance. The only hope he could see was to hold the position he had taken and force the P.G.s to offer terms—general amnesty, perhaps, for the insurrectionists.

Nowlein still thought he might get into town by the *mauka* route. If not, he could at least make a stand somewhere along Waiʻalae Road and prevent Wilcox' force from being taken from the rear. Wilcox agreed. He would post a few men, he said, on top of Diamond Head. From there, as soon as it was light, they could reconnoiter the government moves in that vicinity and, looking *mauka*, gauge the success of Nowlein's thrust toward the city.

There was plenty the leaders could have quarreled about— Nowlein's inexcusably late arrival and Wilcox' failure to control his men—but if sharp words passed between the two, no one recorded them. About midnight Wilcox went back to post his men on Diamond Head, and Nowlein issued marching orders to his depleted command.

Considering everything, the array as the rebels left Kāhala was impressive: first a skirmish line under Charles Warren, then Nowlein on the horse Greig had brought from the stables, and behind him the rest of the men divided into two squads, both commanded by Widemann. Extra guns, ammunition, and the poi barrel had been loaded into a cart which went between the squads; but because there had not been room for all the rifles, six or seven of the Japanese woodcutters trudged along unwillingly, carrying Winchesters and cartridge belts.

Thus they marched to Wai'alae Road, then west toward town until they were opposite Kaimukī. There, abruptly, Nowlein halted his company. For four hours his men idled along the road, leaned against the stone walls that bordered it, sprawled on the ground, talked together in Hawaiian. The loaded cart stood in the center of the roadway. The Japanese threw down the extra guns and started for their homes. The night wore on.

"Lurking place of the rebels Nowlein, Wilcox, and others at area near Old Waialae Road, January 7, 1895." Photo by Prof. Albert B. Lyons, taken on the day of the rebellion. (This spot is now, in 1976, at approximately the intersection of King Street and Kapi'olani Boulevard.)

"Mauumae battleground, January 7, 1895. Diamond Head beyond." Photo by Prof. Albert B. Lyons, taken on the day of the rebellion.

"Rebel rifle pit, Mauumae, January 7, 1895." Photo by Prof. Albert B. Lyons, taken on the day of the rebellion.

Defeat

At daybreak Nowlein had the men empty the cart, lifting and tossing its contents over the *mauka* wall. With the dawn he had found that directly opposite his night's position the ground rose steeply toward the rocky height called Mau'umae, which not only would be difficult for the enemy to assail but would give Nowlein, once he was entrenched there, a long view of the country in all directions. He proposed, therefore, to establish a line running *mauka* from near the road up the incline to the heights. Most of the men in his command were strangers to him, willing but utterly untrained and undisciplined. He could see that they would never stand and fight without cover; he must teach them to stretch themselves along the ground behind boulders or to build up little rock piles in front for protection.

The poi was running low, but the men had milk for breakfast. They halted one of Paul Isenberg's dairy carts, forced the driver to drink first to prove the milk was not poisoned, and then cured hunger and thirst in eager gulps. When they had unloaded all the cans, they sent the boy and his wagon back to the ranch.

Even more cheering than the milk was the arrival of reinforcements from Ka'alāwai, led by Marshall, Greig, and Bipikāne. Wilcox, they said, had told them to turn the prisoners loose and to empty the camp at Rosa's. He would hold the culvert *makai* of Diamond Head as long as he could. With close to sixty men now, Nowlein was ready to make a stand. But how different it all was from the way he had planned it: a thousand men marching swiftly, quietly along this Wai'alae Road, into the city on Beretania Street, dividing into two corps—one under Wilcox to join with Tom Walker and his company to seize the station house, the other, Nowlein's own, surrounding the palace, immobilizing the government regulars, shooting down the gunners who tried to man the cannon in the grounds, starving out the garrison if it did not choose to surrender immediately; haole royalists running armed from their dark houses to lead bands of loyal natives to street intersections, so that the volunteer companies and the Citizens' Guard could not muster, and arresting helpless P.G. officials in their homes; the very young and the very old and halt gathering at Washington Place to help protect the queen until, on the utter collapse of the government, he, Samuel Nowlein, could lay at her feet as a gift the kingdom the Americans had stolen from her in 1893. It had been a most happy dream.

At midnight Sunday, Robert Wilcox took a handful of his men up the ridge near the signal station to the rim of Diamond Head and posted them at four points. The largest number, ten or twelve under Lot Lane, were at the summit, and there in the gray of dawn they sighted a gathering of government troops in Kapiʻolani Park. When the enemy brought up a fieldpiece and began shelling their position, Lane's men let out a defiant cheer. "Move forward," they yelled in Hawaiian, "and we'll shoot you."

Shells continued to pepper the mountainside, throwing dirt in the defenders' faces. One shot went over the hill and fell into the ocean at Kaʻalāwai, but on Diamond Head no one was wounded. They had no food, but they drank from pools in the crater where the wild cattle drank, and their spirits revived.

Below at the culvert Joe Clark had been on guard all night,

Government troops shelling the rebel stronghold on Diamond Head from the road near Sans Souci. Sketch (from a photo taken on the day of the rebellion) published in the San Francisco *Examiner*, January 19, 1895.

walking to and fro with Pūkila, his lieutenant, while the other boys by turns snatched some rest. At four he called reveille and had the boys kneel on the hard ground while Pūkila prayed in Hawaiian, asking that their enemies be delivered into their hands, and that every man be given a stout heart to fight for the independence of his country. Then Joe gave a heartening speech, like one the Duke of Wellington—so he had learned in school—delivered before Waterloo: ". . . let us all stand shoulder to shoulder, of one heart and one mind; let us be like Richard with the heart of the lion." The boys cheered him, then took their places in line only minutes before the first enemy bullets whizzed over.

Government soldiers, stationed near Bertelmann's through a quiet night, had begun to advance eastward into the Beckley premises; but since it was not yet light enough for the excited rebels to see them, Clark told his men to hold their fire awhile. He instructed them how to use their gunsights to find the range of Beckley's pink stucco house, some six or seven hundred yards away, and how to fire deliberately and with true aim. He also told them to move quickly to right or left after firing, so that enemy bullets, aimed at puffs of smoke, would miss them. When the rebels began shooting again, they could see from the stir among the P.G.s at Beckley's that they were coming close to their mark. So Clark had them fire singly and in volleys until the enemy retreated into Bertelmann's yard. He then extended his line forward along the flank of the hill, scrambling over the lava ridges, until his right was *mauka* of the road above Bertelmann's. By 8:30 he had driven the P.G.s back into the park, where, among the *kiawe* trees, they were out of sight and out of range. For a time the shooting ceased.

Yet Joe Clark was grave. He knew the handicap of having no artillery. When he joined the movement he had been assured that there would be plenty of rifles and two or three cannon. On his arrival yesterday—was it only yesterday?—he had asked at once to see the big guns, and, finding none at Ka'alāwai, had wanted to ride over to Kāhala to inspect what was there. Now he knew that the rebels had no artillery, that their men were too few, and that the lack of a wise overall command meant the waste of what troops they had. But he would try.

He put Io'ela Kiakahi in command with Mahuka under him. "Hold fast," he called to the boys as he passed them on his way back to Rosa's. "I'll bring you ammunition and perhaps reinforcements."

Within sight of the house he met a young Hawaiian on horseback. Greig and Marshall, who now commanded at Ka'alāwai, wanted ten more of Clark's men for Nowlein; or, if Clark thought best, they would take the whole of his force over to Kaimukī, where Sam was making a decisive stand. Grimly Joe Clark yielded the men.

It was about eleven o'clock Monday morning when Sam Nowlein's company, crouching behind boulders on Mau'umae, caught glimpses through the trees of P.G. men marching eastward on Wai'alae Road. They waited, tense, for almost an hour before they spotted skirmishers in the open field, *mauka* of the road, advancing unprotected toward their position. A volley from Mau'umae sent the attackers scurrying over the wall into the road, and continued fire drove them back out of range and presently out of sight.

Another hour passed before anything else happened. Then it was uniformed men who deployed up Pālolo Road, crouched behind its eastern wall, and fired deliberately and well. Yet they could not get the range; most of their bullets fell behind Nowlein's men, who, unhurt, returned the fire. There was plenty of ammunition on Mau'umae, and the rocky hill was as impregnable as a fort. The rebels were doing better now; their bullets were dropping all around the enemy. But the enemy, too, knew how to take cover after each shot.

Sam Nowlein knew that the P.G.s could flank him by climbing the eastern rim of the valley, *mauka* of his position; so presently he sent Hoa Casabianca Ulukou with two others up Pālolo ridge to signal if any of the enemy came that way. But before the flanking movement developed, a more menacing attack came from Wai'alae Road. A fieldpiece, its polished brass reflecting the afternoon sun, wheeled into range and began pounding Mau'umae. Dust and rocks flew all around. The rebels disappeared by twos and threes into the tangle of the lantana,

Government officials watching the action at Kaimukī from the palace tower. Sketch (from a photo taken on the day of the rebellion) published in the San Francisco *Examiner*, January 19, 1895.

some working up Pālolo and some climbing over the ridge into Wai'alae Valley. The big gun moved nearer.

Nowlein had a fleeting intention of calling for volunteers to go down and hide behind the wall next to the road, then jump out and capture the cannon when it came along. But the men who had not already gone cowered in panic and spoke hoarsely of surrender. Shots began to come from the ridge above. Casabianca, the watchman, had not stood his ground; he had deserted, leaving his gun and cartridge belt behind. Bipikāne had fled, carrying a half-filled milk can. Charley Warren, too, seeing the hopelessness of the fight, had made off toward Wai'alae, sending a messenger to tell Nowlein to retreat that way. If the P.G.s held Makapu'u pass, Warren said, he would build a bonfire on the hillside to notify his commander. But there was no need for such service, for an orderly retreat was no more to be had than a victory. Convinced of this, Nowlein, too, escaped into the brush. Widemann, Greig, and Marshall went with him.

Now the P.G. fire came from all sides, from ridge and road, and the leaderless rebels who remained in the Mau'umae fort, quickly making themselves truce flags out of handkerchiefs or poi wrappers, began to march out. Government men waded into the lantana to meet them and accept their surrender. Thirty-nine, in the end, were disarmed and sent off to town. The battle was over.

From the top of Diamond Head, Robert Wilcox had watched Nowlein's command as it entrenched itself on Mauʻumae, and the government troops as they tried to dislodge it. About three o'clock in the afternoon he ordered both the men on the crest and those in charge of Ioʻela below to go as rapidly as possible and join Nowlein. If they could snatch a little food from the banana patch east of Lēʻahi, so much the better.

By that time the tug *Eleu*, with a cannon and a detail of sharpshooters on board, was steaming along Waikīkī and Diamond Head, firing at the rebels on the flank of the hill, and the government skirmish line was advancing eastward, slowly, steadily. Ioʻela and his handful of men circled around to Kaʻalāwai to take away the extra rifles left in Antone Rosa's house, but a native woman told him her neighbors had already hidden the guns. As the *Eleu* was now bombarding the house and grounds with grapeshot, he did not linger to look for them.

So the last of the force that had mustered at Kaʻalāwai scurried in confusion across the thorny plain and over Kaimukī, trying to find Samuel Nowlein's disintegrating army. They heard shots now and then, but whether from government soldiers combing the area or from their own frantic fellows they could not tell. Stone walls afforded intermittent shelter. By nightfall bands of seven, ten, or thirteen had made their way beyond the Waiʻalae Road and bedded down, hungry and thirsty, in the brush at the foot of the valleys that grooved the Koʻolau range. It was then that Robert Wilcox ceased to map strategies and began to think only of escape. With Lot Lane, Robert Hakuʻole Sylva, and seven others, he climbed the west ridge of Pālolo Valley, found his way to an unoccupied house, and settled down for the night. Water the refugees had brought with them from Pālolo Stream, after relieving their day-long thirst, but there was no food except the remnants of a bunch of bananas. Wilcox spoke quietly. He said he had not wanted to get into this thing. He had known from the start that it was badly planned and not properly led. He had no doubt that by now martial law had been proclaimed in town. "We are men condemned," he said. "If we are taken, we will be put to death at once. We must fight now for our lives."

He proposed that they cross through the upper end of the valleys—there were trails that only a native could find—and come down in Moanalua or Waipi'o, beyond danger. But what had become of Nowlein? of Greig? of Widemann and Marshall? How could almost a hundred men have disappeared? Would not morning bring a reunion of rebel forces and perhaps a fresh, desperate stand against the enemy?

Before sunup Robert went down the ridge and, prowling through the lantana, roused ten or so of the scattered rebels. He ordered Lot Lane to find a bullock for breakfast. While they were roasting the meat, others came—Io'ela and Pūkila among them— until their party numbered fifty. Five Hawaiians from the region joined them now, and one of these, Kupihe, brought his wife. They were *aloha 'āina* people, but they had not heard the word to turn out on Sunday. Now they said they would guide the refugees, and by going along they would save their own skins in case the P.G.s came back to the region.

To give his scouts time to round up all the stragglers in the valley, Wilcox maintained camp near the house until midafternoon Tuesday. So he knew that the government troops had searched Mau'umae and the adjoining wilderness for men and arms and that they had moved on toward Kāhala and Diamond Head. And he guessed that P.G.s would be stationed in lower Mānoa, expecting the rebels to cross from Pālolo and come down that way.

Late in the day, Wilcox led his men far up the valley and climbed the ridge toward Mānoa after dark. When it was too foggy to go farther, they found a hollow, made a fire, cooked beef and green bananas, and set guards—three watches during the night. Again Wilcox slept little. He was planning the next day's movements, foreseeing their need for food that could be eaten on the march. Tomorrow there would be no time for kindling fires and roasting meat; tomorrow there would be steep climbing and, in all probability, pursuit.

At four o'clock he roused Manuel Rosa and two others and

sent them ahead into Mānoa to buy whatever they could from friendly residents. Six hours later, dirty, tattered, unshaven, but on the whole cheerful, the fifty-odd rebels straggled down into the valley, well toward its upper end, and ate eagerly the cooked rice that Rosa dealt out of a bag, a small handful to each person. When, a little later, they came upon a Chinese farmer planting bananas, they took up a collection—pennies, dimes, and quarters that totaled five dollars—and gave it to the man to buy them food. He was to deliver it that evening on the heights toward Nuʻuanu, back of Tantalus.

Meanwhile the going was rough and slow, and the ascent steep. The insurgents had long since broken up into small bands, each trying to keep an eye on at least one other group. About noon a scout sighted uniformed men marching up the valley, pausing to search houses and explore copses and thickets. It was doubtful now that the rebels could reach the pass at Kealaʻeli without being seen and fired on.

Mānoa Valley ends in "the pen." Rocky, wooded ridges enclose it to right and left, and straight ahead is the black, sheer face of Kōnāhuanui. The rebels were approaching this cul-de-sac at its *makai*, or southern, angle, along the stream called ʻAihualama. The trail into Nuʻuanu opened at its upper left, or northwestern, angle. Here was a good path for a *kamaʻāina* going alone from valley to valley, though it was no place for a skirmish line.

They had worked into the triangle before the firing began at midafternoon. With the first shot, Robert Wilcox rallied his weary men, deploying them where they could see and not be seen. They still had plenty of ammunition, they were on higher ground than the enemy, and at first they behaved with spirit. But when the sharpshooters came up, matters took a different turn. These experienced men mounted the low ridges to east and west, advanced boldly on spurs and cliffs, and raked the triangle with cross fire. For the first time rebels were wounded—one fatally, another slightly. Up went a white handerchief, dangling from a stick. Ioʻela and Lot Lane shouted angry protests, and from somewhere in the pen came potshots at the weakening ones. As the government fire ceased, Moehau, whose ear was bleeding, and his comrade who bore the flag of truce stumbled down the slope to surrender.

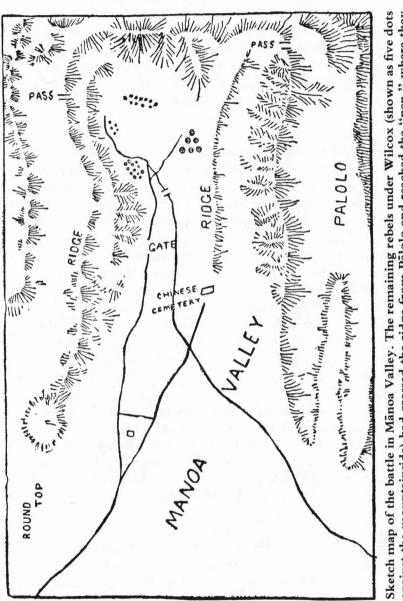

Sketch map of the battle in Mānoa Valley. The remaining rebels under Wilcox (shown as five dots against the mountainside) had crossed the ridge from Pālolo and reached the "pen," where they were caught between the sharpshooters (to the right) and two contingents of military (to the left), who had approached along Mānoa Road. From the San Francisco *Morning Call*, January 19, 1895.

Pūkila, who had prayed for a stout heart, lay dead in the bushes.

For ten minutes the guns were silent, and during that interval a good many of Wilcox' men made for the trail, dodging among the *kukui* trees. When fire resumed from the ridges, only a few scattering shots gave answer. The forlorn force was trickling over Kealaʻeli into Pauoa and Nuʻuanu. Robert Wilcox, with Ioʻela, Kupihe, and Kupihewahine, was among the last to cross. From the crest he fired in sheer bravado a farewell volley.

For the government boys the war of 1895 was more exciting than dangerous. Except for Charles Carter, who died early Monday morning of the wounds received at Bertelmann's, and Lieutenant Ludewig, who, grazed in the leg at Mauʻumae, was out of action less than a day, there were no casualties, though many a man later astonished his family with tales of bullets that buzzed past his ears or sang over his head. In some instances, shoes that had been worn to church on Sunday evening split their uppers and lost their soles on the stony ground at Mōʻiliʻili or Diamond Head; but town was only a few miles off, and anybody who was in real distress with his footwear could do something about it. As to clothes, the Citizens' Guard fared worst, for they had no uniforms. Though some of them got into old togs before responding to the call, many sacrificed their go-to-meeting coats or their best business trousers in the lantana. And lucky was he who wore a brimmed hat, be it of straw or felt. The regulars, in Companies E and F, who had smart soldier caps to go with their white trousers and blue jackets, reddened painfully in the noon sun at Mauʻumae.

Food, too, was somewhat uncertain at first. More than one squad was ordered to the front without breakfast, and more than one officer, turning his command over to the next in rank, appeared at the executive building to pound on somebody's desk and insist that his men be fed at once. Company B's chow wagon got lost in a fog, and Company A's camp stove took six hours to bring coffee water to a boil. But by Wednesday the companies up in the valleys were receiving not only regular rations from a well-organized commissary but sandwiches, pie, fruit, chocolate, sauerkraut and speck, fresh homemade rolls, peanuts, bologna, and roast turkey from the republican homes near which they were encamped. To drive up in a break or phaeton with a milk can of hot coffee and a huge basket of buns or doughnuts became the fashion among the ladies. Such arrivals were invariably hailed with "three cheers and a tiger."

Downtown, where squads and companies guarded public buildings and escorted prisoners, the women, glad of something to do, prepared breakfasts and lunches and evening treats. At Central Union Church, where the sharpshooters were billeted, wives, mothers, and sweethearts, using a new kitchen range designed to cook church suppers, earned the accolade of "best providers anywhere." Mrs. Afong, of the rich and prominent Chinese family, sent ginger ale and apples to Company D at the barracks.

And food was not all. Canteens and rubber coats, blankets and tents—things the government could not afford on its $10,000-

Guard in front of the executive building ('Iolani Palace), January 11, 1895. Sketch made from a photo and published in the San Francisco *Examiner*, January 20, 1895.

per-day budget—found their way into the camps from private donors. Company A's handsome flag was the gift of Lieutenant Rowald's family. Company F, when finally it broke camp, came home garlanded in leis.

These were the amenities that were noted at the time in the newspapers and recounted by old men when other war memories had faded. But until the rebel leaders were captured, apprehension and uncertainty, if not fear, permeated the oddly assorted ranks and chilled Honolulu. Nobody knew how much of the Wilcox army had escaped or when Sam Nowlein might appear with fresh forces from Ko'olau or Maui. Nobody knew how many guns and giant-powder bombs were concealed in cellars on King Street or carriage houses along Beretania. Nobody knew how many white royalists waited in town for a chance to rise.

Every important street corner was guarded. Only persons who had passes could go about the city. The *Alameda* from San Francisco docked under guard with no crowds to welcome her passengers. Accustomed to phoning their friends at the slightest hint of excitement, women felt isolated and panicky now that central refused all but official calls. So they sat on their verandas or hung on their fences, waylaying those who came by, begging for news from downtown or the front. Some of them thought only of their own safety or that of their men who had gone off to fight. Some of them felt only grief that the splendid venture toward "good government" and democracy had come to this pass—neighbor fighting neighbor and in some cases relatives taking opposite sides. A few were fierce in their resentment against those they thought responsible for fomenting the outbreak.

At Central Union Church the exuberant sharpshooters—"we good Americans," one of them called the troop—marked their return from the skirmish in Mānoa Valley by petitioning the government for the prompt arrest of Lili'uokalani. The resolution had four "whereases," the fourth reading: "Whereas, we believe that the action of the Government in not arresting and imprisoning her, is calculated to affect injuriously good Government and the success of our present struggle to put down rebellion; now therefore . . ."

The resolution itself "respectfully" asked "her immediate

arrest and imprisonment in Oahu Prison, like any other common felon." But the men of the executive council viewed the matter more soberly and less vindictively.

At the Hawaiian Hotel a handful of tourists, booked for trips to other islands, fretted at the government for thwarting their plans. Among *kama'āina*s, concern mounted lest any day one of the incoming interisland steamers might turn out to be loaded with royalists from Maui or Hawai'i, ready to rush ashore and shed blood in Honolulu.

On Tuesday the government sent H. P. Baldwin on the *Ke Au Hou* to touch by night at Kahului and Māhukona and, without revealing the state of affairs on O'ahu, to learn from dependable persons what was going on elsewhere. "Everything quiet," Baldwin reported two days later. "Sugar mills grinding without interruption." But speculation was rife to windward, Baldwin said, because the interisland steamer had failed to arrive on schedule from Honolulu. Royalists were predicting that news, when it came, would tell of the queen's restoration.

12. ARREST AND ABDICATION

The arrest of those known or believed to have worked for the downfall of the republic began on Monday as soon as martial law took effect. At the prison, James Low, warden, sweated to make ready for these political prisoners as they came from the station house. Ordinarily the grim coral-block structure on the beach at Iwilei had room and to spare for whatever thieves, arsonists, or brawlers had shattered the calm of a generally law-abiding city. On Sunday, January 6, warden Low was guarding and feeding one hundred sixty run-of-the-mill inmates. By Wednesday evening he had received some forty war prisoners, taken in the field, and thirty civilians suspected of complicity in the uprising. By the close of the week, as arrests went on apace, he had three hundred on his hands, and the end was not yet. To a branch prison in the old barracks, back of the palace, he transferred sixty of his "most harmless and reliable" regular charges and added, as they came in, one hundred fifty others. Company D was set to guard them.

Among the first were the editors and sponsors of *Holomua*, the newspaper that had rallied the queen's partisans and kept them heartened through the days of waiting. For a long time, government officials had had an eye on these journalists.

There were a dozen or more Britishers—contractors, auctioneers, small merchants, draymen—whose royalist sympathies were well known. They had been noisy and talkative, but what, if anything, they had done to further this particular revolt remained to be discovered.

There were the handful of Germans, who two years before, as members of the Drei Hundert, had rushed to defend the Provisional Government, but who later, grumbling because they did not get the offices they coveted, had joined or encouraged the monarchists.

There was Captain Davis of the *Waimanalo*, who on Friday had congratulated himself that he was through with the affair of the guns; there were host George Lycurgus of Sans Souci and two of his "guests"—Arthur Peterson and Charles Creighton. (Of Lili'uokalani's last cabinet only Peterson was arrested. Billy Cornwell, whose name had appeared so often in the marshal's mail, had sailed about the end of November for California—"to make an extended stay." Sam Parker had not been found in conspirators' ranks since September, and John Colburn apparently had shunned intrigue all along.)

There were Charles Clark, second in command under Nowlein at Washington Place, and Joseph Heleluhe, a long-time retainer of the queen. Much to their own surprise there were four of the Stand 290 hack drivers who had conveyed royalists hither and yon and delivered their messages.

There were Prince Jonah Kūhiō Kalaniana'ole and his *hapa haole* friend John Wise, concerning whose visits to the Ka'alāwai and Kāhala camps war prisoners soon testified. There was John Lane, arrested after dark on January 6 in Kapi'olani Park. A policeman had ordered him out of his hack when Lane said he was on his way to Bertelmann's "because I like to go there."

There were Johnny Kahoeka of Waimānalo (Cummins' "boy") and a few other Ko'olau lads, among them Kaulī and Kawelo of the Rabbit Island watch. Captain Robert Parker had arrested them late Monday between Makapuʻu and Waiʻalae. Admitting that the poi they carried in a calabash was intended for the rebel soldiers, they said they did not know that part of the country and had lost their way.

There were the Ashford brothers, Clarence W. and Volney V. Early on Monday, when telephone messages brought them news of the fiasco at Diamond Head, they had gone to register with Minister Wodehouse as British subjects, so that, along with other apprehensive denizens, they could claim aid and protection from their mother country.

There were J. Cranstoun and A. E. W. Mueller, partners in a feed business, who in their few months' residence in Honolulu had turned the Schuetzen Club—if reports were true—from an organization supporting the government into one that threatened and menaced it. Mueller's alleged dynamite plots filled many a bizarre page in the marshal's file, attested by police officers he had tried to seduce.

There was J. B. Johnstone, a mild-mannered Scotchman, who had served ten months in the government's secret service. Under the pseudonym "J. B. Adams" he had assured the republic again and again that the royalists had "no intention of rising." From his cell he wrote in protest to the marshal: "I fondly hoped I would be allowed to serve with the military . . ., but behold, here I am in durance vile. . . . Do you think I would join the Royalists? Sooner would I lose my right arm than oppose, in any way, the employer whose bread I have eaten." But it was a long time since Old Man Hitchcock had taken any of Johnstone's wily words for truth.

First of those who later were called the Big Four was W. H. Rickard, British-born planter and naturalized citizen of Hawaiʻi. Next was Major W. T. Seward, who lived with John A. Cummins and had gone with him to Washington. Cummins' son-in-law, Thomas Beresford Walker, was the third. He was arrested, brush in hand, whitewashing his fence at Pāwaʻa. It was common talk in Honolulu that he had supervised the making of dynamite bombs for the rebels. The fourth of the big haole leaders was Charles T. Gulick. For months before the uprising, the government had watched his house on King Street as a suspected meeting place of the queen's friends.

So all over the city the marshal's men went about seizing citizens, denizens, and aliens whose open talk or covert behavior had linked them with the royalists. They took most of them in their homes, for all except the most indispensable of the business houses remained closed, and, without warrant or formal charge, herded them into the "Reef" for safekeeping until the day of trial. At the entrance, jailor Low had them searched for knives, pencils, and toothpicks, then sent them to their cells—cubicles six feet wide and eight feet long—each of which, as the number of inmates mounted, housed two or three or even more men. To each person the attendants issued a hammock, a blanket, and a covered bucket, and, if the arrival was after supper, a ration of crackers and tea to tide him over until breakfast time.

They came with hearts full of anger and resentment, these royalists who had thought to keep clear of the uprising until it was successful. A few of them had probably subscribed money for the purchase of arms, although it was never established just who had done so; many of them had pledged their hunting rifles or pistols to the cause of restoration; some of them had agreed to lead or join the march on the police station, the telephone exchange, or the executive building; several of them had helped plan the queen's new government and had hoped for places of power in the re-established monarchy. But since they had not committed overt acts of rebellion, they hardly had expected to be lodged in the damp and malodorous Reef; to sleep in a sailor's hammock under a blanket, which, though clean, might be as full of holes as a sieve; to use a stinking pail for sanitary purposes; and to have only a few short periods of liberty each day in the yard.

In the main, the political prisoners were quartered in a different corridor from the prisoners of war, but occasionally mistakes were made and a fastidious haole found himself bunking with a "dirty *kanaka*" whose clothes were tattered and whose scratched feet were caked with dust and dried blood.

Harassed warden Low did his best. For newcomers he telephoned friends to bring in mattresses, bedding, and clothing, and after the first day or so he stationed a deputy in the yard with pencils, paper, and envelopes, so that those who wished to write home for comforts could do so. As to visitors, they were indeed

O'ahu Prison (the "Reef"), 1895.

a problem. From morning till night throngs of women and children, armed with passes from the marshal or someone of equal authority, waited outside the walls. Clearly, they could not be allowed to storm in all at once to console their husbands and fathers; so warden Low kept them waiting several days, admitting at first only persons who came on matters of business, usually at the request of the prisoners. Whatever the families brought for the use of their menfolk the warden took from the visitors and conveyed to the cells, and by the end of the week he had organized a schedule of calls. But no one was happy; everyone felt abominably treated, insulted, and put upon.

For political prisoners the food was abundant if not tasty— one routine breakfast consisted of cooked beef, potatoes, onions, rice, taro, and tea—but the haole royalists ate it in bitterness. As for the Hawaiians, they needed so much poi that the regular supplier rebelled and withdrew from his contract. It was with great difficulty that the warden kept his native charges from going hungry.

Though many of the insurgents had been captured at the battle of Pālolo, afterward in the mountains, or as they filtered back into town and returned to their homes, the active leaders were still at large a week after the rebellion broke. Scouts from the National Guard and mounted patrolmen from the police force searched the valleys and guarded the passes, and in the station house the marshal's men grilled the war prisoners for hints of their officers' whereabouts.

On Sunday evening, January 13, Captain Robert Parker telephoned from Wai'alae to Marshal Hitchcock. "Get Pae'āina Nālua," Parker said. "He knows, sure." Monday morning Nālua, brought from his home at Mō'ili'ili, sat squirming under the piercing eyes and persistent questioning of Chief Justice Judd and attorney William Kinney. For a quarter of an hour he answered "no" to every question. Then with a shy smile he asked to be forgiven for his lies. As a church member, he said, he knew that "there is nothing which shall not be manifested" nor "anything kept secret."

Men had come on Monday night, he said, and knocked at the

door of Haliaka, his daughter, just *mauka* of his own house. Haliaka had recognized Sam Nowlein. There were three men with him, and they were hungry. Haliaka and her children had made a fire and boiled some salmon for the men to eat with their poi, and afterward they had had some coffee. The men slept there that night. But Nālua and his wife were frightened. They thought the P.G.s would come and burn the houses; so they carried their trunks and some articles they prized out into the bush and hid them. The P.G.s did not come then—they went away toward Kaimukī—and next day when Nowlein gave him money, Nālua went to town and bought food—beef, onions, cabbage, bread, and sugar—and had his son deliver them to Haliaka's. But the things he had heard in Honolulu had convinced Pae'āina Nālua that there was still danger in harboring the men. He had heard how the P.G.s in both Pālolo and upper Mānoa were arresting native residents who would not talk, keeping them under guard in an empty house until the last of the leaders should be taken. It was a wonder to Nālua that they had not visited his dwelling or Haliaka's.

So he had found a place in the thick growth below Kānewai Spring where the fugitives could hide through the day. Until Saturday they came indoors to sleep; after that they stayed in the bush all the time, and the young folks carried food to them. On Wednesday "Nowlena" said they wanted to borrow a boat and get away from O'ahu. Reluctantly Nālua went to Niu, to William Auld, who lived by the sea. But the government had seized all of Auld's boats; he had only a canoe just large enough for one person. Nālua came back at midnight, crawled into the refuge and broke the news to Nowlein. He saw then that he would have the four unwelcome visitors on his hands for a long time.

It was Auld who told about the request for a boat, after Robert Parker had pressed him hard. This was no time for a royalist to deny cooperation, with martial law in effect and the prison overflowing. So Marshal Hitchcock and Henry Waterhouse rode out to Niu at three o'clock Monday morning to get the whole story from Auld. There was, as Nālua had said, "nothing hid."

Will Kinney, supported by a force of police, confronted Nālua *wahine* in her cottage near Kānewai Spring a little before midday Monday. "The lives of your husband and son depend on your telling us where these men are," he said. The woman did not seem greatly disturbed by the pistol in Kinney's hand, and she showed no deep reluctance to give the information, though she said she would like to talk first with "her neighbor," Haliaka. A few minutes later Kinney passed the word outside that the rebels were hidden in a thicket near the spring. Government men encircled Kānewai and sent young Nālua and his sister in with a message: "We have you surrounded." Along the trail where they had carried food to the refugees, the boy and girl returned in three minutes, followed immediately by Sam Nowlein, Will Greig, Carl Widemann, and Louis Marshall, their arms stretched upward. Henry Waterhouse placed a hand on Nowlein's shoulder and said gently, "We accept your surrender."

By the time the party had reached the station house, the news had gone around Honolulu and a crowd had gathered in the noonday glare; but it was a quiet, restrained crowd, for these were, after all, their fellow townsmen and neighbors. The captives walked steadily and squared their shoulders, but their faces were sober; the weight of failure was upon them. Only Louis Marshall whistled, smiled, and shrugged as nonchalantly as if he had merely lost a cycling race.

Deputy Marshal Brown said, "Well, my boy, you've got yourself into a pretty bad scrape."

Marshall admitted, "I suppose I have, but I can't help that now." To a representative of the *Honolulu Star* a moment later, he said, "Yes, we are tired of it."

Samuel Nowlein was already indicating a willingness to write off the whole lost cause and to talk as freely as his captors might wish, provided he could win clemency for himself by doing so. Carl Widemann could think only of his father and his sisters and the grief his arrest would be to them. Would his next-door neighbor, Professor W. D. Alexander, break the news to his father? Carl asked. Professor Alexander did. Just a week ago he had borne to Charles Carter's mother the word of her son's death. There was something about this grave, humane, and scholarly man that made evil tidings bearable when he brought them.

George Townsend had been taken at Black Point and Charles

Warren, Pālau, and Bipikāne at Niu. Joe Clark had been brought over from the Kāne'ohe jail. Every day a few more scratched and ragged rebels in the upper reaches of the valleys said "*pau.*" But Robert Wilcox, Io'ela Kiakahi, Robert Haku'ole Sylva, and Lot Lane were still at large when Nowlein surrendered. As long as Wilcox was out, the rebels in the prison and those who were cowering in their homes could dream of a sudden reversal in which recruits from the outer islands or filibusterers from the mainland, having landed at some unwatched point, would march down Nu'uanu or gather back of Punchbowl and bombard the town with smuggled-in cannon. As long as Wilcox was out, the republican forces and the civilians in the suburbs could not feel quite sure that the war was over. Some of the captives estimated that he had led fifty men to safety.

But by the time he had crossed through Keala'eli to the junction of Pauoa and Nu'uanu, his band had shrunk to eight, including Kupihe, the guide, and Kupihewahine. All the others had made off across the wooded slopes, seeing clearly that the time had come for each man to look out for himself, lest the devil take him as the hindmost.

All day Thursday those who had stayed with Wilcox were working their way across Nu'uanu and up the western side. There, since Kiakahi was *kama'āina* in that area, the guides—Kupihe and his wife—could leave them to return home. When the fugitives came *makai* in Kalihi, looking for a place to cross the government road, there were but six of them. They had had little sleep for many nights and only bananas and guavas to eat. Near Kalihi Bridge, at the house of Nai'apoepoe, they had food enough to revive them; but they dared not linger, for they knew the valley was patrolled. Indeed, as they crossed the bridge in the dark of Friday evening, they heard shots and ran *mauka*, losing each other in the gloom.

Only Io'ela and Wilcox stayed together. Moving stealthily down the valley, hiding in the lantana by night and in the taller bushes by day, the two of them lived through a miserable forty-eight hours without food. On Sunday at dusk they came out on the beach, helped themselves to a canoe, and put off to the home of Charles Hopkins. A royalist but not a rebel, Hopkins gave the bedraggled pair something to eat and a place to sleep in an outhouse. Monday morning, when he carried them breakfast, he spoke firmly. The uprising had been a failure. Most of the native participants and many haole royalists were in jail. There was martial law. The harbors were watched. Government scouts were everywhere. He could not shield them any longer. He must report their presence on his premises. He would advise them to give themselves up.

When C. A. Brown came late that afternoon with two hack-loads of sharpshooters, the rebel leader met him with a wan smile. "I am glad you take me," Wilcox said. "We have been friends, and I know you will protect me." Till the end he had thought he would be shot by the first P.G. who set eyes on him.

The *Honolulu Star* published an extra. "The war is over," it announced. "The chase is ended. Wilcox is in jail."

Only Lot Lane remained in the hills. Some said he had thirty men with him, but most Honoluluans thought there could not still be that many rebels at large. As a matter of fact, he was alone and had been ever since the Wilcox party scattered after escaping from the Mānoa "pen." He had thrown away his gun and painfully on bare feet had climbed up a small gulch to keep away from the government soldiers, whose tents he could see well up Pauoa Valley. He had only ferns to eat. Sometimes he heard the voices of officers, giving orders to their men; sometimes he could see the men prowling up and down the valley, scouting for refugees; but they did not come into his gulch.

Suddenly after a week of hiding, Lane woke to find the tents gone. A little later there came the boom of a cannon from downtown. "It is the end of martial law," he thought. "I will go down to my nephew, John Long, and get food and clothes"—his old ones were in shreds—"and find out what is going on." But it was January 17, and the cannon had boomed to celebrate the second anniversary of the overthrow of the monarchy. Martial law was still in force, and Lot Lane's nephew and his family were clearly uneasy to have a rebel on their hands. They prepared to rush him into town without a moment's delay, but Lane begged them to feed him first. On second thought, they let him have time to shave and to change into one of Long's suits. At 9:30 that night they delivered him to the police station, the last prominent rebel to be accounted for. The big Hawaiian spoke quietly. He said he had gone into the fight with his eyes open, as a matter of principle. Now that the movement was a failure, he could only hope that he had not hurt anybody.

Captain Ziegler of Company F sat down beside him and began to compare notes on the campaign. Lot's scratched face brightened as he entered into the discussion.

At Washington Place, Lili'uokalani waited, unhappy and fearful. Of the details of the uprising her partisans had told her little. From the details of the catastrophe too they had shielded her. But the great bitter fact she knew: the attempt had failed. A small fragment of concrete lay on her desk, suitable perhaps for a paperweight. No one had told her where it came from, but she must have guessed that it was from one of the shells discarded many months ago in the making of bombs for the protection of Washington Place. Now the counterrevolution itself was as shattered and futile.

Though they had brought her no news from Diamond Head or Pālolo, friends shared with her almost hourly the gossip of the station house and the Reef. She knew that Samuel Nowlein was in jail and that he was talking. She knew that Robert Wilcox had been taken. Perhaps he too would talk. She had trusted Nowlein, and Nowlein had failed. There was something about the "missionaries" that made all their projects succeed. They knew when to move suddenly and when to hold fast. Now, in spite of native loyalty and haole support, she was at their mercy. Her informants had warned her that the executive council was discussing her arrest. She thought of sending a message that she was willing to agree to anything, to sign any document, if in so doing she could purchase pardon for her friends. But she decided to wait a little longer.

On Wednesday morning, January 16, Deputy Marshal Brown and Police Captain Robert Parker received an order from the office of the adjutant general: "Arrest Lili'uokalani Dominis forthwith, and deliver her to Lieutenant Colonel Fisher, commanding the military, at the Executive Building."

The guards at Washington Place did not challenge the re-

GENERAL HEADQUARTERS

REPUBLIC OF HAWAII

⸰⸝⸰

Adjutant-General's Office.

Honolulu H. I. Jany 16 1895

E. G. Hitchcock Esq

Marshal of the Republic of Hawaii

Sir:

You are hereby directed forthwith to arrest Liliuokalani and to deliver her to the Commander of the Military Forces at the Executive Building.

By order of the Commander in Chief

Jno H C Soper

Adjutant General

Warrant of arrest of Liliʻuokalani. Facsimile published in the San Francisco *Examiner*, February 6, 1895.

public's officers. The lady-in-waiting, Mrs. Charles Clark, said that the queen was lying down. She would call her. The men had little time to wonder what resistance or tears they must face before Liliʻuokalani entered, as regal in a simple morning dress as she had ever been in gala attire. She heard their announcement calmly, giving no sign of surprise, and answered quietly, "I will go."

A few minutes later she came again from her bedroom, dressed entirely in black and without luggage. Mrs. Clark, whose husband was already under arrest, followed, carrying a small handbag. Through the bright morning sunshine two hacks—one conveying the royal captive and the officers, the other, only the lady-in-waiting—traversed the few blocks to the Richards Street gate, entered the grounds, and drew up at ʻIolani. The palace, which she had left with a protest just two years ago, hoping always to return in triumph, was now to be her prison.

Colonel J. H. Fisher came down the steps to receive her and lead her into the central hall, then up the magnificent *koa* staircase. On the second floor, Liliʻuokalani the prisoner, came face to face with a life-sized portrait of Liliʻuokalani the queen. A flick of her white handkerchief across her cheek was the only sign she gave as she turned to enter the room that had once been Prince David's.

Across the hall the cabinet interrupted its morning's business to stand silent in the doorway of the council chamber and regret the need almost as much as it rejoiced in the power to imprison the last Hawaiian monarch.

The room was not uncomfortable; electric lights had been installed in Kalākaua's day, and some of the old royal bedroom furniture had been reassembled.

"Colonel Fisher spoke very kindly as he left me there," Liliʻuokalani wrote afterward; "if there was anything I wanted I had only to mention it to the officer and it should be provided."

She had brought a small Book of Common Prayer and invited Mrs. Clark to join her in devotions appropriate to the evening. Then they lay down, but the queen did not find it easy to sleep. The monotonous sound of footsteps as guards paced the hall and the veranda was hard to bear. No other night had ever seemed so long.

At noon on January 17, Chief Justice Albert Francis Judd, who had been commissioned by President Dole to examine the former queen's papers for evidence useful in the coming trials, entered the study at Washington Place, where so recently Lili'uokalani had sat considering renunciation, and began to take from crowded pigeonholes and drawers the letters, notebooks, and documents that had been accumulating there for two years. The contents of the desk and of the small safe at the end of the hall suggested that the queen had to the very end felt secure in Washington Place.

The papers filled two large grain sacks when Judge Judd, having spent more than four hours on his first cursory inspection, gathered them up to take them to the judiciary building. The Washington Place guard, their chief officer already in jail, came and went about the house and grounds like so many dazed shadows. They had made no effort to stay the arrest of their queen, and they made none now to prevent the searching of the place.

Long after dark, Captain Robert Parker came with two native policemen and a wagon. At the back of the garden he unloaded spades and lanterns and began to dig. Four feet down he found what he was looking for—what one of the prisoners had said he would find—twenty-one homemade bombs; thirty-four rifles, a little rusty but usable; eleven large pistols; upwards of a thousand cartridges in belts or boxes; and five fine swords.

A squad of the Citizens' Guard had been thrown around the grounds. In the morning Captain McStocker and three others arrested the native guardsmen. Washington Place had fallen to the republic.

On the morning after her arrest, Lili'uokalani insisted that Mrs. Clark should "go home to her children." Mrs. Charles B. Wilson, who before her marriage had been known as "pretty Kitty Townsend" (she was Red George's sister), came willingly to attend the captive queen; and her husband, with government consent, became the agent through whom Lili'uokalani could communicate with the world outside.

Gravely and accurately, Wilson carried Lili'uokalani's messages to the government and brought her the only information of the outside world she was allowed. Newspapers were forbidden and visitors restricted to those whose business the republic approved. Trials by a military court began on the second day of Lili'uokalani's imprisonment. On the fourth day attorney Paul Neumann came by permission of the government to tender his services. Wilson and Neumann between them persuaded Lili'uokalani to abdicate. Her wisest friends, they said, naming them, advised the move. She would still have to face the court, possibly on a charge of treason, the sentence for which was death; but the gesture could do no harm, since the monarch's cause was hopeless, and it might mitigate the plight of her fellow prisoners.

When, two years later she looked back at this time of decision, she recorded bitterly that the act of abdication had been "drawn out for the men in power by their own lawyer, Mr. A. S. Hartwell." "I knew nothing at all of such a transaction," she wrote then, "until they sent ... the insulting proposition written in abject terms. For myself, I would have chosen death ... but it was represented to me that by signing this paper all the persons who had been arrested, all my people now in trouble by reason of their love and loyalty towards me, would be immediately released."

There is ample evidence, however, that it was Lili'uokalani's friends—William G. Irwin, H. A. Widemann, Samuel Parker, Neumann, and Wilson—who had asked A. S. Hartwell, dean of Honolulu attorneys, to draft a document that would fit the sorry situation.

After full and free consultation with my personal friends and with my legal advisers ... [the statement said], and acting in conformity with their advice, and also upon my own free volition, and in pursuance of my ... understanding of my duty to the people of Hawaii, and to their highest and best interests, ... and without any claim that I shall become entitled, by reason of anything that I may now say or do, to any other or different treatment or consideration at the hands of the Government than I otherwise could and might legally receive, I ... do hereby make known ...

There followed six amply worded assertions: first, that the Republic of Hawai'i was the only lawful government of the Islands, and that the late Hawaiian monarchy was "forever ended";

second, that for herself and her heirs and successors she renounced forever all claims to the "late throne," all "rights, . . . demands, privileges, honors, emoluments, titles and prerogatives whatsoever," save only such rights and privileges as belonged to her in common with all private citizens of the republic; third, that she implored for "such misguided Hawaiians and others as [had] been concerned in the late rebellion . . . such degree of executive clemency as the Government may deem to be consistent with its duty to the community, and such as a due regard for its violated laws may permit"; fourth, that it was her sincere desire henceforth to live in privacy and retirement; fifth, that she offered therewith her duly certified oath of allegiance to the Republic of Hawaiʻi; and sixth, that she had caused the foregoing statement to be prepared and that she now signed it without having received the slightest suggestion from the president of Hawaiʻi or from any member of the government concerning any part of it.

That her friends pressed her hard, and that she signed in humiliation and helplessness and with little comprehension of the legal phraseology—so well larded with herebys and whatsoevers, with henceforths and forevers—is beyond doubt; that her advisers stood about to witness her agony and then to subscribe their own names below hers is a matter of record. Just how much such realists as Paul Neumann and C. B. Wilson expected from the third section—the one that sought executive clemency for the late rebels—it is hard to say. But that anyone in the room that afternoon, except perhaps Liliʻuokalani, thought that all prisoners would be "immediately released" is extremely unlikely.

On January 29, after both the executive and the advisory councils had pondered Liliʻuokalani's communication, Attorney General W. O. Smith wrote a reply. Before accepting and placing her statement on file, Smith said, the government desired to make clear its views, "in order that no misunderstanding might hereafter arise." The execution of the document, he went on, could not be taken to exempt Liliʻuokalani from "personal and individual liability" for "such complicity as due investigation and trial [might] show that she had had in the conspiracy." It could not be conceded, the answer further noted, that such rights and claims as Liliʻuokalani now voluntarily relinquished had had any legal existence since January 14, 1893. So far as the communication might be taken as a notice to the "disaffected" that she desired them to recognize the republic as the "sole and lawful government of the country," it was, the attorney general said, "fully appreciated," and its "unselfish appeal for clemency" would receive full consideration.

Whatever the words about clemency meant, the trials went on. A week later, on February 5, Lili'uokalani herself faced the military court on charge of misprision of treason.

13. TRIALS

Except for the crystal chandeliers, every trace of
grandeur had departed from the throne room
at 'Iolani. The gold and crimson chairs were gone, and the costly
crowns, the lofty *kāhilis*, the velvet draperies, the portraits of
kings and queens. The chamber was as spare as a New England
church and as orderly as a banking house. For what would take
place there in the next six weeks was no splendid pageant; it was
business, grim and sober. To be just but not vindictive, to be safe
but not harsh, to draw the fine line between treason and misprision
of treason, to distinguish a man's right to hate the government
from his crime in plotting against it—this was the task of the
republic, lately rescued from overthrow.

Long and earnestly the cabinet had discussed the form of the
trials. To use the civil courts would have meant to try all Hawaiians
and part-Hawaiians before native juries; and native juries in times
of racial tension had been known to ignore the evidence and yield
to their hearts. Better to have no trials at all, the cabinet had argued,

than to run the danger of farce and mockery. And how could a native panel have been assembled, when civil law admitted to jury duty only those who had sworn allegiance to the republic?

But under martial law, which still prevailed, Commander-in-Chief Dole had appointed a military commission—a president, a judge advocate, and six members from the National Guard. William Austin Whiting—who once had served the queen as attorney general, and who as judge of the circuit court had kept away from the controversy of the last two years—would preside. Dole had commissioned him a colonel and Judge Advocate William A. Kinney a captain. The others were Lieutenant Colonel J. H. Fisher, who commanded the First (and only) Regiment of the Guard; Captains C. W. Ziegler (Company F), J. M. Camara, Jr. (Company C), J. W. Pratt (adjutant), W. C. Wilder, Jr. (Company D); and First Lieutenant J. W. Jones (Company D). An hour before the opening of the court on January 17, they met, grave-faced, in the foreign minister's office to discuss their procedures.

When the doors opened, a detail of soldiers stood guard within the chamber. The officers of the court came downstairs and took their places at the table at the *mauka* end; the gentlemen of the press laid out their pencils and copy paper on a smaller stand to the right near the chairs reserved for the prisoners. Cabinet members and foreign representatives sat at the court's left. Visitors —all haoles—filled the *makai* half of the hall.

The prisoners came at eleven, walking two by two, surrounded by a hollow square of regulars under Captain Coyne. There were thirteen in today's contingent, Robert Wilcox and James Lane in the lead. Though he had come most recently from the field, Wilcox was the most sprucely dressed, in a light gray suit, white shirt, and white lawn tie. His right hand, badly scratched in the mountains, was bound in a handkerchief. Several prisoners wore boutonnieres of carnations and fern—tributes from their admirers. As they came along Merchant Street from the station house and across the square to the King Street gate, throngs of natives cheered them. There had been plenty of muttered criticism of one leader and another since the failure of the uprising; but now, as they marched with dignity to confront the "missionary" court, all were heroes.

A brisk walk at midday, even a short one, leaves a man thirsty. Belowstairs in the hallway of the basement a lively corporal with pail and dipper hurried among them until everybody was refreshed. Then the guard led the prisoners to the chamber, and the silence as they entered was as palpable as when mourners gather for a funeral. Presently, Judge Advocate Kinney rose to read the order by which Commander-in-Chief Dole had convened the court "to meet at Honolulu, Island of Oahu, on the 17th day of January A.D. 1895, at 10 A.M. and thereafter from day to day for the trial of such prisoners as may be brought before it on the charges and specifications to be presented by the Judge Advocate."

That the defendants might have time to consult their counsel, the court adjourned at noon. As the guard marched the prisoners through the grounds, cannon boomed and the band played in honor of the second anniversary of the overthrow. Hawaiian and American flags flew from all the staffs. Warm as it was, Charles Gulick drew his faded cape overcoat around him and shuddered. Major Seward's face was paper-white. Robert Wilcox looked haughty and defiant. Only Samuel Nowlein and Henry Bertelmann appeared at ease; pleading guilty, they had turned state's evidence and had little to fear from the court.

At the station house Judge Advocate Kinney and his assistants —the young lawyers A. G. W. Robertson and Alfred Carter, and the seasoned attorney W. R. Castle—worked feverishly to prepare their cases. They had been at the job for more than a week, and during that time they had not gone to their homes at all. On the hard cots at police headquarters they had snatched a little sleep as they could, spelling one another in a round-the-clock interrogation of prisoners. They combed the marshal's file for clues, checked one story against another, and pressed each man to tell all, hinting strongly that the court would deal leniently with those who gave valuable testimony.

Many of the earlier interviews brought forth only denials or fabrications. Kaulī of Waimānalo said at first that he had never heard of an arms-bearing schooner and had most certainly not gone out in a boat to one. William Pua, his dark hair still long on his shoulders, told a completely fictitious tale about going fishing with a party of strangers on the night of January 3. The queen's coachman, Joe Heleluhe, lied so brazenly about recent events that the authorities clapped him into a dark cell for twenty-four hours to help him recover his memory.

Major Seward denied that he had taken any part in securing the arms or sent any letter to the captain of the schooner.

"I don't know of any such letter," he said. "I don't know anything about it. . . . I don't know anything about a schooner being off there."

"Didn't you know that guns had been bought over at the Coast?"

"No sir I didn't. . . ."

But George Townsend had talked freely, and Charles Warren, too, after a little preliminary reluctance. So had Captain Davis of the *Waimanalo*, disgruntled to find himself, not richer by $10,000, but in mortal jeopardy. Once the queen was taken away, Charles Clark, second in command at Washington Place, was willing to discuss bombs and hidden guns; and Henry Bertelmann, who had been brought in on January 6, hugging his prayer book as if he expected instant death, had early agreed to cooperate with the prosecution. Nowlein, captured in his Kānewai hideout on the fifteenth, belched information like a volcano in eruption. Robert Wilcox, on the other hand, would not seek immunity by helping the prosecution. The investigators did not press him; they did not need to.

Hour after hour, the judge advocate and his assistants questioned the natives who had surrendered in the field and the haoles whom the government had scooped up in its net; they decided on the order of the hearings and the groups in which the defendants should be tried; they worded specifications and charges, and listed witnesses. But chiefly they sought to break down the denials and the stories that did not ring true.

"You better tell the truth here," an investigator would say. "This is a big *pilikia* [trouble] for you fellows and if you lie about it, it will be all the worse for you. You just tell the truth, all you know about it. Everybody else is telling what they know, so we can tell if you lie or not."

Before long, Kinney came to the conclusion that the republic's most dangerous enemies had been at home on the night of January 6, and that they were haoles. "... cowards of the most malignant type," he called them; "white-skinned and villainous individuals who were not in the front ranks ... but skulking in their holes." If human law could reach them, he vowed, they would be treated without mercy.

On Friday, January 18, the defendants having had time to consult their counsel, an interpreter and two court stenographers were sworn in and the trials were under way.

For the leaders who had been at Diamond Head, whether their plea was guilty or not guilty, there was little to hope for but clemency after conviction. The facts were not in dispute. The men had been there where the rebels had gathered, and they admitted—indeed, they almost boasted—that they had intended to destroy the republic. But Paul Neumann, chief counsel for the defense, was not without resources. If legal stratagems, passionate pleadings, and appeals to the hearts and consciences of the court could win advantage for his clients, he was prepared to use them. For each defendant separately he filed a formal written protest against the court's jurisdiction. Suspending the writ of habeas corpus, he maintained, had not abrogated the law of the regular courts. "Mere delaying tactics," scoffed the *Star*; but Neumann held his ground. On the basis of these signed documents he hoped to start civil suits for the release of the condemned when marshal law had ended.

When three days of testimony were over and the first summing up began, Neumann called powerfully for leniency. He asked that mercy be shown those who had been "misled into rebellion," whose love of country had "blinded their judgment." Though their crime might be named treason, he insisted, surely it did not merit death.

"... able & eloquent," a "missionary" observer commented. "He ... spoke with dignity and admirable tact, and deep feeling, to save the lives of his clients."

The Big Four—Seward, Rickard, Gulick, and Walker—though arraigned with the others on the seventeenth, were not brought again to the courtroom until the twenty-first. Of these,

Paul Neumann (standing, left) addressing the military court on behalf of the conspirators. Clockwise from left around the table: attorney Walter Jones, Capt. W. A. Kinney, Lt. Col. J. H. Fisher, Capt. Ziegler, Capt. F. S. Pratt, attorney A. Brown, Capt. Wilder. Seated at right, from left: C. Wilson, C. Gulick, T. Walker, J. F. Bowler, Capt. Davies, W. H. Rickard, and V. V. Ashford (front, in uniform). San Francisco *Examiner*, February 7, 1895.

only Tom Walker had pleaded guilty. The other three still believed the republic could not produce enough evidence to convict them. They had heard that Nowlein was talking, but his unsupported word would not go far, they thought, against their bold denials.

To their dismay, one witness after another took the stand to tell, under questioning and cross-questioning, the tangled story—of the *Wahlberg* and the watch at Rabbit Island; of the *Waimanalo's* voyage and the landing of arms at Diamond Head; of meetings at Gulick's, "generally once a week for four or five months," lately oftener; of communications between Rickard and Gulick about guns and boats; of bombshells made of cement or iron and filled with giant powder; of what went on at Bertelmann's on January 3. Not only Sam Nowlein but a hack driver from Stand 290, who had carried messages between Gulick and Rickard; a grocer and one of his clerks, who had noted every click of Gulick's front gate opposite their store; the queen's secretary, who had recognized Gulick's handwriting on some incriminating documents; Henry Bertelmann, in whose dining room Rickard had penned a note at midnight; the men who had been on the *Waimanalo* when Rickard went aboard her that same evening—all these helped to link to the conspiracy the haole royalists who had thought themselves secure.

"Things are looking pretty dark for me," Rickard sighed on January 21, as he returned to the police station after one day in court. He gulped down a fid of whiskey and wondered if he must give his life for the cause in which he had already spent thousands of dollars. The dollars he had felt sure would come back to him when the monarchy flourished again; a life was something else.

White-haired John A. Cummins, looking old and bemused, acknowledged that he had known of Major Seward's purchase of arms at the Coast; that he had interpreted for the major in conversations with Kaulī—conversations about guns and boats and devices for signaling; that he had telephoned John Liʻiliʻi Kahoeka at the major's request about some pistols landed at Waimānalo from a schooner. "I would like to tell the whole story—everything," Cummins said after a few of Kinney's sharp questions, "but this skipping makes it bad for me." Kinney let him take his own course, and when he had finished, it was useless for Seward to go on protesting his innocence.

Tom Walker, learning that his young son was to be called against him, took the stand himself to tell about his bombmaking. "I charged these nine," Walker said, "and put them in a pail and sent them down to Nowlein by my boy. They were covered over, he not knowing what they were. . . . Mr. Nowlein had promised to come for them but had not come."

Nor were these the first giant-powder bombs Walker had made. He told about manufacturing some with cement shells in the fall of 1893 and going out to Mōʻiliʻili with Sam Nowlein to test them. They were to have been used to protect Washington Place when it was thought there might be fighting between U.S. marines and P.G. soldiers. It was the broken shell of such a bomb that lay on the queen's desk after she had been arrested and taken to the palace.

Three of the Big Four had now ceased to hope, but Charles T. Gulick still believed he could extricate himself. He wrote a long statement, which the judge advocate read to the court. He had been ill for several months, Gulick said, and his friends had called only to cheer him up. As to the queen, he had done some legal business for her, and he had written out a constitution and some proclamations at Nowlein's request. But he had known nothing— absolutely nothing—about the purchase of arms or the recruiting of rebel forces. The meetings "at which plans, commissions, martial law orders and the like" were said to have been discussed had never taken place. The outbreak of the revolution was as much a surprise to him, Gulick wrote, as to any stranger. "I had neither a knowledge of it, nor any expectation that it would take place."

Neumann argued the Big Four case for two hours. For Seward and Rickard he found little to say—except to deny Judge Advocate Kinney's assumption that a white man was necessarily guiltier than a native; except to sneer at Nowlein, who "with the promise of a whole skin becomes communicative and useful"; except to suggest that Nowlein's skin "might be stuffed and placed in the Bishop Museum as an example of Hawaiian valor."

As far as Walker was concerned, Neumann could only beg the court not to be unduly horrified by the mention of giant powder. Bombs were not illegitimate weapons, he said; they often had been used in sieges and to repel attack. He reminded the court that loyal citizens had used dynamite in 1889 to drive the Wilcox rebels out of the palace bungalow.

But for Gulick, Neumann fought valiantly. "There is no gunpowder in words," he said. "The planning of a new government—call it 'Kingdom Come' or what you will—is not treason." He referred to Charles Gulick's long and honorable record as a citizen of Honolulu; to the time in '73 when, during a mutiny in the king's barracks, Gulick had risked his life in an attempt to restore order; to how in '74, when Queen Emma's partisans had rioted over an election, Gulick had been one to go among them and try to quell the mob. The word of such a man, Paul Neumann asserted, was worthy to be trusted far above that of Nowlein.

It remained to be seen whether the court would agree.

As each group of cases concluded, the commission met privately to agree on the verdicts and to pass sentence on the guilty. But their decisions were not made public nor conveyed to the defendants. Instead, they were laid before Sanford Dole, commander-in-chief, for review. The great question was whether to condemn to death any of those convicted of treason. A statute passed by the councils of the Provisional Government in 1893 allowed the court an option—capital punishment or fine and long imprisonment—according to the gravity of the offense.

Public clamor was loud for the death penalty—not for the common natives who had fought at Diamond Head or Mauʻumae, but for the white and half-caste leaders. All Paul Neumann could say about giant powder did not calm citizens who believed that bombs were to have exploded among them. As the trials brought out details, people shuddered to think of the blood that would have flowed had Nowlein and Wilcox marched on an unsuspecting city in the middle of the night. The republic's irascible soldiers, who had risked their lives among the badly aimed bullets, were vociferous in their demand that Wilcox and Nowlein should hang, along with whoever their accomplices proved to be. And Liliʻu-okalani? Well, let her be banished. Nothing less would satisfy the relentless ones. American Leaguers, always ready to upbraid the government on any count, shouted peevishly that the marshal could have their guns; they would not shoulder them again for the damned republic if the culprits were let off.

W. O. Smith wrote to Lorrin Thurston in Washington that "very many of our best men feel it imperative for our future safety that some examples should be made." The republic's foreign minister, F. M. Hatch, told the same story: "There is the most intense feeling . . . that some capital sentences should be imposed and carried out. The feeling does not seem to be that of revenge but is the cool judgment of those who went to the front that some examples are necessary to prevent a recurrence . . . of similar attempts. The police and loyal natives are most strongly of this opinion. I cannot at present make up my mind that they are not right."

But even before the trials began, there had been pressure for leniency. Both British Commissioner Hawes and American Minister Willis had tried to exact a promise that there would not be capital sentences, and, failing, had telegraphed their governments, via San Francisco, for directives. Gresham's answer came as promptly as wire and steamer could bring it: "If American citizens were condemned to death by the military tribunal, not for actual participation in the reported revolution, but for complicity only, or if condemned to death by such tribunal for actual participation, but not after an open and fair trial, with an opportunity for defense, demand a delay of execution. In either case report to your Government the evidence relied upon to support death sentence."

Lorrin Thurston, aware of the temper of Washington, wrote, "I do not think that it is going to injure the government to reprieve all implicated from capital punishment."

By January 26 the military commission had sentenced Robert Wilcox, Samuel Nowlein, Henry Bertelmann, Charles T. Gulick, William H. Rickard, and William T. Seward to be hanged "at such time and place" as the commander-in-chief should direct; Thomas B. Walker and Carl Widemann to imprisonment for life; and fourteen others to various fines and terms of imprisonment. But the man who must make the final decision—Sanford Dole— moved cautiously. He laid the reports before his cabinet; discussed them with the advisory council; conferred with Ministers Willis and Hawes; received the friends, relatives, and legal counselors of the prisoners; and listened gravely and patiently to what each had to say. Above all, he read the transcripts of the trials—hundreds of pages of testimony—working at night until he was often too weary and troubled to sleep.

It did not help matters when early in February the *Star* gave out the commission's sentences, still unconfirmed. Minister Willis communicated them to Washington without explaining that they were not final. In the foreign capitals anger flamed anew against the government. Pleas and protests doubled; Californian Joaquin Miller, who had commended the republic's soldiers for their bravery and the republic's leaders for their wisdom, suddenly changed sides and sent home violently antirepublic dispatches; secret meetings resumed among the royalists; the marshal's detectives reported threats of a jail delivery. Editor Towse was called before the commission to explain the unauthorized publication.

On February 11 the first ten sentences were approved and delivered. Kauaʻi, Apelehama, Lot Lane, Tom Poole, Pālau, Bipikāne, Kiliona, Joe Clark, William Widdifield, and Ioʻela Kiakahi, called into jailor Low's office at the prison, heard Major Potter of the National Guard read the sentences in English, and Marshal Hitchcock translate them, one at a time, into Hawaiian. Terms of imprisonment ranged from five to ten years; because these were all poor men, the $5,000 fines had been remitted.

Decision on the capital cases came almost a fortnight later. On the evening of February 22, after day-long council meetings, Majors Potter and McLeod entered the marshal's office, their hands full of papers. The death sentences had been commuted to long terms of imprisonment at hard labor. Execution of the sentences of Nowlein, Bertelmann, and Captain Davis was suspended because "they each became witnesses for the government and gave testimony of great value." The prisoners concerned learned of their reprieve the next morning.

In groups of from twelve to twenty-five, native war prisoners continued to be brought before the court. They were scrubbed

Permission is hereby granted to ....

Dr. N. B. Emerson,

to visit R. Palau, W. Widdifield, Joe Clark
Geo Townsend.
at Oahu Prison

A. M. Robertson

for *Marshal of the Republic of Hawaii.*

Honolulu Feb 5 1895

J. A. Low Esq
   Jailor Oahu Prison
Dear Sir.

   You will please allow Dr.
Emerson to have an interview with
Joela Kiaitahi.

   Yours

A. M. Robertson
Dep Atty Genl.

29

Passes issued to Dr. N. B. Emerson to interview prisoners at Oʻahu Prison.

and shaven and wore the new clothes their "folks" had brought to the prison or, washed and mended, the ones they had worn when captured. As they sat in the dock, following alertly every move of the commission, some looked eager and piquant, some rueful and pensive; but there was not a sullen face among them. Most of them had already told their stories, and were not averse to telling them again, either because they were proud of their proven patriotism or because they believed themselves innocent of offense against a government they had never sworn to uphold. A fair number of them had been in court before—as defendants, witnesses, or spectators—and they thought of a trial as a game in which quick-witted defendants could score points against the prosecution and win laughter and applause from the audience. Even the strict decorum of a military court did not overawe them; they still played a heroic role and felt no great fear of the consequences.

They did not all take the opportunity, as had Lot Lane, to make patriotic speeches; but even those who said they had turned out, deceived, for a *lūʻau* or a fishing party offered these excuses in a pert, saucy manner, as if they did not expect to be believed, nor much care. They did not seem greatly dashed by the failure of the movement, nor ashamed of their surrender. It was as if they said, "We made a good try, didn't we?"

Many pleaded guilty, making no defense at all. A few thought they were not guilty because they had fired no shots at Pālolo. Few of the natives asked for counsel, but they seized readily the opportunity to question the government's witnesses.

"Did you see me out there at that house?"

"What was I doing?"

"What did I go there for?"

"Do you know whether I fired my gun or not?"

"How far was I from you when you saw me?"

"Now all these lies that you have been telling the Court, do you mean to say that that is the truth?"

A good many made long statements in their own behalf. They began: "Pukila came to my house and proposed that we go to Waikiki together." Or, "Sunday morning I was in town, got back to Waialae somewhere about 11 or 12 o'clock; I had something to eat and then I went to sleep; by and by, after a while, Kauai and Apelehama came there; they asked me about Aloha Aina." Or, "Saturday morning I and my cousin we both came down town to look for work. . . . we met some friends and went up to one of the saloons and got in there and were drinking till late in the afternoon. Then along between 6 and 7 in the evening William Pua said he was going out to a feast at Waikiki."

They ended: ". . . the people on the road kept firing at us. We laid down among the bushes . . . and by and by when the firing stopped we tied our handkerchiefs on a stick and . . . I finally surrendered." Or, "I wanted to surrender but I had no handkerchief. . . . I tore off a piece of my shirt tail, I put the rag on the end of a stick and waved it over my head." Or, "I went up Palolo Valley and stopped in a cave and waited there until Wednesday morning and I went back to Waialae." Or, "I got away over there to Pauoa and I stayed there ten days . . . in the mountains feeding on guavas and then on Wednesday morning I made up my mind to go down, if the Government soldiers would capture me or shoot me that is all right. I came right down and got home safe. Then I came down and reported myself to the Marshal."

On the morning when Kawelo, one of the Rabbit Island boat boys, was just finishing his testimony, a large chunk of plaster fell from the ceiling to the table, barely missing Colonel Whiting and his colleagues. Eyes twinkled when the commission's portly president, his fine uniform covered with white dust, rose to say, "I guess we'll take a short recess." Hawaiians told each other, "The *kahunas* are working for us!"

But for all the storybook quality of some of these hearings, a grimness settled over each of them as it neared its close. "Treason for that the said _____, while owing alegiance to the Republic of Hawaii, did engage in open rebellion against the Government of Hawaii, and did attempt by force and arms to overthrow and destroy the same and did levy war against the same . . . ,"—so ran the charge, and there was no doubt that the men on trial, however ineffectively, had so engaged and so attempted. The sentence, except for those who had recruited others, was the minimum for treason: five years at hard labor and a fine of $5,000. Commander-in-Chief Dole remitted the fines.

"I do not know how to answer," John A. Cummins said when he had heard the charge and the specifications. Distress showed in every line of his wrinkled face. He could not deny what he had done, he said. He knew now that he had made a terrible mistake, but he had not deliberately committed treason. At the time he did not at all realize the seriousness of the matter. He wiped away the sweat that gathered on his forehead and looked at his lawyer, J. Alfred Magoon.

Young Magoon advised a plea of guilty to the charge and one specification: "... did commit treason by procuring and providing munitions of war, arms and forces to be used and which were used in levying war against the Republic of Hawaii."

Cummins' story was already on record. He was not made to repeat it. The argument began at once. "One of Hawaii's most conspicuous sons stands before you ... for sentence ...," said Magoon. "He has pleaded guilty but his guilt is so slight that it just brings him within the law and that is all. ... I submit there are several matters ... which palliate his offense. ... the Government of his native land had been overthrown and ... he could not be expected, being an Hawaiian, to give up his love for the former Government ... and loving it he had no place in his heart for its successor."

Magoon spoke of Cummins' duty to protect "even a most worthless" son-in-law and of the claim Seward—his "eyes and ears ... in communication with the world"—had upon Cummins' friendship. He noted that Cummins was broken in health, and that to imprison him even for a short time would bring death. As to a fine, Mr. Cummins was not a rich man; he had once had plenty and to spare, but in his old age he found himself burdened with debt and "face to face with the stern realities of life."

Judge Advocate Kinney, when his turn came, said, "I submit to the Commission that the law is this and nothing else: every man that raises his finger in the carrying out of a treasonable plot is guilty of treason, no matter how small a part he took. A great many have to participate in the bringing of arms, some have to supply money, some have to make the arrangements, boats have to be rowed, arms have to be concealed; in this case someone had to act as ... interpreter; every man from the first to the last who assists in any way ... is guilty of treason. ...

"But it was a small part that Cummins played; ... and ... I don't think there is a man in this community who feels hardly towards him, and if this Commission has any recommendation to make, why, by all means make it; ... I think that no one will complain."

The commission, finding Cummins guilty, listed seven extenuating factors and recommended "the exercise of extreme clemency." It advised, moreover, that "imprisonment, if any be enforced," be served without hard labor.

A little more than three weeks later Cummins was sentenced to pay a fine of $5,000. Imprisonment had been remitted. It took Alfred Magoon less than twenty-four hours to raise the money. On March 1 the white-haired chief went free.

Slowly the trials went forward. The court worked with as much dispatch as, in its judgment, comported with justice. But in the prison, men against whom no charge had yet been made fumed and cursed. These were the haoles whose loud anti-government talk had long ago got them into the marshal's book, but whose connection with the uprising of January 6 could be established only with difficulty if at all. Yet so snarled were the strands of conspiracy and so intricate the revelations of each day's work at the station house that the judge advocate was unwilling to release men against whom he might eventually make a case.

If, however, the discontented ones would agree to leave Hawai'i, never to return without the government's permission, such exile would solve, to some extent, everybody's problem. By the end of January inklings had reached Kinney that some of the prisoners were ready to do anything to free themselves from irksome confinement. Without making a direct offer, he had them sounded out, and eventually came to an agreement with them.

"... it being understood and agreed by me that said charge is in no wise withdrawn nor in any sense discontinued ...," read the document such persons signed. This was a bitter pill, and many of the signers maintained to the ends of their lives that they were innocent and had been unjustly arrested and held. But almost-solitary confinement, with twenty hours out of every twenty-four spent in the cell, had made them ready, as Charles Creighton said, to "say anything, sign anything, even to signing away ... life," to get "out in the free air again."

". . . not that we had anything in particular to complain of in the way of food or accommodations," Creighton told an *Advertiser* reporter. ". . . Mr. Low made it as pleasant as he could for us consistently with his duty as jailor. . . . But the weariness of that cell life is indescribable."

The first of the exiles left on Saturday, February 23. They had been released a few days earlier, so that they might make business arrangements, pack their belongings, and say their farewells. The marshal's spies watched them and reported all their moves. Their friends came to the wharf with them and draped them in leis as if they were pleasure bound, but there were no tears and no demonstrations. The government band played with spirit, handkerchiefs waved, last messages were shouted back and forth from deck to dock. Then, as the steamer pulled slowly into the channel, the exiles tossed their flowers overboard. The traveler whose lei drifts back to land is sure, a tourist tradition has it, to come again to the Islands. Most of these men would in time return—the first of them in less than three months.

With jailor J. A. Low at Oʻahu prison the departing inmates had left a gift. "This little memento is presented to you," said the letter that accompanied it, "by your friends who so lately sojourned with you, as a mark of their individual good will toward you for the many little acts of kindness received at your hands during the trying times and under the circumstances in which we were all placed; we wish you to consider this entirely a personal matter, and no other significance is to be attached thereto."

The gift—a cane of *kauila* wood with silver ferule and gold-mounted head—had been on hand in a Honolulu jeweler's shop since August 1893, when the Hui Aloha ʻĀina had ordered it as a farewell present to Commissioner Blount. The commissioner, quite properly, had refused it. Now the jeweler had buffed off Blount's name and inscribed the cane to "J. A. Low, from his friends, Honolulu, Feb. 23, 1895." The time would come when, as claimants for damages, these men and others would give at least silent assent to stories of mistreatment in Oʻahu Prison. Whipped up by California reporters, who did not always bother to interview the exiles they quoted, the falsehood would flourish that extreme torture had been a part of the program at the Reef. When A. P. Peterson died of pneumonia in a San Francisco hospital only a month after his release, his friends, bitter and angry, laid the blame at the government's door. Affidavits by ex-prisoners and officials, sufficient for legal purposes, were not enough to prevent the growth of a legend of abuse. But to the end of his days James A. Low had his handsome *kauila* cane as evidence that he had done what a man could do under difficulties.

How much had V. V. Ashford—aggressive Reformer in '87, reluctant defender of the "missionary" cabinet in '89, conspirator and exile in '92—known of royalist plans in 1895? That was the question before the court when, late in January, the trials began of those charged with misprision of treason.

Since his return to Hawaiʻi after the overthrow in '93, V. V. had made one thing clear: Though he was strong for annexation (to Blount he had said, "It will be a sorry day for both America and Hawaii if annexation should now be deferred"), he had no use for the men in power. "Their attempted monopoly of politics," he had told Blount, "their alternative subservience and hostility to monarchy, according to their hold on office for the day; . . . their contemptible airs of superiority over those not so rich as themselves, and their continually repeated efforts to grind the natives to inferior political position have alienated all classes against them." Here was the bitter fruit of an 1887 quarrel.

Annexation failed, and V. V. Ashford became a man without a party, with, as he put it, "nothing to gain by restoration and nothing to expect from the present regime." For a long time he stayed away from politics, but as the outbreak neared, Sam Nowlein would not let him alone. According to the testimony Nowlein gave, it was V.V. whom he had asked to help him plan the strategy for the landing of arms and the attack on the city on January 3. Nowlein did not claim that Ashford had assisted him in any way; he merely pointed to him as one who had known the uprising was imminent. To have known, and yet not to have informed the government of its danger, constituted the crime with which Ashford was charged.

Besides Nowlein, the prosecution called Lee Tong, a hack driver who said he had taken Ashford to a rendezvous with Nowlein on the Waikīkī road; Sing Fook, Ashford's clerk, who had seen Nowlein come again and again into the law office; and Captain Davis, who said V.V. had quizzed him like one who knew a good deal about the royalists' plans and wanted to know more.

Wan and anguished, for he was a sick man, V. V. Ashford dragged himself to the stand to testify in his own behalf.

". . . we spoke of this and that," he said, referring to a January 2 conversation with Nowlein, "and he asked me what I thought of the political situation . . . and I told him about what I tell everybody that talks with me; . . . that I didn't think that we would have any satisfactory condition of affairs here until annexation was finally settled. . . . he asked me if I didn't think there was a chance for the restoration of the monarchy; I told him that it was perfectly dead, and had been ever since the queen had refused to accede to the American minister's terms; that was her last chance."

There was a question from the judge advocate: "At any time [when] he [Nowlein] approached you . . . did you dally with him and give him to understand that perhaps you might take a hand?"

"No. My Heavens, no," V.V. answered. "I never dreamed that such a thing would take place or that such an inference would be drawn. I supposed him to be a friend and we were talking about the general situation."

Kinney, in summing up, painted Ashford as one who had balanced himself on the fence and waited "cynically and coolly" for the storm to break upon the town, with no other object than "that in the turn of the wheel . . . fortune would come his way," and that "at least he would not be injured either way the die turned."

The court found V. V. Ashford guilty of misprision of treason and sentenced him to a fine of $1,000 and a year at hard labor. In view of his illness the labor was remitted. On February 14 his appearance in black-and-white striped prison garments shocked his brother Clarence into angry, futile protest. Soon afterward, Clarence Ashford yielded to his wife's entreaties and accepted exile in preference to the trial that was scheduled to begin on the twenty-fourth.

In May, feeble and pain-racked, V.V. was granted a conditional pardon and joined his brother in California.

Among others convicted of misprision of treason by the court were John Wise and Prince Kūhiō. If Wise had told in 1895 even a fraction of what he put into an affidavit twenty-nine years later, they would have been charged, not with misprision, but with treason. Only their presence near the rebel camp on the afternoon before the outbreak was mentioned in the testimony. By common consent witnesses who might have incriminated Kūhiō shielded him.

There was the faintest hint of swagger in the prince's manner as he took the stand in his own defense. The warm smile he bestowed on the whole assemblage was ingratiating and confident. It was almost as if he could read the future and see that the persons now arrayed against him would unite in a few years with his royalist friends to send him time after time to represent the Territory of Hawai'i as delegate to Congress.

Lili'uokalani wore black—a becoming dress of rich material—and a small flower-trimmed bonnet. Violets and maidenhair fern trimmed her *lauhala* fan. She was wholly composed, completely dignified, alert, and calm—a queen in manner though no longer in fact.

Some of her royalist advisers had intimated that if the charge were altered from treason to misprision of treason, Lili'uokalani would plead guilty. The charge had been altered; but when she was called upon, she said firmly, "I decline to plead." The president of the court directed a plea of "not guilty" to be entered.

Next day the prosecution began the difficult task of convincing the commission that Lili'uokalani had been aware not merely of vague hopes and promises of action in her behalf, but of the preparation for one particular rebellion, that of January 6.

And that day Paul Neumann and Will Kinney joined battle as never before—a battle of wits, of forensics, and of legal tactics.

Even Sam Nowlein did not claim that he had consulted Lili'uokalani about details or confided in her all his star-crossed plans, but on the stand he reported conversations that went far to show—if they were accepted as fact—that there was an understanding between them.

"I went to the queen that morning," he said, speaking of January 4, "and I told her I was sorry the thing we undertook to do that night did not come off and she said, I have heard of it, and I said that Warren and Townsend had just reported to me that they had landed arms and ammunition beyond Diamond Head; then she looked at me but didn't say anything."

Charles Clark's testimony was similar. He had been speaking with Her Majesty at Washington Place on Sunday night: "I told her Nowlein had told me the time had come for the movement that was going to be made. She told me that Nowlein had told her the same thing and that she hoped it would be a success . . . and then I went in later on and told her we were surrounded, the government had got on to it and the troops were out. . . . That was about 9 o'clock."

Ka'auwai, a daytime guard at Washington Place had said to the queen, so he testified, "Our work did not get along very well last night." That was on Friday morning, January 4. The queen had answered, "Yes."

Lili'uokalani's own diary, taken from Washington Place after her arrest, was put in evidence. "Signed eleven commissions today," she had written on December 28. William Ka'ae, her secretary, repeated testimony he had given earlier. He had prepared the commissions; also, he had engrossed a new constitution, a proclamation of martial law, and another proclamation calling on all loyal subjects to rally to the support of the restored monarchy. Asked what had become of these secret papers, he said the prisoner had told him that she destroyed them, along with the book that listed the visitors at Washington Place.

Lili'uokalani gave all her testimony in Hawaiian. She denied that the conversations reported by the prosecution had taken place. She had not seen Charles Clark on Sunday night; Nowlein had not told her anything on Friday morning; she had never talked with Ka'auwai about such matters; she had not known that the guards around her house were armed on Thursday night; she had thought the only arms on the place were the antique ones her husband had collected and kept in a cottage at the rear.

At midafternoon on the third day of the trial, Paul Neumann filed for his client a long written statement in which Lili'uokalani again reviewed events since January 17, 1893, and asserted that the "movement undertaken by the Hawaiians last month" was "absolutely commenced" without her "knowledge, sanction, consent or assistance, directly or indirectly." "I received," she said, "no information from anyone in regard to arms which were procured, nor of any men who were induced to join in any such uprising."

Again Lili'uokalani had used Hawaiian, though the court interpreter had provided a translation of the statement. It was as if she wished to plead her cause, not before the military commission, most of whom understood only English, but before her native friends. Or as if she took this way of making fully her own the phrases and ideas her attorney had suggested.

The court straightway adjourned to study the document. In the morning the commission ordered half a dozen paragraphs stricken out—such statements as "A minority of the foreign population made my action the pretext for overthrowing the monarchy, and, *aided by the United States naval forces and representatives* established a new government"; and such assertions as "The United States *having first interfered in the interest of those founding the government of 1893 upon the basis of revolution* concluded to leave to the Hawaiian people the selection of their own form of government." [italics added]

Never again would the government consent to receive, as it had on January 17, 1893, a document embodying this version of the overthrow. Neumann objected to the withdrawal of any section unless the whole was canceled. He was overruled, and the expurgated statement went into the court records. Unexpurgated, it had gone abroad by yesterday's steamer. Many republicans thought Neumann had devised it to influence world opinion rather than President Whiting and his colleagues.

When the question of deletions had been settled, attorney Neumann began his argument. He made no appeal to sentiment; he was all cold steel, hacking at the case of the prosecution. First came the old issue of jurisdiction: "I say that her offense, if she be guilty of any offense, was ... committed and ended before the proclamation of martial law and she is amenable to the law of the land and to the civil courts as much as though martial law had never been proclaimed."

Not only that, the attorney went on, but "no matter how wide the powers of a military ... tribunal," the existence of the court should end with "the cessation of the necessity." That the necessity had ceased he thought no one could deny. There had been only "a riot commenced ... by about 92 persons partially armed resisting the search of a house for arms"—no battle fought (Captain Ziegler must have been astonished to hear this), no rebel forces in the field (there were men in the audience who might have questioned this—the men who had been at Mauʻumae and in the Mānoa "pen"); in short, "there never was any war, and if there

Paul Neumann speaking on behalf of Liliʻuokalani at her trial in the palace. San Francisco *Examiner*, February 6, 1895.

was any necessity for martial law it had long ceased to exist."

Next, there was no such crime as the one charged. Under Hawai'i's statutes there was no such offense as misprision of felony, no law to force a citizen to "divulge either the wrongdoer or the deed itself." Duty—yes. It might be one's duty to report what he knew, but there was no law on the books that said he must do so.

Let that pass. Far more important was the matter of evidence. "You have stated here upon your word of honor," he reminded the commission, "that you would try this case impartially, justly, without bias or prejudice and upon evidence; I ask you to redeem your word."

Then Neumann reviewed the testimony of Clark, Ka'auwai, and Nowlein. In none of the conversations, he maintained, was there a word about anything that was to be done, nowhere had a witness told of imparting information to the prisoner about the uprising. Nowlein, to be sure, had said something about Warren and Townsend and their landing of arms at Diamond Head; but nothing at all about what was to be done with these arms, whether they were to be used for an outbreak or not.

"You may believe the queen knew what those arms were for." Here he fixed the court with an accusing eye. "Your belief gentlemen does not weigh one particle in the matter . . . you have got to find from the evidence."

And he must remind the commission that the prisoner had denied that these conversations occurred and that there was no reason to doubt her veracity. The prosecution's witnesses, on the other hand, were largely suspect. Nothing would be easier, he scoffed, than to "pay tribute to the infamy" of Charles Clark, "a man who had been eating the bread of charity . . . for two years and now lies to gain a favor." But he would refrain. Instead, he had something to say about Ka'auwai, who, in jail, had been threatened, told that he was under arrest for treason, that the punishment might be death, that the best thing he could do for his own interest was to tell "the truth." "That," said Paul Neumann, "is a way of eliciting truth that borders on the incredible." It could not, he thought, be called anything but suborning testimony by threats.

As to the revelations of William Ka'ae, the prisoner had

freely admitted signing the commissions. And had she not the right to do so? Her signing of a constitution, if she chose to sign one, was not treason. To make it treason the constitution must have been promulgated and the commissions must have been delivered and accepted. She could have signed a thousand commissions as long as they remained silent. The signing was "totally immaterial."

At last Paul's deep, guttural voice fell silent. He had argued that the court had no jurisdiction, that the offense charged did not exist at law, that, above all, there was no evidence upon which to convict.

At the beginning of the trials William A. Kinney had seemed by comparison with his adversary a trifle lackluster. Today he blazed. He sneered; he jibed—not at the woman who sat quiet and inscrutable in the prisoner's chair, but at the defense her attorney had devised for her. Today he earned anew the description Lorrin Thurston once gave of him as "the most intense man I have ever known."

He plied the commission with arch questions: "It is unfortunate, is it not [,] that out of the eleven that were commissioned legitimately and as a matter of right, nine are now in jail . . . , unfortunate . . . that that new constitution came direct from the hands of three of the leading conspirators who had charge of this rebellion.

"It is strange [,] is it not [,] and unfortunate that . . . those proclamations . . . were drawn in the hands of C. T. Gulick and found their way into the hands of innocence we know not how or when. It is certainly astonishing [,] is it not [,] that these documents should have passed from the hands of the accused just at the right time into the hands of traitors, men who had a musket in one hand and the new constitution and these declarations in the other. Unhappy coincidence, strange coincidence [,] is it not?

"It is an unfortunate circumstance [,] is it not [,] that in 1889 out of the premises of this accused, marched Wilcox and his men from Palama. Unfortunate coincidence, strange coincidence! An easy going public accepted the declaration that her premises were used without her knowledge or authority, but when the thing comes back again in the shape of Washington Place turned into an arsenal without her knowledge [,] consent or approval—and while she was engaged in the . . . pursuit of peace and diplomatic discussion—if this Commission can swallow it, well and good, but . . . God knows what would have happened if the lady really [had] turned her mind to war instead of . . . peace."

The judge advocate continued to elaborate his theme. "It is unfortunate in conjunction with other unfortunate circumstances that the lady after having indulged in . . . innocent recreation, legitimate recreation, her right, claimed in open court by the learned counsel, should have then a very few days after this uprising . . . lost all interest in believing these possibilities, and lost them so securely that even that lynx-eyed marshal of ours who discovered bombs growing in a flower garden, and rifles in a rubbish pile, has not been able to find a trace. . . .

"It is unfortunate that as to her diary which recorded the visits of the faithful . . . it was found necessary to . . . commit it to ashes in the back yard before her arrest. . . ." The burning of documents of that kind, Kinney said, growing suddenly serious, "is one of those stumbling blocks I submit the Commission must face. I submit that the undisputed facts raise an irresistible presumption that she knew what was going on."

He was still serious when he looked toward Lili'uokalani. "The lady knows, as all men know, that the object of this government is not to gratify any personal vengeance or spite against her, but simply to prevent a repetition during the next two years"—here for an instant the bantering manner returned—"of the pursuit of peace and diplomatic discussion such as she has pursued during the past two years . . . and that outside of that they do not intend to raise their hand to do her any harm.

"The government are looking for peace, with eyes still . . . turned to the Mother Country . . . with the belief that ere long . . . she will take us to herself and . . . give to us all that is right and just and restore prosperity and peace in the land. . . .

"I submit to the commission that by all the rules of evidence Liliuokalani is guilty of the charge preferred against her and that it should be so found."

The trial was over—not the last but in some ways the most important of the series. Guards and attendants escorted the prisoner up the *koa* staircase to her chamber. The spectators went their way,

remembering not only the clever and caustic words of the em-
battled lawyers, but the wise and moving ones of Liliʻuokalani
in the document they had heard yesterday: "The happiness and
prosperity of Hawaii are henceforth in your hands alone as its
rulers," she had said. "You are commencing a new era in its
history. May the Divine Providence grant you the wisdom to lead
the nation into paths of forbearance, forgiveness and peace, and
to create and consolidate a united people ever anxious to advance
in the way of civilization outlined by the American fathers of
liberty and religion."

At two o'clock on the afternoon of February 28—three
weeks after the close of her trial—Major Potter, Major McLeod,
Charles B. Wilson, and Mrs. Wilson were admitted to the queen's
apartment. Liliʻuokalani knew why they had come. She started
to rise, but at Major Potter's softly spoken suggestion she remained
seated. The sentence was the maximum for misprision of treason
—a fine of $5,000 and five years' imprisonment. President Dole
had remitted the labor. Her room in the palace would continue
to be her cell.

The trials had been over for a fortnight when, on March 19,
martial law ended and the military commission adjourned *sine die*.
Altogether 190 prisoners had come before the court—37 charged
with "treason and open rebellion," 141 with "treason," and 12
with "misprision of treason." Five had been acquitted; five had
received suspended sentences. The rest had begun serving their
terms, with or without hard labor, with or without fines.

Three aliens had been deported to Vancouver. Twenty-two
citizens had gone into exile in California rather than wait out the
tedious hearings and almost certain convictions. Twenty-seven
others, still untried when the commission adjourned, were
released. At any time, they were warned, they might be haled
into circuit court to explain their complicity in the uprising; but
they never were. The prosecutors, overcome by a great weariness,
let well enough alone.

Samuel Nowlein, his sentence suspended, bought himself an
expensive new suit and, with a nosegay in his buttonhole, went
jauntily about, hailing his old friends and admirers. But people

looked busily elsewhere when he approached. Now and then a woman stared at him with fierce hate. Sam began to imagine things said behind his back by persons whose sons or brothers had been condemned to hard labor. A week after his release he asked, and was granted, permission to spend the night in the station house. Early next morning he boarded the *W. G. Hall* for Lahaina. It was said that his relatives on Maui were more understanding.

EPILOGUE: HAWAI'I, U.S.A.

Honolulu was at peace again. The citizen-soldiers had gone back to their everyday jobs. The circuit court calendar held only such charges as arson, drunkenness, vagrancy, disturbing the quiet of the night, and "furious and heedless" driving. In the marshal's office someone stuck up a sign, quoting Shakespeare, not quite accurately:

> Grim-visaged war hath smoothed his wrinkled front
> And all the clouds that lowered upon our house
> Are in the deep bosom of the ocean buried.

In late January the almost forgotten cases of Bush, Nawahī, and Crick came to trial amid public apathy. The testimony of Marshal Hitchcock's agent, repeated from the December hearing, was no more piquant than last week's half-warmed *laulau*. Convicted of conspiracy, Crick, the *malihini*, was given the option of leaving the country. Bush and Nawahī went free on parole, Nawahī to refrain from politics through the few months he still

216

had to live, Bush—so strangely do loyalties alter—to become an ally of the government.

Lili'uokalani in her palace prison saw no visitors except Charles Wilson. Letters arrived in abundance, but always the government had opened them. Baskets of fruit, bouquets of flowers, cakes and jellies came daily from friends, and hibiscus and lilies from her own garden. That she need not fear poison—as Hawaiians invariably did—her meals were cooked at Washington Place and brought in covered dishes to her door. Mrs. Wilson was her faithful attendant.

She could have books, but not newspapers. Her hunger to know what was going on in Honolulu—how the other prisoners were faring and what the *aloha 'āina* people were doing—was not satisfied by Wilson's meager communications. But the former marshal was true to his instructions; when bouquets came wrapped in newsprint, he removed the damp, crumpled sheets before he handed the flowers to his wife to arrange.

Days were long, from Captain Good's eight-o'clock inquiry after her health and comfort until five, when she could walk on the veranda—or, as time went on, in the grounds, provided she did not go close to the iron fence. Again, as when she had waited at Washington Place for words of encouragement from America, she found real solace in her music. She practiced on her auto harp and her guitar, and, drawing on blank paper the lines of the staff, she recorded old tunes and composed new ones.

Her mood at this time can best be judged from the words she wrote and set to music in March:

> 'O kou aloha no
> Aia i ka lani,
> A 'o kou 'oia 'i 'o
> He hemolele ho 'i.

> Your love
> Is in heaven
> And your truth
> So perfect.

In the remaining stanzas she continued to speak of her sorrow, her forgiveness, and her faith.

For Whom Are the Stars?

I live in sorrow
Imprisoned,
You are my light,
Your glory my support.

Behold not with malevolence
The sins of men,
But forgive
And cleanse.

And so, O Lord,
Beneath your wings
Be our peace
Forever more.

She "lovingly dedicated" the hymn to her niece Ka'iulani. It is known today as "The Queen's Prayer."

Certain former royalists, at last convinced that monarchy was a blind alley, set out that spring among the Hawaiians to organize them into an annexation league. The queen's abdication had removed the last feeling of obligation from such men as Samuel Parker, John Colburn, and Antone Rosa, and left them free to seek the one outcome that seemed now to promise a future for their people.

"Speaking ... for myself," Colburn wrote Lorrin Thurston on January 20, "I am for annexation and will use my best endeavors ... to bring it about as soon as possible, the sooner the better." Thurston's answer was friendly but reserved. He reminded Colburn that, under existing conditions in Washington, annexation might be long delayed; he hoped that there would not be discouragement and backsliding in case no immediate result was obtained.

It was not strange that the new patriots—eager to sign petitions, to become voters and campaigners and even soldiers for the republic—thought that all that was needed to bring speedy annexation was for a few hundred Hawaiians to rally to the cause. For so long they had been told that the great American nation sought only to fulfill their wishes; they could not understand that in Washington the fate of the Islands had become a shuttlecock between two powerful and stubborn political parties, and that what happened in Hawai'i now had little to do with the outcome.

Epilogue: Hawai'i, U.S.A.

Most Hawaiians, on the other hand, clung to the hope of restoration. Leaders of the Hui Aloha 'Āina asserted again and again that the exiles on the Coast soon would return in strength, that the natives on the outer islands still thirsted for action, that "next time" royalists could count on the American League, the Germans, and the Portuguese. The sight of the convicts in their stripes, passing along the streets to their labor at the quarry, inflamed many a Hawaiian. When thirty-five of the prisoners departed by the *Kinau* to Hilo to work on the roads of the Big Island, friends on the dock wept and moaned and shouted until the scene was like the mourning in olden times at the death of a chief. "*Auwē!*" they cried, "*Auwē! Auwē!*" Some of the women had made themselves *holokus* and hats of striped material to match the prison suits. They wore them about town for several days afterward.

When the trials had been over only two months, royalist supporters began to petition for a general amnesty. The first appeal, signed by many Hawaiians, came to President Dole on his birthday in April. Having discussed the matter with cabinet and council, Dole wrote a personal letter to the woman who had started the action, telling her that it was the wish and intention of the government to show clemency, but that its exercise must be conditional on "the interests of the community, on the conduct of the prisoners, and on the course of their friends." As Fourth of July approached, the hope grew that the president's ambiguous words were a promise of parole for all on the holiday. But when the pitifully expectant company gathered under the *kamani* tree in the yard at the Reef, it was only the five-year prisoners who heard the good news of release. The reduction of the major sentences by ten years each seemed to the long-termers and their friends, not clemency, but insult.

By September, however, the president and his advisers felt secure enough to grant conditional pardons to Lili'uokalani, Prince Kūhiō, Carl Widemann, and forty-six others. Louis Marshall and Will Greig, because they were ailing, had been released in August—Marshall to go home to Massachusetts; Greig to sail for Australia and a new start in life.

Rickard, Walker, and five more received pardons on Thanksgiving Day that year. This left but eight, among them Robert Wilcox, C. T. Gulick, and W. H. Seward. Hundreds of Hawaiians signed petitions for their release. The men themselves sent in letters of appeal. To Attorney General Smith, Robert Wilcox wrote: "I will not abet or join any more to any move of any sort against the Republic. But I am willing to accept the situation, to conciliate the natives and to uphold the ... welfare of the Republic of Hawaii."

Freed in the last group, on December 31, Robert kept his word. The man who had called himself a professional revolutionist did not lift his hand again against the republic. He welcomed annexation when it came and threw himself into the effort to obtain manhood suffrage for the new territory. Hawai'i elected him her first (nonvoting) delegate to Congress.

On the afternoon of September 6, 1895, Lili'uokalani went home to Washington Place, from which she had been absent more than seven months. Here she must live, the government had decreed; she must not change her residence without official permission; she could receive only those visitors whom the government approved. Charles Wilson locked the gates and saw that the rules were obeyed.

In February 1896, Lili'uokalani was set free to go where she would on O'ahu and to see whom she would at her home; in October 1896, came complete release, absolute pardon, and restoration of civil rights. Almost two years before annexation the government ceased to restrict her. In December the foreign office issued her a passport, and she sailed for the United States, where she stayed until the summer of 1898. Spending much of her time in Washington, she did all in her power to defeat annexation. Part of her effort was the writing, with the help of a Bostonian, Captain Julius A. Palmer, of *Hawaii's Story by Hawaii's Queen*, published early in 1898.

Oh, honest Americans [she wrote in her closing chapter] as Christians hear me for my down-trodden people! Their form of government is as dear to them as yours is precious to you. Quite as warmly as you love your country, so they love theirs.... The people to whom your fathers told of the living God, ... and whom the sons now seek to despoil and destroy, are crying aloud to Him in their time of trouble....

Epilogue: Hawai'i, U.S.A.

It is for them that I would give the last drop of my blood; it is for them that I would spend, nay, am spending, everything belonging to me. Will it be in vain?

But when, in 1898, a Hui Aloha 'Āina anti-annexation delegation returned to Honolulu from the American capital, one of its members told the Honolulu press, "Queen Liliuokalani want only money. She print a big book to sell for money for herself. . . . She did not help our delegation.

"We do not want her. We want our young Princess. . . . it will be told to all our society people from Hawaii to Niihau. It is the Princess we will hold out for."

It took another war to bring annexation—not a little war along a few rods of stone fence and across a few acres of lantana-clad plain and rock-strewn valley; not a miniature war that cost but two lives and a mere hundred thousand dollars; not a pygmy war fought with two cannon by land and a funny old tug by sea; not something Washington could laugh off as a "Sunday afternoon riot." This was a mighty, far-flung conflict—altruistic or jingoistic as one saw it—but by the standards of its day, colossal.

How soon annexation would have come without the Spanish-American War is hard to say. At least it had not come by the spring of '98 despite the change of administration at Washington. The treaty of 1897, ratified with exuberance in Hawai'i and sent to the United States Senate with strong endorsement by President McKinley, had lain there, unable to command a two-thrids vote. In January of 1898 debate on it had resumed, but a month later its chances still looked so dubious that expansionists began to talk of substituting a joint resolution.

So matters stood when the declaration of war against Spain and the May Day entrance of Admiral Dewey into Manila Bay suddenly pushed the American frontier almost five thousand miles to the west of Hawai'i and made coal piles along Honolulu's esplanade worth their weight in gold.

The strategic importance of the Islands to the United States, just emerging as a naval power, was widely recognized. Senator Henry Cabot Lodge pointed out that Uncle Sam should have "taken" them long ago. A joint resolution for annexation was brought before the House early in May; Speaker Reed, through his control of the Committee on Rules, blocked a vote until June 15; then the measure passed 209 to 91. Debate on the House-approved resolution began in the Senate on June 20. President McKinley brought all his influence to bear in favor of its passage, but a small number of anti-expansionists—men who had stood with Cleveland and who still opposed acquisition of Hawai'i as the first step in imperialism—filibustered against it for sixteen days.

The *Coptic* brought the news on July 13. Forty-two to twenty-one, on July 6, the Senate had passed the Newlands resolution; President McKinley had signed it on the seventh. The Pacific Mail steamship had made the crossing in six and a half days, to signal with flags while it was still off the harbor: Annexation!

Again thousands went to the waterfront; again the streets filled with ecstatic haoles—laughing, weeping. A salute of one hundred guns roared across the bay; factory whistles blew and firebells clanged. The band blared its way to the quay and then, followed by the crowd, marched back to the palace grounds, where it played the "Star Spangled Banner."

Next morning the *Advertiser*'s dateline read: "Honolulu, H.I., U.S.A."

The *Gaelic*, bringing Lili'uokalani home, appeared off Koko Head past midnight on August 1. Quickly the word went among the Hawaiians. Some had been waiting, awake, for the call. Others jumped up from their beds and rubbed the sleep from their eyes. By the hundreds they hurried to the waterfront. The Princess Ka'iulani was there, and the princes David and Kūhiō. And so were the men and women of Hui Aloha 'Āina, forgetting what their leaders had said not so long ago.

One by one the channel buoys came alive. The pilot boat chugged out. Then the running lights and afterward the huge black hulk of the steamer crept into view. As the *Gaelic* eased into her berth, loving eyes searched the deck and found the queen, standing in a little enclosure of canvas that sheltered her from the other passengers. Crassly the Americans on board shouted to their friends ashore, but the Hawaiians made no sound. Even when women began to weep, they clung together and smothered their sobs in one another's *holokus*. Even when Prince David brought Lili'uokalani down the gangplank, there was a stillness like death.

The queen looked, amazed, at the upturned faces. "Aloha," she said softly, smiling at them. "Aloha!"

"Alo-o-ha!" cried a thousand voices, and the crowd surged forward as if to embrace her all at once. Then a wizened old woman lifted her arms and began an ancient chant. There on the electrically lighted pier among the cranes and hoists, the ropes and the capstans, Mahoe sang in weird, repetitive cadences of *malos* and calabashes and feather mantles and the beautiful, mountainous land of Kamehameha, of heroes and gods and battles and the beloved *ali'i* of whom Lili'uokalani was one.

The queen and her attendants and Prince David entered Ka'iulani's carriage. There was a nodding of heads to left and right and more calls of aloha as the white horses pranced off along the esplanade and then *mauka* toward Washington Place. At the mansion liveried chamberlains, in black broadcloth and tall silk hats with fluttering white rosettes, stood at the gates and alongside the front steps with flaring, pungent *kukui* torches. They were old men, who had served the Kalākaua or the Dominis family through the years, but they stood stiff and straight and steady at their posts. Garlands of *maile* and ferns decked the window frames and veranda pillars and traced *"Pumehana"* (a warm welcome) above the open door. Light streamed out upon the men and women who had followed from the wharf and who now squatted on the ground, where they could see through the French windows as Lili'uokalani, seated at table in the dining room, refreshed herself with fruit and fish and poi. They could see that vanity and self-will had gone from her face, leaving it noble and strong and kind. Young girls, dressed in white, waved white *kāhili*s slowly above her.

The chanter began again with her *oli*s, the chants recounting old-time deeds of valor. Sometimes others took up the refrain, the women's voices blending in harmony, the men wailing as for the dead. On and on the singing went for hours. When the meal was finished, the queen's old retainers—those who had lived on her bounty at Mu'ulaulani or Hamohamo or here at Washington Place—went before her to pay their respects. They came through the front yard between the ranks of singers, and at the steps of the veranda fell on their knees and inched their way humbly to her feet. Lili'uokalani called each subject by name as he touched her hand, dropping tears upon it. Then, still on their knees, each one backed away to give place to the next in line. Later there were those of higher degree who were permitted to kiss the royal hand without kneeling, and a favored few of the women who remained near the queen in a circle and talked quietly with her about the sad, irrevocable things that had happened while they were apart.

Toward dawn Mahoe began working herself into a frenzy and ran about as she sang. An old man joined her, and, as if they read each other's thoughts, they swung together into a hula, twisting their bodies and rippling their wrinkled arms in wild, seductive rhythms. It seemed as if there would never be an end; but when the sun was fully up, the singing faded away and the people began to withdraw. For the day that was dawning would see them coming back with their *ho'okupu*—their gifts of ti-wrapped taro, live chickens, squealing pigs, and a dozen kinds of fruit and flowers.

Hawai'i's crown had fallen; the scepter had departed. But in thousands of hearts Lili'uokalani was still a queen. The land had gone from the Hawaiians, and soon their flag would come down. But above in the heavens the stars still shone, just as they had shone when the first Kamehameha ventured forth to unite the Islands into a great and glorious kingdom.

So long as they had voices for the chants, and feet and hands for the dances; so long as they had memories to treasure what their ancestors had told them, old Hawai'i would live on. It had not been taken from them—nor ever could be.

BIBLIOGRAPHY

Abbreviations

AH: Public Archives of Hawai'i
BPBM: Bernice P. Bishop Museum Library
FO: British Foreign Office
HHS: Hawaiian Historical Society Library
HMCS: Hawaiian Mission Children's Society Library
UMSC: Spaulding Collection, University of Michigan Library,
        Ann Arbor

Alexander, W. D. Papers. Mary Alexander Smith collection.
———— *History of the Later Years of the Hawaiian Monarchy and the Revolution of 1893.* Honolulu, 1896.
American and British Claims Arbitration Tribunal, Claim No. 84, Hawaiian Claims; Answer of the United States, with appendix. Washington, 1924.
An Accurate Version of Historical Truths. A Plain Narrative of Startling Facts. Details of the Conspiracy that Led to the Overthrow of the Monarchy, Its Inception and Consummation. Revised and reprinted from the *Independent.* Honolulu, 1897.
Ashford, C. W. "Last Days of the Hawaiian Monarchy." In *Twenty-seventh Annual Report, Hawaiian Historical Society.* Honolulu, 1919.
Attorney General's Insurrection File. AH.
Bemis, S. F., ed. *The American Secretaries of State and Their Diplomacy, 1776–1925.* New York, 1928.
Bishop, Sereno E. Letters. HHS.
———— "The Hawaiian Queen and Her Kingdom." *Review of Reviews,* September 1891.

Bibliography

Carpenter, E. J. *America in Hawaii; a History of United States Influence in the Hawaiian Islands.* Boston, 1899.

Carter, Charles L. *The Hawaiian Question. An Open Letter to Secretary Gresham.* Honolulu, 1893. UMSC.

Carter, Joseph L. *Reminiscences of Company A, HNG.* Honolulu, 1895. HHS.

Castle, W. R. "American Annexation of Hawaii." Typescript. HMCS. (Also published in *Reminiscences of William Richards Castle.* Honolulu, 1960. Privately printed.)

Chambers, H. E. *Constitutional History of Hawaii.* Johns Hopkins University Studies in History and Political Science. Baltimore, 1896.

Claims of Certain British Subjects. Correspondence between the Government of the Republic of Hawaii and Her Britannic Majesty's Government in Relation to the Claims of British Subjects for Complicity in the Insurrection of 1895 in the Hawaiian Islands. Honolulu, 1899.

Cleghorn, A. S. Papers. AH.

Coleman, Harriet Castle. "How It Looks in Honolulu." Extracts from a private letter from Mrs. Coleman. *Life and Light,* May 1893. HHS.

Cooley, T. M. "Grave Obstacles to Hawaiian Annexation." *Forum,* June 1893.

Craft, Mabel Clare (Deering). *Hawaii Nei.* San Francisco, 1899.

Damon, Ethel M. *Sanford Ballard Dole and His Hawaii.* Palo Alto, California, 1957.

Davies, Theo H. *Letters upon the Political Crisis in Hawaii, Jan. 1893 to Jan. 1894.* Honolulu, 1894. HHS.

"Designs of United States on Pearl River, 1886–1888." F. O. 58. British Foreign Office file relating to the Pacific Islands. Ms. Public Record Office, London.

"Designs of United States on Hawaii, 1888–1898." F. O. 58. British Foreign Office file relating to the Pacific Islands. Ms. Public Record Office, London.

Diplomatic Correspondence, Jan. 1892 to Feb. 1893. Foreign Office and Executive File (Kingdom of Hawaii). AH.

Dole, Sanford B. Letters. Robert E. Van Dyke collection.

———— "Evolution of Hawaiian Land Tenures." *Papers of the Hawaiian Historical Society,* 3. December 1892.

———— *Memoirs of the Hawaiian Revolution.* Edited by Andrew Farrell. Honolulu, 1936.

Emerson, Nathaniel B. "The Revolution in Hawaii; Brief Resume of the Facts and Affairs of the Hawaiian Rebellion of January, 1895." Ms. Robert E. Van Dyke collection.

———— Papers. Six notebooks, containing statements by twenty-five

Bibliography

persons involved in the counterrevolution of 1895. Robert E. Van Dyke collection. (Typed copies, made with Van Dyke's permission, in HMCS.)

Evening Bulletin. Newspaper. Honolulu.

Frear, W. F. "The Evolution of the Hawaiian Judiciary." *Papers of the Hawaiian Historical Society,* 7. June 1894.

Gilles, J. A. *The Hawaiian Incident; an Examination of Mr. Cleveland's Attitude toward the Revolution of 1893.* Boston, 1897.

Girvin, J. W. *The Cummins Case.* Honolulu, 1905. AH.

Hatch, F. M. "The Constitutional Convention of 1894." In *Twenty-third Annual Report, Hawaiian Historical Society,* 1915.

Hawaiian Commission. *Message from the President of the United States, Transmitting the Report of the Hawaiian Commission, Appointed in Pursuance of the "Joint Resolution to Provide for Annexing the Hawaiian Islands to the United States."* Washington, 1898. UMSC.

Hawaiian Star. Newspaper. Honolulu.

Hobbs, Jean. *Hawaii, a Pageant of the Soil.* Palo Alto, 1935.

Independent. Newspaper. Honolulu. AH.

Judd, A. F., Jr. "A Boy and a Revolution." Paper read to the Social Science Association of Honolulu, April 2, 1934. Ms. BPBM.

Krout, Mary H. *Hawaii and a Revolution; the Personal Experiences of a Correspondent in the Sandwich Islands during the Crisis of 1893 and Subsequently.* New York, 1898.

Kuykendall, R. S. "Constitutions of the Hawaiian Kingdom." *Papers of the Hawaiian Historical Society,* 21. 1940.

—————— *Hawaiian Diplomatic Correspondence in the Bureau of Indexes and Archives of the Department of State, Washington, D.C.* Honolulu, 1926.

—————— *The Hawaiian Kingdom.* Vol. 3. *The Kalakaua Dynasty, 1874–1893.* Honolulu, 1967.

—————— "Negotiation of the Hawaiian Annexation Treaty of 1893." In *Fifty-first Annual Report, Hawaiian Historical Society.* Honolulu, 1943.

Liberal. Newspaper. Honolulu. HHS.

Liliuokalani Collection. AH.

Liliuokalani. Diary. BPBM and AH.

—————— *Hawaii's Story by Hawaii's Queen.* Boston, 1898.

Lodge, H. C. "Our Blundering Foreign Policy." *Forum,* March 1895.

Lydecker, R. C. comp. *Roster of Legislatures of Hawaii, 1841–1918; Constitutions of Monarchy and Republic; Speeches of Sovereigns and President.* Honolulu, 1918.

Madden, H. M., ed. "Letters of Sanford B. Dole and John W. Burgess." *Pacific Historical Review,* 5:71–75. 1936.

Marx, B. L. *Recollections of the Republic of Hawaii.* Honolulu, 1935.

Bibliography

Memoranda of conversations with the Secretary of State, 1893–1898, relating to Hawaiian affairs, copied from the originals in the archives of the State Department, Washington. UMSC.

Moore, L. A. "Veteran Resident Recalls Days of Wilcox Revolution." *Honolulu Star-Bulletin*, April 25, 1940.

Moreno, Celso Caesar. *The Hawaiian Question or the Position of Men and Affairs in Hawaii, Most Respectfully and Earnestly, in Homage to Truth, Justice and Equity, Submitted to the Senate and House of Representatives in Congress Assembled*. Washington, D.C., 1894.

Nevins, Allan, ed. *Letters of Grover Cleveland, 1850–1908*. Boston, 1933.

Nielson, Fred K. *American and British Claims, Arbitration under the Special Agreement Concluded between the United States and Great Britain, August 18, 1910*. Washington, D. C., 1926.

Pacific Commercial Advertiser. Newspaper. Honolulu.

Palmer, Julius A., Jr. *Again in Hawaii*. Boston, 1895.

―――― *Memories of Hawaii and Hawaiian Correspondence*. Boston, 1894.

Pratt, Julius W. *Expansionists of 1898*. Baltimore, 1936.

―――― "The Hawaiian Revolution: A Reinterpretation." *Pacific Historical Review*, 1:273–294. 1932.

Proceedings of the Executive and Advisory Councils of the Provisional Government of the Hawaiian Islands, 1893–1895. AH.

Russ, W. A. *The Hawaiian Revolution*. Selinsgrove, Pa., 1959.

―――― *The Hawaiian Republic*. Selinsgrove, Pa., 1961.

―――― "Hawaiian Labor and Immigration Problems before Annexation." *Journal of Modern History*, 15:207–222. 1943.

Schurz, Carl. "Manifest Destiny." *Harpers New Monthly Magazine*, October 1893.

Smith, W. O. "Statement of Events prior to January 17th, 1893." Ms. AH.

Soper, William. "Saw Kingdom Fade and Die." *Honolulu Star-Bulletin*, November 17, 1936.

Spaulding, T. M. "Cabinet Government in Hawaii, 1887–1893." *University of Hawaii Occasional Papers*, 12. Honolulu, 1924.

Stevens, John L., and Oleson, W. B. *Picturesque Hawaii. A Charming Description of Her Unique History, Strange People, Exquisite Climate, Wondrous Volcanoes, Luxurious Productions, Beautiful Cities, Corrupt Monarchy, Recent Revolution and Provisional Government*. Philadelphia, 1894.

Taylor, A. P. "How Overthrow of Hawaiian Rule Thirty Years Ago Was Precipitated by a Pistol Shot." *Honolulu Advertiser*, January 14, 1923.

Taylor, Clarice B. "Tales about Hawaii." Series of articles about John Adams Cummins. *Honolulu Star-Bulletin*, 1955.

Thurston, Lorrin Andrews. *A Handbook of the Annexation of Hawaii*. St. Joseph, Mich., 1897.

Bibliography

———— *Memoirs of the Hawaiian Revolution*. Edited by Andrew Farrell. Honolulu, 1936.

Towse, E. *The Rebellion of 1895*. Honolulu, 1895.

Two Weeks of Hawaiian History, Being a Brief Sketch of the Hawaiian Revolution of 1893. Honolulu, 1893.

U.S. Congress. Senate. Executive Documents nos. 45, 57, 76, and 77. 52nd Congress, 2nd session, 1893. Papers and documents relating to the Hawaiian Islands. UMSC.

U.S. Congress. Senate. Executive Document no. 16. 53rd Congress, 2nd session, 1894. Report of Rear Admiral J. G. Walker on situation in Hawaii. UMSC.

U.S. Congress. Senate. *Hawaiian Islands: Report of the Committee on Foreign Relations*, with accompanying testimony and executive documents, transmitted to Congress from January 1, 1893 to March 10, 1894. Washington, D.C., 1894.

U.S. Department of State. Papers relating to the mission of James H. Blount, United States Commissioner to the Hawaiian Islands. UMSC.

Unpublished Correspondence Pertaining to the Report of Queen Liliuokalani's Commissioners in 1894. Honolulu, 1898. AH.

Wall, Charles Ormand, and Wall, Walter. Letters concerning the counterrevolution of 1895. Ms. Robert Van Dyke collection.

Whitney, Caspar. *Hawaiian America; Something of Its History, Resources and Prospects*. New York, 1899.

Young, Lucien (USN). *The Real Hawaii, Its History and Present Condition, Including the True Story of the Revolution*. A revised and enlarged edition of *The Boston at Hawaii*. New York, 1899.

Ziegler, C. W. "Revolution and Intrigue: Col. Ziegler Recalls Old Guard Days." *Honolulu Star-Bulletin*, August 22, 1936.

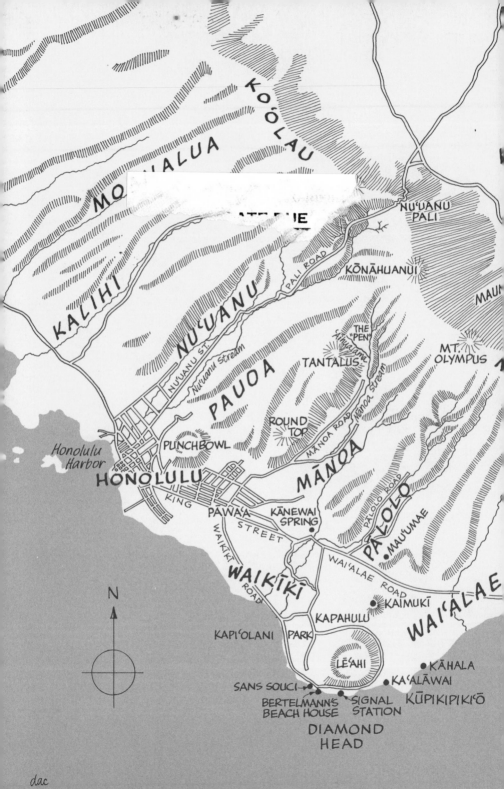

KO‘OLAU

MOANALUA

NU‘UANU
PALI

PALI ROAD

KALIHI

KŌNĀHUANUI

NU‘UANU

NU‘UANU ST.

NU‘UANU Stream

PAUOA

TANTALUS

THE
"PEN"

Waiakeakua

Mānoa Stream

MT.
OLYMPUS

MAUM

MAN

ROUND
TOP

MĀNOA ROAD

MĀNOA

PALOLO ROAD

PALOLO

Honolulu
Harbor

PUNCHBOWL

HONOLULU

KING

PĀWA‘A

STREET

KĀNEWAI
SPRING

MAU‘UMAE

WAI‘ALAE ROAD

WAIKĪKĪ
ROAD

WAIKĪKĪ

KAIMUKĪ

WAI‘ALAE

N

KAPAHULU

KAPI‘OLANI PARK

LĒ‘AHI

KĀHALA

KA‘ALĀWAI

KŪPIKIPIKI‘Ō

SANS SOUCI

BERTELMANN'S
BEACH HOUSE

SIGNAL
STATION

DIAMOND
HEAD

dac